COMPARATIVE JUDICIAL SYSTEMS

ADVANCES IN POLITICAL SCIENCE
An International Series
Published in cooperation with the International Political Science Association

Volumes published in this series:

1. THE EMERGING INTERNATIONAL ECONOMIC ORDER: Dynamic Processes, Constraints, and Opportunities (edited by Harold K. Jackobson and Dusan Sidjanski)

2. MANAGING INTERNATIONAL CRISES (edited by Daniel Frei)

3. WHY GOVERNMENTS GROW: Measuring Public Sector Size (edited by Charles Lewis Taylor)

4. INNOVATION IN THE PUBLIC SECTOR (edited by Richard L. Merritt and Anna J. Merritt)

5. COMMUNICATION AND INTERACTION IN GLOBAL POLITICS (edited by Claudio Cioffi-Revilla, Richard L. Merritt, and Dina A. Zinnes)

COMPARATIVE JUDICIAL SYSTEMS

Challenging Frontiers in Conceptual and Empirical Analysis

John R. Schmidhauser
Editor

Butterworths
London Boston Durban Singapore Sydney Toronto Wellington

First published 1987

British Library Cataloguing in Publication Data

Comparative judicial systems: challenging frontiers
in conceptual and empirical analysis. — (Advances
in political science)
1. Law and politics 2. Comparative law
I. Schmidhauser, John R. II. Series
342 K3165

ISBN 0-408-03165-4

Library of Congress Cataloging-in-Data

Comparative judicial systems.

(Advances in political science; [6])
In part based on papers presented at the conference organized by the Research Committee for Comparative Judicial Studies of the International Political Science Association and held at Mansfield College, Oxford University, April 6–8, 1981.
Bibliography: p.
1. Courts—Congresses. 2. Judicial review—Congresses. 3. Judicial process—Congresses.
I. Schmidhauser, John R. (John Richard), 1922–
II. International Political Science Association. Research Committee for Comparative Judicial Studies.
III. Series.
K2100.A55 1981 347′.012 87–13151

ISBN 0–408–03165–4 342.712

Phototypesetting by En to En, Tunbridge Wells
Printed and bound in Great Britain by Anchor Brendon Ltd, Tiptree, Essex

CONTENTS

FROM THE SERIES EDITOR

Advances in Political Science: An International Series reflects the aims and intellectual traditions of the International Political Science Association: the generation and dissemination of rigorous political inquiry free of any subdisciplinary or other orthodoxy. Along with its quarterly companion publication, the *International Political Science Review,* the series seeks to present the best work being done today (1) on the central and critical controversial themes of politics and/or (2) in new areas of inquiry where political scientists, alone or in conjunction with other scholars, are shaping innovative concepts and methodologies of political analysis.

Political science as an intellectual discipline has burgeoned in recent decades. With the enormous growth in the number of publications and papers and their increasing sophistication, however, has also come a tendency toward parochialism along national, subdisciplinary, and other lines. It was to counteract these tendencies that political scientists from a handful of countries created IPSA in 1949. Through roundtables organized by its research committees and study groups, at its triennial world congresses (the next of which takes place in August 1988 in Washington, DC), and through its organizational work, IPSA has sought to encourage the creation of both an international-minded science of politics and a body of scholars from many nations (now from more than forty national or regional associations), who approach their research and interactions with other scholars from an international perspective.

Comparative Judicial Systems: Challenging Frontiers in Conceptual and Empirical Analysis, edited by John R. Schmidhauser, is the sixth volume in *Advances in Political Science: An International Series.* Like its predecessors, it comprises original papers which focus in an integrated manner on a single, important topic – in this case, comparative judicial structures and processes – and its authors, from various countries and social systems, take differing approaches to the central theme. The volume itself represents a particular aspect of the International Political Science Association's research program: the chapters were first presented at a conference organized at Mansfield College, Oxford University, by the IPSA Research Committee for Comparative Judicial Studies.

Richard L. Merritt

FOREWORD

The Conference by the Research Committee for Comparative Judicial Studies of the International Political Science Association – held at Mansfield College of Oxford University from April 6–8, 1981 – which gave birth to many of the papers incorporated into this volume, proved to be a genuine, indeed an outstanding success. That success represents a tribute to its leading organizer, John R. Schmidhauser of the University of Southern California; its local host-manager, John Boal and the scholars of the Centre for Socio-Legal Studies, Wolfson College, Oxford University; and to the twenty-one diverse participants. The latter, having travelled from all over the world[1] to a delightfully hospitable, if dreary, rainy, and raw Oxfordshire, delivered thirteen formal papers and six *viva voce* presentations in six extended sessions, characterized by lively and informed debate.

Of the high scholarship and, in a good many instances, pioneering on the still all-too-neglected front of Comparative Judicial Studies, the quality of the papers speaks for itself. To one who was among a handful of American political scientists who met in a Dallas hotel in 1964, in an admittedly humble endeavor to give birth to a more or less organized attempt to incorporate the study of Comparative Judicial Studies into political science curricula in the United States, the Mansfield Conference's achievement provided a genuine source of pride and satisfaction. It had been a long road from that Dallas meeting – involving a "small band of brothers", to wit, the quintet of Professors Becker, Danelski, Fleming, Schubert, and myself. Traffic on that road was aided by diverse individual pre-Dallas efforts on the comparative studies front by such scholars as Professors Cappelletti, Cole, Corry, Ehrmann, Friedrich, Kirchheimer, Loewenstein, McWhinney, and Tingsten. It would be joined in post-Dallas days by the significant contributions of such diverse "traditionalists", "conventionalists", and "behavioralists" as Professors Gadbois, Galanter, Grossman, Jacob, Kommers, Krislov, Nagel, Pritchett, W. F. Murphy, Schmidhauser, Steamer, Tanenhaus, Ulmer, and others.

The scholar's quest ought to be for the attainment of learning and understanding, here that of the diverse theories and practices that inform judicial processes throughout the world, coupled with their derivative application and, conceivably, adaption or adoption within the parameters of the "art of the possible". The latter is what the political and judicial process is all about. Thus, scholars seek answers to the three basic questions political scientists in public law perpetually do, and must, ask. These were neatly summarized by professors Murphy and Tanenhaus, as follows: "(1) How *can* the judiciary operate? . . . (2) How *does* the judiciary operate? . . . (3) How *should* the judiciary operate? (1972:20)". The scholarly assemblage of the Mansfield Conference provided sundry lessons, some that may even prove to be seminal, within that aforementioned "art of the possible". It may be useful to attempt to elucidate some of these lessons by way of identifying references to the papers and commentaries that provided the *sine qua non* of the three days of that so useful enterprise:

1. Although the fact of life may be more implicit than explicit, in the final analysis the Comparative Judicial Process in democratic or *soi-disant* democratic states finds a gravitation toward similarities rather than differences, at least in terms of ultimate, rather than penultimate, impact and effect upon the governmental process in a free, or relatively free society.

2. While the appellate structure in general and the highest appellate tribunal in particular still hold what is perhaps majority fascination, we have indubitably come to recognize that we wish to, indeed that we must, study more than legal *systems;* that functional analysis without more does not render a complete picture of the Comparative Judicial Process. In short, we are dealing with considerably more than just conflict resolution.

3. Indeed, the concept of "comparative" government is at last coming to be recognized as a veritably broad one. No longer conceptionally or linguistically confined to a study of diverse states or nations and their cultures, it is a concept that may well be profitably applied vertically as well as horizontally; or, to put it differently, *intra* as well as *inter* state, country, or division.

4. Although there is no doubt that the study of the Comparative Judicial Process evinces roles and results that are tending to pinpoint similarities rather than differences in governmental impact, the very real differences that *a priori* characterize the nature of the judicial process within separate states and their societies nonetheless must be researched, examined, and understood.

5. Given man's increasing striving toward and assertion of the goals of freedom of the person and absence of excessive governmental restraint, both the interest in and analysis of the state of that freedom, of the lines and limits of liberty and equality, happily characterized a good many, perhaps most, of the Conference's papers as well as the purposes of the sub-discipline.

6. Judicial review which, whatever its genesis – arguably Greek, Roman, French, or even English – is still demonstrably present, at least in theory, in some sixty sovereign states (although it may be truly effective in probably no more than a dozen, if that many) *will* and indeed *should* continue to occupy our most acute, arguably central, concern and attention. One may well note the spate of books on judicial review and "line-drawing" on the parameters of the judicial role that have appeared since 1976 in the United States alone: Berger, Choper, Ely, Gabin, Lusky, A.S. Miller, and Perry. Judicial review and its inter-organ dispute-results were thus fortunately not neglected by the Conference's members.

7. A viable theoretical mold remains elusive, as does a foolproof model: there is a patent need for a social theory, a political theory. The quest is neither facile nor predictable. But scholarly assemblies such as the 1981 Mansfield College Conference on Comparative judicial Studies may go a considerable way toward realizing that desirable goal. As the pages of this remarkable collection of essays demonstrate, that Conference constitutes a significant effort; its contributions are indeed of high quality and promise.

Henry J. Abraham
University of Virginia

Charlottesville, Virginia

NOTES

1. The following countries were represented at the Conference: Bangladesh, Canada, England, India, Italy, the Netherlands, Scotland, Sweden, and the United States.

References

MURPHY, W. F. and J. TANENHAUS (1972). *The Study of Public Law.* New York: Random House.

PREFACE

Comparative Judicial Systems: Challenging Frontiers in Conceptual and Empirical Analysis comprises a comprehensive and cohesive collection of investigative essays by a group of well-qualified scholars who are significant contributors in the field of comparative judicial institutions and politics.

The essays are organized in accordance with the progression of scientific inquiry in the field. Part 1 deals with comparative models, conceptual frameworks, and the problems inherent in developing them. Part 2 treats a wide variety of single nation analyses, most of which are devoted to efforts at mapping the bases for scientific investigation of comparative judicial politics. Part 3 comprises a number of multi-nation analyses. These begin with imaginative descriptive conventional pairing of the judicial characteristics of more than one nation and extend to serious efforts at rigorously developing and applying criteria for conceptual equivalence of such characteristics.

This book builds upon the pioneering efforts of the fine scholars noted among the pre- and post-Dallas contributors by Professor Abraham in his Foreword. Yet in a more immediate sense it is the outgrowth of the intense, critical exchanges which characterized three international conferences, the panel discussions of the 1979 IPSA meeting in Moscow, USSR, the 1981 conference of the Research Committee on Comparative Judicial Studies at Mansfield College, Oxford, England, and the 1982 IPSA meeting in Rio de Janeiro, Brazil.

I should like to thank two universities for the opportunity to participate and edit this volume – my own institution, the University of Southern California, and the University of Virginia, which provided an intellectually stimulating setting for a visiting professorship in the academic year, 1982–1983.

John R. Schmidhauser

PART I

COMPARATIVE MODELS AND CONCEPTUAL FRAMEWORKS

Introduction

Are the characteristics of a nation's legal profession and judicial system largely determined by indigenous factors which may be unique to a particular society or by attributes which are universal? The great 18th century founder of comparative law, Charles-Louis de Secondat, Baron Montesquieu, set the stage for an intellectual debate on this issue which, in certain respects, has endured for centuries. Montesquieu developed a conceptual approach which emphasized the uniqueness of the law of individual nations. Such uniqueness was determined by a number of "causes" such as climate or religion (Montesquieu, 1977). In the 19th century, Jeremy Bentham posited the contradictory proposition that since nations shared in common similar problems in law, solutions for these problems should be developed by universally adopted legal reforms. In the 1960s sociologist Wilbert E. Moore asserted that "the world . . . is a singular system" in which virtually all professionals, lawyers or otherwise, regardless of nation or region, share similar educational, economic, and ideological characteristics, especially a "rather remarkable concurrence in the ideology of economic development" (Moore, 1966). In a number of important respects many members of the Research Committee on Comparative Judicial Studies have attempted to systematically examine the propositions of contemporary advocates of Montesquieu, Bentham, Moore, and many others.

The development of categories of research committees under the auspices of the International Political Science Association has provided significant impetus to comparative analysis of national legal and judicial systems and their personnel. As Henry Abraham pointed out in the Foreword to this volume, contemporary contributors to comparative legal and judicial scholarship owe an enduring debt of gratitude to those pioneering scholars who contributed the basic initial investigations and provided encouragement to successive generations of scholars. The originators and subsequent chairmen of the IPSA Research Committee for Comparative Judicial Studies, notable among them Joseph Tanenhaus, Donald Kommers, and Joel Grossman, in addition to their substantial published contributions, provided significant leadership for all of the scholars comprising the Committee. The agenda they set has, indeed, also provided inspiration and guidance for the contributors to this volume.

For approximately two decades, the Research Committee for Comparative Judicial Studies has sought to fulfill the goals projected by its own members and by the leaders of the International Political Science Association. The subject matter emphasis reflected, in large part, the interests and goals of the participating scholars on the Research Committee. The Committee's intellectual mission comprises the conduct of investigations of national, subnational, or transnational judicial systems, procedures, and elites, and includes conceptualization and theory building as well as empirical studies. The organizational emphasis of this Research Committee, conversely, represents both the concomitant intellectual goals of the Research Committee members as well as the broad organizational imperatives of the leadership of the International Political Science Association. Regarding the latter, two of the most important objectives are national diversity in Research Committee memberships (Article 3.a) and what is referred to under Article 2 as "equitable composition with respect to schools of thought". The Research Committee for Comparative Judicial Studies has over one hundred members from twenty nations, namely Brazil, Botswana, Canada, Great Britain, Hong Kong, Hungary, Italy, India, Japan, Malaysia, Nigeria, Norway, the Netherlands, the Peoples Republic of China, Peru, Sweden, Switzerland, the USSR, the United States, and West Germany. The "schools of thought" comprise very diverse approaches and emphases both conceptually, theoretically, and methodologically. In short, the range of intellectual interests and resultant scholarly contributions is very broad. This volume contains contributions by a number of the participants in the Research Committee which represent excellent illustrations of this diversity. Regretably, the tyranny of space limitations and the logic of cumulative scientific development in comparative judicial studies made impossible the inclusion of several well researched works. For example, Professor Giovanni Bognetti of the University of Milan contributed an appraisal of the development of public law and the judicial process in the academic culture of major Italian universities from what he called "the age of positivism and formalism" in the nineteenth century to the contemporary emphasis upon "norm-oriented" comparison. A series of well researched "progress reports" of the quality of Professor Bognetti's analysis of Italy would be of significant value to judicial comparativists, identifying key developments and disciplinary trends throughout the world. This volume, of necessity, eschews a nation by nation appraisal of the state of the subdiscipline and, instead, comprises empirical investigations and conceptual analyses of one or more judicial systems. Ideally, this collection of essays should be organized in accordance with the progression of scientific inquiry in comparative judicial systems and behaviour. In 1969, Professor Glendon Schubert had summed up the state of professional development in comparative judicial behavior in his incisive chapter entitled "From Area Study to Mathematical Theory". Nearly two decades have passed since that important year of comparative judicial productivity and publication, the highlights of which were Glendon Schubert and David J. Danelski's *Comparative Judicial Behavior* and the section on "Foreign Judicial Systems" in Joel B. Grossman and Joseph Tanenhaus, *Frontiers of Judicial Research* (1969). Unfortunately, despite some additional contributions of great intellectual rigor and analytical skill, among them the seminal two-volume work of Glendon Schubert, *Political Culture and Judicial Behavior* (1985), progress toward the goals posited in 1969 is, at best, very slow. As is true in every subfield of the profession, there is considerable disagreement over the definition of progress and, on occasion, over the goals themselves. The contributors of this volume are not seriously divided over the ultimate goals of comparative cross-national judicial inquiry, but many found that progress toward fulfillment of such goals was, to put it mildly, very uneven. Thus while not a single contributor engaged in traditional area study descriptive analysis, many found it desirable to concentrate upon a single nation's judiciary, appropriately treated in a comparative cross-national context.

This volume is organized in three major sections. Part I comprises two chapters treating Comparative Models and Conceptual Frameworks. Part II consists of five chapters which employ single nation judicial analysis as a basis for mapping the fundamentals of comparative cross-national analysis. Part III embodies four chapters which incorporate multi-national comparative approaches.

In Part I, Chapter 1, Professor C. Neal Tate provides a challenging inventory of leading works and a critical appraisal of the approaches and prospects for integrating courts into the comparative study of politics. Not surprisingly, Tate found little cumulative research which was truly cross-national. But he did find several individual national studies of substantial theoretical interest and elegant methodological rigor. Professor John R. Schmidhauser undertook the initiation of empirical examination and scientific testing of two alternative frameworks relating to competing conceptions of law in macro political and economic power relationships throughout the world. One, a neo-Weberian framework conceptualizes law as impartial dispute resolution, but also posits a model designed to create the optimum conditions for the development of capitalism. Thus from the perspective of world system analysts and dependency theorists, who frequently view the world as an economic system in which capitalism currently dominates, but faces competition from socialism, the neo-Weberian model is not value free. Conversely, the neo-Weberian advocates often view the legal corollary of the Wallersteinian world economic system as excessively power-oriented and candidly, but unacceptably partisan. These contrasting perspectives on law, judiciaries, and legal professions afford conceptual frameworks for serious investigation of legal systems in a macro political-economic context.

References

GROSSMAN, J. B., AND J. TANENHAUS (1969). *Frontiers of Judicial Research.* New York: John Wiley and Sons, Inc.

MONTESQUIEU (1977). *The Spirit of the Laws,* **27**, 287–297 (Berkeley: University of California Press).

MOORE, W. E. (1966). "Global Sociology: the World as a Singular System." *American Journal of Sociology,* **72.**

SCHUBERT, G. and DANELSKI, D. J. (1969). *Comparative Judicial Behavior: Cross-Cultural Studies of Political Decision-Making in the East and West.* New York: Oxford University Press.

SCHUBERT, G. (1985). *Political Culture and Judicial Behavior* (2 vol.) Lanham, Maryland: University Press of America.

CHAPTER 1

JUDICIAL INSTITUTIONS IN CROSS-NATIONAL PERSPECTIVE: TOWARD INTEGRATING COURTS INTO THE COMPARATIVE STUDY OF POLITICS

C. NEAL TATE
NORTH TEXAS STATE UNIVERSITY

This chapter focuses upon the role and significance of judiciaries as political institutions. It seeks to take some initial steps toward integrating the study of courts into the study of comparative politics. It suggests that such integration may best be accomplished by research which is cross-national, i.e. by research which attempts to delineate and operationalize the basic concepts or dimensions on which courts can and should be compared across the population of current and past national political systems.

A question which should be addressed before proceeding is a simple one: *Why* should the study of courts be integrated with the study of comparative politics? Preferring not to leave the desirability of such an integration as a matter of faith, I would suggest two answers. First, scholars of comparative politics would benefit. As I shall attempt to demonstrate, such scholars have generally ignored the existence of courts in their descriptions and analyses of the politics of nations. They appear to have assumed that courts are not inherently political institutions, do not exercise significant political power, and are not significant determiners of public policy outside the borders of the United States. Integrating the study of judicial institutions into the study of comparative politics will force the attention of comparative politics scholars to the fact that in a fairly large number of nations, courts are indeed politically powerful institutions whose operation can be understood in the same terms as that of other political institutions, and whose public policy role can be quite significant. It might even direct their attention to determining why this is so in those societies and not in others.

Integrating the study of courts into the study of comparative politics should also be beneficial to scholars of public law and judicial politics. To the extent that such schlolars have studied courts in a variety of national political systems, they have often failed to put their research into the comparative political context which is essential for developing broad generalizations about courts, their operation, and political and policy significance in societies. Problems with which the comparativist constantly attempts to cope – equivalence of language, concepts, and operationalizations and measurements – may well be ignored by public law scholars who concentrate only on the legal doctrines and constitutional and statutory environments which affect and are affected by the courts which interest them. Judicial politics and behavior scholars who never get beyond comparing judges with themselves or, at best, with other judges within the same society, must inevitably face some constraints imposed by their inability to put judges into a comparative context including other political actors.

I do not mean to overstate my case. There have been scholars of comparative politics who appreciated the actual or potential significance of judicial institutions. Similarly, there have been public law and judicial process scholars who have recognized the similarity between judicial and other kinds of politics. But the plain fact is that research in these two areas of the political and social sciences has proceeded along parallel, rarely converging paths.

The chapter begins with a review of several suggested conceptual frameworks which might be used to guide the cross-national study of judicial institutions. In bringing together for discussion and comparison a number of such frameworks, the review may have some educative value for students of courts and judiciaries. However, the primary purpose of the review will be to analyze the frameworks with respect to their utility for guiding data collection and theory-building on the political/institutional roles of courts. The review of the conceptual frameworks will try to identify the crucial variables on which we appear to need information if comparative courts research is to progress. It will then focus on the difficulties likely to be encountered in operationalization and measurement of these crucial variables.

Where possible, it will suggest what data sources might be utilized to create the necessary measurements.

Following the discussion of the conceptual frameworks is a brief survey of the data available in a number of cross-national data collections produced by scholars from several disciplines. The purpose of the survey will be to ransack these data sets for measurements of the variables which appear important in cross-national courts research.

Conceptual frameworks

The review of conceptual frameworks to be undertaken in this section will begin with a discussion of the sources from which such frameworks potentially may be drawn. The discussion of sources will be followed by a review of a number of frameworks which are noteworthy for their clarity, comprehensiveness, and comparative focus. The review of each framework will attempt to highlight its major concepts and comment on their utility for cross-national courts research, noting especially the ease or difficulty of the operationalization and measurement of the concepts, and the apparent breadth of their applicability to the universe of the world's court systems.

SOURCES

There are three major bodies of social scientific literature which suggest themselves as potential sources for conceptual frameworks for cross-national courts research: the works of comparative politics scholars concerned with providing summary or more detailed treatments of political institutions and their significance in the contemporary world; the works of public law and judicial process scholars concerned with extending the applicability of their research beyond the traditionally legalistic and ordinarily nation-specific contexts with which it arose; the works of scholars in disciplines outside political science, especially those of scholars most clearly identified with the "law and society" approach.

Comparative Government and Politics Sources Although it is still true, it is no longer novel to note that comparative government and politics textbooks, which usually devote a considerable amount of their attention to concepts crucial to the understanding of the political roles of executive, bureaucratic, and legislative institutions, typically virtually (or literally!) ignore the courts and their associated legal institutions (for this complaint, see Becker, 1970: 136; Tate, 1974;

Beller, 1981). For example, Joseph LaPalombara's excellent, institutions-focused text *Politics Within Nations* lacks a chapter dealing with courts, but has five dealing specifically with legislatures, executives, and bureaucracies (see LaPalombara, 1974). Indeed LaPalombara's neglect of the political role of courts seems to be total: there is no reference to courts, judiciaries, adjudication, or any other related topic in the thorough index to *Politics Within Nations.* This total neglect of courts, the judicial process, or adjudication is also true of a number of other survey textbooks with which I am familiar. Although they are intended to inform introductory students of comparative government and politics of the basic institutions and processes underlying the politics of contemporary nation-states, they all leave the impression that courts are political institutions which are simply not worthy of attention (see Roth and Wilson, 1980; Cattell and Sisson, 1978; Gorden, 1972; Mayer and Burnett, 1977).

The total neglect of courts and related topics is not actually typical of comparative government and politics texts. Most survey textbooks at least mention courts, judiciaries, or possibly "judicial review" in their indexes and devote from a line to a few pages to these topics (see Feit, 1978; Finer, 1971; Hagopian, 1978; Rasmussen, 1969; Sarkesian and Buck, 1979 for examples of texts providing index listings on one or more of these topics but little else; see Almond and Powell, 1978, 1981; Groth, 1971; Irish and Frank, 1972; McClennan, 1975; Palmer and Thompson, 1978 for examples of texts which devote a few pages to these topics). However, such treatment as courts do receive in these volumes is often remarkably legalistic or even naive, standing in sharp contrast to the treatments afforded other institutions.

Only a few comparative politics-related texts provide a continuous, systematic discussion of the courts which is of chapter or at least major section length. Among these are the introductory texts by Barnes *et al.* (1980). Hitchner and Levine (1981), McClennan (1980), Merkl (1970, 1977), Wahlke and Dragnich (1971), the more restricted effort to focus on "political institutions" by Fried (1966), and, especially, the upper-level text by Blondel (1969).[1] In addition, there is the volume by Henry Ehrmann, a scholar whose roots are in comparative politics, which makes an extended effort to discuss aspects of "legal culture", including courts, from a broad comparative perspective (Ehrmann, 1976).[2]

Of the comparative politics volumes mentioned above, only the ones by Blondel (1969) and Fried (1966) present conceptual frameworks of sufficient significance to merit discussion here. However, the Ehrmann

(1976) treatise will also prove to be of use as a source of suggestions for variables on which comparative data needs to be gathered.

Public Law and Judicial Process Sources The second major source of conceptual frameworks to be reviewed is the work of political scientists whose roots are in public law and the study of the judicial process, rather than in comparative politics. The emergence in the 1950s of the "judicial politics" and "judicial behavior" approaches to the study of public law carried with it the necessary implication that courts were significant political institutions, performing political as well as narrowly legal roles. By the late 1960s the perspective of the new approach(es) had been broadened beyond the United States, and books urging the study of *Comparative Judicial Politics* and *Comparative Judicial Behavior* appeared (see Becker, 1970; Schubert and Danelski, 1969). The 1970s saw a number of efforts to outline explicit conceptual frameworks for the comparative analysis of courts and legal processes. The contributions of Becker (1970), Shapiro (1975), and Schmidhauser (1978) appear to be the clearest and most comprehensive of these. They will be discussed here.

Non-Political Science Sources The study of courts and their roles and significance has long been a concern of scholars in disciplines other than political science. Anthropologists, for example, have produced a number of monographs about the cultures and political processes of simple societies which have analyzed the legal and judicial institutions associated with the societies in very perceptive ways. Law professors with a sociological orientation and their colleagues in legal sociology have endeavored to provide broad summaries of the role of law and legal institutions in societies.[3] Many of these works have manifest or latent implications for the cross-national study of courts as political institutions. However, for two broad reasons no representative work from this body of literature is reviewed here:

(1) their approaches are often so broadly focused on the law and the legal system as a whole that they pay little attention to courts and their social and political roles and significance.
(2) their most significant politically-relevant concepts have been well integrated into the work of the political scientists cited above.

The conceptual frameworks to be reviewed are thus restricted to those put forward by political scientists. Explicitly, the remainder of this review section will discuss the conceptual work of Becker (1970),

Blondel (1969), Shapiro (1975), Fried (1966), and Schmidhauser (1978).

BECKER

The first conceptual framework to be reviewed is that suggested by Theodore Becker in his *Comparative Judicial Politics: The Political Functioning of Courts* (1970). The subtitle of Becker's book suggests its relevance for the present endeavor. Its contents include discussions of a number of concepts which, Becker maintains, should underlie comparative research on courts.

The key to Becker's approach lies in his elaborate and rather restrictive definition of "court". He defines a court (1970: 13) as:

> (1) a [person or body of persons] (2) with power to decide a dispute, (3) before whom the parties to the dispute or their advocates or their surrogates present the facts of the dispute and cite existent, expressed, primary normative principles (in statutes, constitutions, rules, previous cases) that (4) are applied by that [person or body of persons] (5) who *believe* that they should listen to the presentation of facts and apply such cited normative principles impartially, objectively, or with detachment . . ., and (6) that they may so decide, and (7) as an independent body.[4]

Becker's definition has been criticized because it attempts to direct research attention toward a "prototype" of court which, allegedly, hardly exists in the real world (Shapiro, 1975: 321). And it is true that Becker's definition would not include as "courts" a great many institutions called by that name or encompass a great portion of the activities engaged in by institutions which would otherwise merit the appellation. Becker acknowledges this effect of his definition, but argues that many of the important questions to be asked about comparative judicial politics have to do with "whether there are courts or not" (Becker, 1970: 98–134).

More broadly, Becker's definition of "court" may be taken as suggesting a number of concepts useful in measuring the institutional role and performance of institutions which in common parlance may be called courts. Specifically, Becker's work suggests that it should be useful to try to compare courts on at least the following dimensions:

(1) number of decision-makers to a court (after Becker's point 1).
(2) amount of dispute-deciding power (after point 2).

(3) extent to which dispute deciding constitutes the total activity of the court (corollary of point 2).
(4) manner of "fact" presentation, e.g. adversary/investigatory or inquisitorial/administrative proceedings (after point 3).
(5) presence/absence of advocates or surrogates for deciding disputes (after point 3).
(6) extent of presentation of existing normative principles as basis for decision in dispute deciding (after point 3).
(7) types of normative principles presented with frequencies of occurence of each type (after point 3).
(8) extent of application of presented normative principles by decision-maker or judge (after point 4).
(9) types of normative principles applied with frequencies of occurence of each type (after point 4).
(10) extent of desirability of impartiablity, objectivity, or detachment in decisions (after point 5).
(11) extent of actual impartiality, objectivity, or detachment in decisions (after point 6).
(12) extent of decision-maker's independence (after point 7).

It should be emphasized that these potential dimensions for comparison are for the most part suggested *by*, not *in* Becker's work. Becker devotes substantial attention to dimensions (11) and (12), but I have no assurance that he would find dimensions (1) through (10) either interesting or significant. Nevertheless, it would appear that attention should be given to each of these dimensions if Becker's approach is to have genuine cross-national utility.

The dimensions listed above vary considerably in their presumed significance, clarity, and ease of operationalization and measurement. Number (1) might appear to be simple, even trivial. Yet counts of the number of decision-makers employed in courts at similar levels of judicial hierarchies in different nations are not readily available, especially over time. The World Peace through Law Center's *Law and Judicial Systems of Nations* (Rhyne, 1978) provides the best available information here, but it is not easy to use for genuine comparative work. In addition, the Stanford Studies in Law and Development volume *Law and Social Change in Mediterranean Europe and Latin America* (Merryman, Clark, and Friedman, 1979) is a useful source of information on this (and related) topics for the (only) six nations included in its data compendium. There appears to be substantial variation on this indicator across nations. That this variation is random, insignificant, and unrelated to other important aspects of political systems and their behaviors remains to be demonstrated. A beginning point for cross-national inquiry on judicial institutions might well be to record and standardize available data on the number of levels and extensiveness of the judicial hierarchies of nations.

The second dimension – amount of dispute deciding power – would appear to be clearly important for the comparative study of courts. Operationalizing and measuring this dimension would be difficult, no doubt. But ways of beginning the operationalization/measurement process can be imagined and perhaps even executed. It might be possible to construct an index of dispute deciding power from formal rules establishing the limits on the size of civil and seriousness of criminal disputes which can be resolved by the courts, or, negatively, debarring the courts from certain types of dispute deciding altogether.

Dimension (3) could be easily operationalized and measured – provided one had full information on the "case loads" and time budgets of the decision makers in the courts. Given such data, it would be a simple matter to calculate relative measures of the extent to which dispute deciding constitutes the activity of the court.[5]

Dimension (4) appears to require a typology of fact presentation methods for its operationalization. Perhaps a beginning would be a simple trichotomy which contrasts "adversary" or "debate", "interrogative" ("investigative") or "inquisitorial", and "report" or "administrative" (see Jones, 1976) styles of fact presentation.

Dimension (5) would require for its operationalization an observation of the relative number of disputes in which the disputing parties were represented in the proceedings by advocates or other surrogate parties. For many courts, this observation would be trivial, since advocates would always be participants in the process of dispute resolution. But outside the Western, industrial nations, there would likely be considerable variation on this dimension.

Dimensions (6) through (9) would require substantial effort for their operationalization. Where relatively complete written records of disputes and their presentation and resolution in courts are available, content analysis procedures could be used to determine the extent, types, and frequencies of normative principles presented as bases for desired decisions. This would be a laborious procedure even under the best of circumstances. Where written records are inadequate, extensive observation of the presentation and resolution of a sample of disputes would provide the same information, at least for current disputes.

Dimensions (10) through (12) are addressed directly by Becker, since they relate to "impartiality" and "independence", the two most central concepts of his work. In his view, operational indicators of the concept of impartiality might include the response of judges to survey items designed to measure their belief in its desirability, the presence of institutions or "trappings" which are designed to promote belief in impartiality, and measures of support for the norm of impartiality derived from content analysis of the writings and speeches of judges and legal scholars (Becker, 1970: 37–41). All of these potential operationalizations are relevant to dimension (10), the extent of desirability of impartiality. None seems relevant to measuring dimension (11), the extent of actual impartiality, and it may be that direct operationalization of this dimension is impossible.

Becker suggests that the independence of judges (dimension 12) can be operationalized and measured through the presence or absence of formal-legal arrangements designed to insure independence, the extent to which judges believe they have independence (as measured by survey items), the number of applications for prerogative writs (mandamus, habeas corpus, etc.), which require a court to consider ordering another governmental institution to do (undo) something it has not done (has done), the amount of attention paid to courts in conversation and in the media (presumably measured through content analytic methods), and the rate at which anti-government decisions are rendered (1970: 145–54, 442). These indicators vary considerably in their face validity and ease of measurement. The first, legal arrangements could be fairly easily obtained from documentary or reference sources. The third and fifth could be discerned from careful samples of actual decisions (see Tate, 1977, for example); the second through an elite survey; the fourth through a mass survey and/or content analysis of mass media.

In addition to the dimensions for the cross-national study of courts suggested by Becker's definition, *Comparative Judicial Politics* contains other concepts which are relevant to such study. Most prominent among these are judicial review and lay participation in decision making. A major dimension for the comparison of courts would be

(13) the extent to which they possess the power of judicial review (a) in law, and (b) in fact.

For nations whose courts do possess some form of judicial review, Becker suggests that the following dimensions for comparison are relevant:

(13.1) nature of the reviewing organs.

(13.2) accessibility to the judicial review structure.
(13.3) scope of the review.

Lay participation in the work of the courts can come through juries, "peoples' courts", and "mixed tribunals" consisting of professional and lay judges. A fourteenth dimension for the comparison of courts thus might be

(14) the extent of lay participation in court decision making through (a) juries. (b) peoples' courts. (c) mixed tribunals.

Operationalizations of the concepts of judicial review and lay participation would be fairly easy to achieve, if one were to rely on formal-legal measures of their existence of extent. However, operationalizing and measuring these concepts in practice, i.e., measuring the extent to which courts actually exercise judicial review, or the actual extent of lay participation, would be considerably more problematic. The research on the exercise of judicial review by the United States Supreme Court shows that operationalization problems are not insuperable. They will just require substantial research efforts.

BLONDEL

The second set of concepts for discussion come from Jean Blondel's *An Introduction to Comparative Government* (1969). Though styled an "introduction", this work is in fact a sophisticated and rather abstract attempt to apply structional-functional analysis to the study of political institutions and processes. Its chapter 22 entitled "Rule Adjudication and the Role of Judges in Government" is one of the clearest extant efforts to suggest a parsimonious set of concepts for the comparison of the political roles of adjudicative institutions. It suggests that the performance of "rule adjudication" by courts can best be compared with respect to three dimensions:

(1) the independence of courts.
(2) the scope of rule adjudication (by courts).
(3) the depth of rule adjudication (by courts).

The independence dimension will presumably be familiar to any student of courts and judicial politics, for it is quite similar to the concept of independence introduced by Becker, for example. However, a careful reading of Blondel's discussion of independence indicates that he includes in the concept the absence of "spontaneous bias" which might deprive a disputant of a "fair hearing" (Blondel,

1969: 436), thus indicating that his concept of independence is also inclusive of the behavior which Becker calls "impartiality". Blondel suggests that the independence of judges might be assessed with respect to two distinct meanings. The first concerns the legal or governmental arrangements designed to insure independence; the second the empirical question of the degree to which judges are independent of social and political pressures. Becker's suggestions of indicators with relevance for measuring independence would also seem adequate to the measurement of Blondel's concept, provided one recognizes that the extent of independence of judges from social and political pressures is not well-operationalized by Becker's indicators.

The scope of rule adjudication refers to the range of subject matters over which the courts are able to pass judgements. "Jurisdiction" is nearly synonymous with "scope", as the latter is defined by Blondel (1969: 436, 438–39, 452–58). The distinction is that Blondel intends scope to refer only to those boundaries around courts' decision making which rest upon basic normative or constitutional principles, rather than merely on rules of jurisdictional convenience. Thus the scope of rule adjudication performance of the courts in a society encompasses all those legal-substantive issues on which the courts are able to assert their right to make decisions on the basis of normative, constitutional, and/or statutory principles.

Becker does not discuss a concept directly analogous to scope. Thus he has no suggestions for appropriate operationalizations for this variable. In other work (Tate, 1974), I have suggested that the scope of a court's decision making might be operationalized and measured by:

(1) the set of formal-legal rules which define its official jurisdiction.
(2) responses to survey items designed to measure judges' beliefs as to the proper substantive limits of their decision-making.
(3) the number and variety of types of cases actually decided by the court.

The depth of a court's decision making is related to the extent to which the judge is allowed to question the rules of the political system. We know that some courts may be restricted to adjudicating only the applicability of a specific rule to a specific case (in principle, at least), without considering the issue of whether the rule is itself consistent with the provisions of other rules alleged to be higher up the rules hierarchy. Other courts apparently have the power to order the invalidation of a specific rule in a specific case without regard to the applicability of the rule to the case simply because the rule is, in their judgements, inconsistent with the provisions of higher-level rules. The concept of "depth" is, of course, closely related to the concept of judicial review. However, the latter, in its stress upon the "power of any court to hold unconstitutional and hence unenforceable any law, any official action based on a law, and any other action by a public official that it deems . . . to be in conflict with the Basic Law" (Abraham, 1968: 283) is clearly narrower than depth. Judicial review, as usually understood, appears to represent the most extreme depth of rule adjudication available to judges. For, as Blondel notes, "if courts come to be allowed to define, interpret, and limit the operation of laws in the name of the constitution, they seem to be in a position to define, interpret, and limit not only the constitution itself, but the powers of the rule-making agencies which exist within the polity" (Blondel, 1969: 440).

Becker's discussion of judicial review suggests indicators which might be used to measure this extreme form of "depth" of courts' decision making. More general operationalizations might include:

(1) formal-legal rules establishing the official depth of the courts' decision-making authority.

(2) responses to survey items probing the judges' beliefs as to whether they can and do consider the consistency of specific laws with higher-level laws in deciding specific cases.

(3) measures of the rates at which courts are requested by disputants to invalidate the actions of government agencies on the grounds they are inconsistent with the requirements of higher-level laws.

(4) measures of the extent to which courts actually do invalidate presumed lawful actions of governmental agencies on the grounds they are allegedly inconsistent with higher-level laws.

I would not wish to maintain that Blondel's conceptual scheme is adequate to guide the full range of inquiries which should be worthwhile in cross-national courts research. It does not include the full range of structural variations which is likely to be of interest, for example. Nevertheles, there is much to be said for the scheme. It is relatively comprehensive in its focus on courts as institutional performers. It is parsimonious. And, it is possible to operationalize each of its concepts by at least one robust but unobtrusive empirical measure. For example, in an earlier tentative exploration of the institutional performance of the Philippine Supreme Court before and after President Marcos' declaration of martial law, I was able to operationalize the Supreme court's independence, scope, and depth of decision making at different times using data coded from a random sample of the Court's decisions (see Tate, 1977). What can be done for a single court at different points in time can, at least in principle, be done for several courts at the same point in time, a requirement for cross-national analysis. Gathering the needed data would be time-consuming, but not really difficult.

SCHMIDHAUSER

In recent work John Schmidhauser (1978) has proposed a "Weberian" conceptual framework to guide comparative judicial research. While I do not doubt Professor Schmidhauser's profession of inspiration by Max Weber's work on legal systems and the emergence of capitalism, the more Weberian aspects of his framework do not impress me as sufficiently closely related to judicial institutions and capable of operationalization to be of much genuine assistance in cross-national inquiry. However, Schmidhauser's attempts to specify "attributes of judicial independence, stability, and probity" which are, in his view, desirable from the Weberian perspective, are quite worthwhile. There are eleven of these attributes, and each is accompanied by a suggested operationalization. The attributes and their suggested operationalizations are (Schmidhauser, 1978: 6–7):

(1) *Functional separation* of the highest judiciary from "political" branches of government such as executive or legislative branches.

operationalization: A Likert-type scale

Total functional separation	Partial Separation	Total Unity

(2) *Tenure* of highest judicial personnel

operationalization:

Total lifetime tenure subject only to impeachment	Tenure for a period of years	Removal at will by executive or legislature

(3) *Irreducibility of salaries* of highest judicial personal

operationalization:

Total salary cannot be reduced and parity of salary guaranteed by automatic cost of living increments	Partial salary guarantee	Salary can be reduced or totally eliminated at the will of executive or legislative leaders

(4) *Compliance* with highest judicial decisions and court orders

operationalization: A Likert-type scale

Total compliance	Partial compliance	Total non-compliance

(5) *Enforcement* of highest judicial decisions or court orders

operationalization:

Courts have total self enforcement authority	Courts are dependent on other enforcement authority	Total non-enforcement

(6) *Nature of the foundation of highest judicial power*

operationalization:

Constitutionally established higher judiciary	Established by statute	Totally dependent upon the day-to-day whims of executive or legislative leaders

(7) *Judicial review* by highest judicial tribunal

operationalization:

Guaranteed by the constitution, overidden only by constitutional amendment	Limited to a few subjects	None

(8) *Cross-cultural representation* on the highest court (where the political system is culturally diverse)

operationalization:

Yes	Partial	No

(9) *High qualitative selection standards* for highest judges or justices

operationalization: Measured by education, professional record, and prior judicial experience

Yes	Partial	No

(10) *Fairness and Objectivity* in internal court procedures and customs

operationalization: A Likert-type scale

High standards	Mixed standards	Low or no standards

(11) *Probity* and standards to prevent unfair financial, family or political influence

operationalization:

Absolute prohibition on bribery, nepotism, and conflicts of interest	Mixed situation	Low or no standards or prohibitions

There are some obvious overlaps between Schmidhauser's eleven attributes and the dimensions for comparison derived from the work of

Becker. For example, Schmidhauser, like Becker, suggests the desirability of comparisons of judicial review and of "fairness and objectivity in internal court procedures and customs", and "probity", which are what is implied by Becker's "impartiality". In addition, Schmidhauser's "functional separation" is linked to Becker and Blondel's concept of "independence", although it need not be the same as independence: independent courts need not be functionally separated, while functionally separated courts need not be independent.

For the most part however, there is relatively little overlap between the attributes suggested by Schmidhauser and the dimensions for comparison derived from the work of Becker and Blondel.

The biggest problem with Schmidhauser's attributes is their capacity for operationalization. The Likert-type scales suggested by Schmidhauser would certainly not be easy to measure, even with the use of expert judges. For example, how are even expert judges to be certain that compliance with the highest judicial decisions and court orders is nearer "total" or "partial" compliance? Of course this is not a problem peculiar to Schmidhauser's operationalizations. It is endemic to all judgement-based scales. (See those in Banks and Textor, 1963, for example.) Furthermore, not all Schmidhauser's operationalizations must be entirely judgement-based. Some, for example the irreducibility of salaries and probity as measured by prohibitions on bribery, can be operationalized at least partially from formal-legal rules. Others, cross-cultural representation and high qualitative selection standards, for example, can be measured by reasonably hard data on the characteristics of the judges who sit on the courts. Schmidhauser's own work has begun the effort to use these attributes in at least roughly empirical studies (see 1978, 1979). Thus I would conclude that Schmidhauser's contribution is a very useful addition to those of Becker and Blondel. Cross-national measurement of his attributes should be a goal of comparative judicial studies.

FRIED

An alternative approach to the comparison of courts and other institutions has been suggested by Robert C. Fried, who focuses on the comparison of institutions in terms of their "share of power in the political system in which they operate" (Fried, 1966: 1). Given this possibly narrow focus, Fried suggests that institutions are best compared in terms of their *resources and handicaps* in securing and exercising power. These are to be measured with respect to a representative, though not necessarily exhaustive, set of *potential sources* of institutional strength/weakness:

(1) information
(2) expertise
(3) social power
(4) popularity
(5) legitimacy
(6) leadership skills
(7) organization
(8) violence
(9) rules
(10) economic power
(11) manpower
(12) office

An assessment of particular institutions' positions with respect to the twelve "sources" should then allow the analyst to rank the institutions into one of a series of seven categories of institutional power:

(1) totalitarian
(2) dictatorial
(3) oligarchic
(4) strong
(5) independent
(6) weak
(7) captive-ceremonial-nil (Fried, 1966: 1–6).

Fried does not attempt to give precise operationalizations for his potential sources of institutional strength/weakness. Nor does he indicate how the twelve resources should be combined to yield an overall measure of institutional power which would allow classification of a particular institution into one of the seven categories of power. But to his credit, Fried does attempt to use his scheme to guide a general discussion of the relative power of seven major institutions, executives, legislatures, courts, bureaucracies, militaries, political parties, and electorates (1966: 7–150).

Unfortunately, the complexity of Fried's categorizations, the difficulty of securing data adequate to support even educated guesses for the relative balance of resources and handicaps possessed by different institutions in different countries, and the possible ambiguities obtained in his categories seem likely to prevent any serious efforts to apply his conceptual scheme in real world research on judicial institutions. Its principal value may be as a "washlist" reminding analysts of the resources which courts may/may not have relative to other institutions.

SHAPIRO

The frameworks discussed to this point have been structurally oriented. A well-known framework suggested by Shapiro (1975) is worth reviewing because it emphasizes the functions performed by the courts, rather than their structures. Shapiro attempts to wrest the focus of scholarly attention away from the court "prototype" which, in his view, will lead to a fruitless "study of courts that is essentially the measurement of deviance from a type that is rarely approximated in the real world" (1975: 321). Shapiro's comments are obviously directed at the sort of definition of court used by Becker, and there is no doubt that his point is well-taken. But if one refuses to view Becker's definition as establishing an ideal type from which one can only measure deviances, and rather chooses to regard it as suggesting a number of important variable continua on which courts can be positioned, then Shapiro's criticism is not necessarily devastating. Nevertheless, there is no doubt that Shapiro is correct in his contention that "courts", as commonly understood, do a great deal which is not accommodated under the "prototype" definitions.

Shapiro sees the basic nature of "courtness" as inherent in the "logic of the triad" in conflict resolution (1975: 321). Parties in conflict have a natural tendency to refer to a third party for assistance in resolving their conflict. Maintaining the viability of the triad depends upon two devices: consent of the conflicting parties and achievement of non-dichotomous or "mediate" solutions. The activities of the third parties in conflict-resolving triads can be categorized into four role types – go-between, mediator, arbitrator, judge – which form a mediatory continuum based on the degree of consent and seeking of mediate solutions which characterize the roles. The *judge,* who presumably presides over a *court,* is the third party who least depends on consent and mediate solutions in resolving conflicts. The lack of freely-given consent is compensated for by the introduction of the concept of "law" and "office" to support judicial resolution of conflicts.

From their origins in the triad in conflict resolution, Shapiro argues courts go on to perform a variety of functions. They are, in his view, best understood as essential segments, or perhaps as tools, of political regimes. As such, they are expected to serve three basic functions:

(1) *to resolve specific conflicts* between individuals and/or groups, including conflicts between individuals or groups and the government, in a manner which may have some chance of being acceptable to even the loser. Obviously this is the function most closely related to the origins of courts.

(2) *to serve as a social controller,* punishing or helping eradicate behaviors defined as undesirable by the regime and its rules.

(3) *to serve as an extension of the administration,* performing a variety of "administrative" tasks (the processing of criminals who plead guilty, for example) which do not involve the inter-personal/group conflict of (1) and (2).

Shapiro suggests that relatively little of what courts do would actually fall into category (1), conflict resolution. Yet it is this function of courts which is very frequently cited, and which underlies the arguments of those who interpret the role of courts in democratic societies as that of defender of the rights of citizens against the abuses of government and other citizens (see, for example, Almond Powell, 1978: 240; Bayley, 1964: 127–29). Shapiro's functional approach to courts is not unique. It is also present in Becker's work. Becker sees courts, at least as he defines them, as producing

(1) internal order or the preservation of the status quo (as in Shapiro's (2);

(2) protection of individual and minority right and liberties (via their conflict resolving role);

(3) justice, fairness, or equity in society (also through conflict resolving?).

There is little doubt that the functional typology of Shapiro and even the more normatively-laden effort of Becker are heuristically valuable. The problem is that they are far from easily operationalizable. One can easily illustrate the performance of the conflict resolution, social control, and administrative processing functions by particular courts: examples will abound. But it will be very difficult to measure the performance of these functions by courts in a manner which will lead to useful cross-national research. Of course the same can be said for Becker's functional products of courts. The principal way of operationalizing the performance of any of these functions would be through the development of rating scales by experts. We shall see, in fact, that useful scales exist for rating nations with respect to the degree of civil liberties and political freedom they allegedly provide their populations. Similar scales which focus directly on the extent to which courts provide such goods would be very valuable, even though there still might be serious doubts about their reliability and validity.

EHRMANN

Henry Ehrmann's *Comparative Legal Cultures* (1976) presents no clear conceptual framework to guide the study of courts across nations. But it does contain a wealth of statements concerning the similarities and differences of courts in a variety of nations from which can be drawn a disparate list of concepts and measurements potentially relevant for cross-national study. Those presented here are drawn in general from *Comparative Legal Cultures.* I have not found it possible to produce specific page citations. In general, then, it might be useful to compare courts cross-nationally with respect to:

(1) their use/non-use of the "political question" doctrine to avoid controversial decisions.
(2) their use of *certiorari* or other devices for discretionary jurisdiction control.
(3) their use of pretrial bargaining or out-of-court settlement in civil and/or criminal cases.
(4) the extent to which the judge is involved in (3), if used.
(5) systems of structural division of the courts, including civil/criminal courts (with same/different personnel), regular/administrative courts, administrative tribunals for certain types of cases.
(6) their "legal culture family".
- (a) Roman-Germanic
- (b) common law
- (c) socialist law
- (d) non-Western law (Islamic, Hindu, indigenous African, etc.)

(7) the prominence of the police role in pretrial hearings.
(8) the types of investigation and indictment in criminal cases, e.g., *juge d'instruction,* grand jury, etc.
(9) judicial selection method
- (a) appointed by Chief Executive with no check from any other institution.
- (b) appointed by Chief Executive with a check by another institution.
- (c) appointed by a judicial executive with Government approval.
- (d) elected
- (e) other

(10) allowance of dissent by judges in multi-judge courts.

(11) actual rates of dissent by judges in multi-judge courts.
(12) degree of acceptance of the mechanical theory of jurisprudence by judges, judicial selection officials, legal profession, and the mass public.
(13) average length of written decisions.

A noteworthy feature of the bases for comparison suggested by Ehrmann's work is their general operationalizability, at least in principle. All thirteen aspects of judicial decision making and institutions can be relatively unambiguously measured by appropriate data which can be gathered, given sufficient dedication, time, and effort. In fact, items number (6), (7), and (9) have been measured to some degree in existing data collections (see below). I would not underestimate the amount of research which would be required to operationalize most of Ehrmann's attributes. Such operationalization would require the coding of the characteristics of judicial documents and decisions in some depth (see numbers (1), (3), and (11), for example), medium to large scale surveys of elite and/or mass populations (number (12)), or possibly detailed observation of a representative sample of courts (numbers (4), (7)). But precisely because the required research may be difficult, tedious, or time-consuming, it is time that scholars were drafting the research proposals to do the work. Without it, comparative judicial studies will make little progress toward the goal of integration into comparative politics, or, indeed, toward the narrower goal of the development of a more general, empirically-based knowledge of the performance and significance of courts, even considered in isolation.

Data Sources

There is no question that measurements of many of the dimensions or attributes of courts described previously will have to be operationalized through painstaking research with documentary and reference sources concerning the judicial institutions and legal systems of individual nations. Others may require survey research work across as many nations as possible with judges, judicial selection officials, the legal profession, and the mass public. Both types of research will be expensive and time-consuming, but they should be begun[6]. In the meantime, the possibility that existing cross-national data collections may provide information relevant to operationalizing some of the concepts discussed here should not be overlooked. In addition, such collections may provide information on important independent variables which may have an impact on the variation nations exhibit in the traits discussed above, or on significant dependent variables which may be affected by variation in the most important characteristics of courts. Thus this section presents first a review of the data in major cross-national collections with a focus on the suitability of this available data for use in cross-national courts research.

CROSS-NATIONAL DATA COLLECTIONS

Since the appearance of the initial *World Handbook of Political and Social Indicators* (Russett *et al.*,1964) (hereafter *"World Handbook")* and of the *Cross Polity Survey* (Banks and Textor, 1963) (CPS), scholars have devoted considerable attention to the generation and archiving of quantified data on the social, economic, and political characteristics of nations.

However, few of the general data collections have contained information at all relevant to courts, their structure, and operation. For example, neither the first nor the second edition of the *World Handbook* (Taylor and Hudson, 1972) contained a single such indicator, despite the fact that the second edition contained many more directly politically relevant and imaginative data series than its predecessor. In part, this was because the general collections consisted mostly of quantitative data drawn from existing international sources which concentrated on economic affairs, not government and politics. But even in the case of the *Cross Polity Survey,* which included many judgement-based ratings of the characteristics of nations' political systems, there was no variable which directly measured any attribute of judicial institutions. The only two variables it contains which relate in any way to legal or judicial systems are a rating of the "role of the police" as either politically "significant" or "not significant", and a classification of the "character of the legal system" (see ICPSR-Banks and Textor, 1968: 29).

The two characteristics just mentioned are of some importance, for they relate well to items (9) ("role of police") and (7) ("legal culture family") in Ehrmann's list of attributes of judicial institutions. In addition, CPS contains a number of other political variables which, while they do not measure attributes of judicial institutions, do measure aspects of national political conditions which are possibly fairly closely related to judicial institutions. Among these are ratings of the national "horizontal distribution of power" (i.e., constitutional separation of powers), "vertical distribution of power" ("federalism"), and freedom of groups to opppose the government.[7] And, in this same connection, it should be noted that *World Handbook II* contains a "Press Freedom Index" useful for investigating the connections between the measured attributes of courts and presence of this political value.

Although not archived, and less well known than the CPS and *World Handbooks,* two data sets created by Jean Blondel for use in his texts are also worth mentioning here because they contain a few variables related to judicial institutions and the most immediate aspects of their environments. In his *Introduction to Comparative Government* (1969), Blondel includes a measure of whether the world's nations have judicial review of legislation, the means of appointment of judges to the judicial review body, and whether there is a separate system of administrative justice. Measuring the presence of judicial review is directly relevant to operationalizing this important concept, one which should be measured for cross-national courts research, according to Becker and Schmidhauser (see above). It also provides a partial operationalization of Blondel's own concept of the "depth" of judicial decision-making. The means of selection of judges to the judicial review body would appear of direct interest in several of the frameworks which have been discussed, since it is directly related to independence. Finally, whether there are administrative courts or not is an attribute on the list drawn from Ehrmann, as well as being related to Blondel's scope of decision making and Shapiro's concept of courts as regular administrative agencies.

Blondel's *Comparative Legislatures* (1973) contains additional indicators useful for purposes of cross-national judicial research. These are whether the nation has a "Constitutional Court" or not, whether the constitution has entrenched clauses protecting minorities (which would be a potential source of political power for courts which wished to play the citizen protector role), and whether the constitution provides for executive emergency powers. The last mentioned attribute would provide a tool for the executive which would allow him or her to withstand attempts at limitation by the courts.

Whether the harvest of indicators just discussed is regarded as bountiful or meager depends upon one's expectations. But in either case, there is no doubt that a basic problem with them is that they are static: each attribute has been measured at only a single point in time, usually the early to mid-1960s. While such measurements are satisfactory as a beginning, and while they have not been fully analyzed yet, continuous measurements of these and other traits of judicial institutions and their immediate environments across long time spans are ultimately essential. There are existing cross-national data collections which do cover from a few to many years of national experience. One set of data which has been generated on an annual basis since the early 1970s is the Comparative Survey of Freedom directed by Raymond Gastil (1979), and partially archived (ICPSR-Gastil, 1977). The Comparative Survey of Freedom contains careful ratings of the relative amount of political and civil rights experienced by national populations in given years, as well as assessments of the overall "Freedom status of the nations". Such measures are relevant to investigating the performance of judicial institutions, although they have nothing directly to do with the characteristics of courts. One study which analyzes the Gastil data (Strouse and Claude, 1976) attempts to predict freedom conditions from a disparate set of socio-economic variables, but makes no effort to include the presumably relevant characteristics of courts as explanatory variables. Given some data on courts and their attributes cross-nationally, the freedom data might be very fruitfully used to investigate hypotheses relating courts to a political value which they are frequently charged with protecting or producing.

The best known set of cross-national data which covers many years of national experience and which contains measurements of political and governmental variables in some quanitity is Arthur Banks Cross-National Time Series Data (ICPSR-Banks, 1977). While this collection covered the period from 1815 to the present for as many nations as possible, and while it contains a large list of measures of the characteristics and effectiveness of legislative and legislative institutions and political parties, unlike CPS, its intellectual predecessor, the Cross-National Time Series contains not a single measure which related to operationalizing any of the court attributes or concepts discussed previously. A large number of the measures it does contain will be useful, however, in analyses which do include measures of the characteristics of judicial institutions, once the latter are available.

There is one cross-national data collection of which I am aware which contains many direct measures of the attributes of national judicial and legal systems across a reasonably long time span. This is the data set resulting from the Stanford Studies in Law and Development (SLADE) project focusing on Mediterranean European and Latin American nations (Merryman, Clark, and Friedman, 1979). Chapters in the volume reporting on the SLADE project contain information useful in operationalizing many of the concepts discussed earlier. For example, various chapters provide indicators of the types and numbers of courts and administrative institutions, the numbers and grouping of "legal actors", including judges, legislators, lawyers, etc., "the types and numbers of processes (e.g., executive and legislative lawmaking; the numbers of contract, tort, divorce, and property cases filed and decided) and the resources consumed by legal institutions and actors (budgets and salaries)" (Merryman, Clark, and Friedman, 1979).

The SLADE project is evidence that good and useful cross-national data judicial institutions can be gathered for different nations across time. It also illustrates the difficulty of the task. Despite a fairly large scale research effort, the project reports data for only six nations: Chile, Colombia, Costa Rica, Italy, Peru, and Spain. Hopefully, this project or another like it will expand the data pool which it has begun.

NOTES

1. I have not included area or country-focused textbooks in this review. Such texts usually do contain some discussion of the courts and legal systems of the nations considered, provided the country sections are not too brief. However, they do not, as a rule, contain summary discussions of the significance or roles for courts which have utility for cross-national analysis. Thus they may prove useful as sources for data, but not as sources for conceptual frameworks or other theoretically relevant formulations.

2. It is intriguing to compare the Ehrmann volume with its companion volume in the Prentice-Hall "Contemporary Comparative Politics Series" dealing with legislatures and the legislative process (Blondel, 1973). The title of Ehrmann's work *(Comparative Legal Cultures)* is much broader that that of Blondel's *(Comparative Legislatures)* and indicates an unwillingness or inability, given the state of our knowledge of courts, to focus on the principal institution of government which directly reflects "legal culture". Blondel's book attempts to gather and utilize available data on legislatures in a genuinely cross-national analysis; Ehrmann's does not. Because of his reliance on available empirical data, Blondel's work is occasionally trite and sometimes overly occupied with documenting the obvious. Because of the lack of a strong basis in empirical data, Ehrmann's book occasionally seems overly abstract and legalistic, even when it is probably not his intention to be so. Blondel's work can be supplemented by less empirical, functionally oriented treatments of legislatures and the legislative process. Ehrmann's work cannot be supplemented by any strongly empirically oriented treatment of courts and judiciaries.

3. See Bohannon (1957), Gluckman (1955), Hoebel (1961), for some classic anthropological studies.

4. I have substituted the phrase "person or body of persons" for Becker's "man or body of men".

5. The American Judicature Society has recently begun publishing the results of their major survey study of the work habits and time budget of American judges. A major report is Ryan (1980). More such work in other nations would be very useful.

6. And they have been. For examples of judge survey work, see Schubert (1981), and Schmidhauser, Green, and Berg (1976). Schubert's data have been archived for public use through the Inter-University Consortium for Political and Social Research (See ICPSR, 1981: 170).

7. For these variables, see Banks and Textor (1963).

References

ABRAHAM, HENRY J. (1968). *The Judicial Process,* 2nd ed. New York: Oxford University Press.

ALMOND, GABRIEL and G. BINGHAM POWELL (1978). *Comparative Politics: System, Process and Policy.* Boston: Little Brown.

—, eds. (1981) *Comparative Politics Today: A World View.* Boston: Little Brown.

BANKS, ARTHUR (1971). *Cross Polity Time Series Data.* Cambridge: M.I.T. Press.

—, and ROBERT B. TEXTOR (1963). *A Cross Polity Survey.* Cambridge: M.I.T. Press.

— (1969. *Cross Polity Survey.* Ann Arbor: University of Michigan.

BARNES, JAMES F., MARSHALL CARTER and MAX J. SKIDMORE (1980). *The World of Politics: A Concise Introduction.* New York: St. Martin's.

BAYLEY, DAVID H. (1964). *Public Liberties in the New States.* Chicago: Rand McNally.

BECKER, THEODORE L. (1970). *Comparative Judicial Politics: The Political Functioning of Courts.* Chicago: Rand McNally.

BELLER, GERALD E. (1981) *"The Political Role of the Indian Judiciary".* Paper presented to the annual meeting of the Southwestern Political Science Association, Dallas, Texas, March 25–28.

BLONDEL, J. (1973). *Comparative Legislatures.* Eaglewood Cliffs, New Jersey: Prentice-Hall.

— (1969). *An Introduction to Comparative Government.* New York: Praeger.

BOHANNON, PAUL (1957). *Justice and Judgement among the Tiv.* Oxford: Oxford University Press.

CATTELL, DAVID and RICHARD SISSON (1978). *Comparative Politics: Institutions, Behavior, and Development.* Palo Alto, California: Mayfield Press.

CLAUDE, RICHARD, ed. (1976). *Comparative Human Rights.* Baltimore: Johns Hopkins University Press.

CURTIS, MICHAEL (1978). *Comparative Government and Politics: An Introductory Essay In Political Science,* 2nd ed. New York: Harper and Row.

EHRMANN, HENRY W. (1976). *Comparative Legal Cultures.* Englewood Cliffs, New Jersey: Prentice-Hall.

FEIT, EDWARD, ed. (1978). *Government and Leaders: An Approach to Comparative Politics.* Dallas, Texas: Houghton-Mifflin.

FINER, S. E. (1971). *Comparative Government.* New York: Basic Books.

FRIED, ROBERT C. (1966). *Comparative Political Institutions.* New York: Macmillan.

GORDON, MORTEN (1971). *Comparative Political Systems: Managing Conflict.* New York: Macmillan.

GLUCKMAN, MAX (1955). *The Judicial Process among the Barotse of Northern Rhodesia.* Glencoe, Illinois: The Free Press of Glencoe.

HAGOPIAN, MARK R. (1978). *Regimes, Movements and Ideologies: A Comparative Introduction to Political Science.* New York: Longman.

HAYAKAWA, TAKEO and JOHN R. SCHMIDHAUSER (1979). "A Comparative Analysis of the Internal Procedures and Customs of the Supreme Courts of Japan and the United States". Paper presented to the XI World Congress of the International Political Science Association, Moscow.

HITCHNER, DELL GILLETTE and CAROL LEVINE (1981). *Comparative Government and Politics,* 2nd ed. New York: Harper and Row.

HOEBEL, E. ADAMSON (1961). "Three Studies in African Law". *Stanford Law Review,* **13:** 418–42.

IRISH, MARIAN D. and ELKE FRANK (1972). *An Introduction to Comparative Politics: Twelve Nation States.* New York: Appleton Century Crofts.

INTER-UNIVERSITY CONSORTIUM FOR POLITICAL RESEARCH (1981). *Guide to Resources and Services.* Ann Arbor: University of Michigan.

ICPR and ARTHUR BANKS (1976). *Cross-National Time Series, 1815–1973.* Ann Arbor: University of Michigan.

JONES, WILLIAM C. (1976). "A Possible Model for the Criminal Trial in the People's Republic of China", *American Journal of Comparative Law,* **24** (Spring): 229–45.

LAPALOMBARA, JOSEPH (1974). *Politics Within Nations.* Englewood Cliffs, New Jersey: Prentice-Hall.

MAYER, LAWRENCE C. and JOHN H. BURNETT (1977). *Politics in Industrial Societies: A Comparative Perspective.* New York: John Wiley.

MCLENNAN, BARBARA (1980). *Comparative Politics and Public Policy.* North Scituate, Massachusetts: Duxbury Press.

— (1975). *Comparative Political Systems: Political Processes in Developed and Developing States.* North Scituate, Massachusetts: Duxbury Press.

MERKL, PETER H. (1977). *Modern Comparative Politics.* Chicago: Holt, Rinehart, and Winston.

MERRYMAN, JOHN HENRY, DAVID S. CLARK and LAWRENCE M. FRIEDMAN (1979). *Law and Social Change in Mediterranean Europe and Latin America.* Stanford Studies in Law and Development. Dobbs Ferry, New York: Oceana Publications (distributors).

PALMER, MONTE and WILLIAM THOMPSON (1978). *The Comparative Study of Politics.* Itasca, Illinois: F. E. Peacock Publishers.

RASMUSSEN, JORGEN (1969). *The Process of Politics.* Chicago: Atherton Books.

RHYNE, CHARLES S. (1978). *Law and Legal Systems of Nations.* Washington, D.C.: World Peace Through Law Center.

ROTH, DAVID and FRANK WILSON (1980). *The Comparative Study of Politics.* Englewood Cliffs, New Jersey: Prentice-Hall.

RUSSETT, BRUCE W., *et al.,* (1964). *World Handbook of Political and Social Indicators.* New Haven: Yale University Press.

RYAN, JOHN PAUL (1980). *American Trial Judges.* New York: Free Press.

SARKESIAN, SAM C. and JAMES H. BUCK (1978). *Comparative Politics: An Introduction.* Sherman Oaks, California: Alfred Publishing Co.

SHAPIRO, MARTIN (1975). "Courts", in Fred Greenstein and Nelson Polsby, eds. *The Handbook of Political Science,* vol. 5, *Governmental Institutions and Processes,* pp. 321–73.

SCHMIDHAUSER, JOHN R. (1978). "A Weberian Conceptual Framework for Comparative Judicial Research". Paper presented to the annual meeting of the Southern Political Science Association, Atlanta, Georgia.

—, JUSTIN J. GREEN and LARRY BERG (1976). "The Comparative Analysis of the Highest Appellate Justices of Twenty-Two Nations". Paper presented to the Xth World Congress of the International Political Science Association, Edinburgh, Scotland.

SCHUBERT, GLENDON (1980). "Subcultural Effects on Judicial Behavior". *Journal of Politics,* 42 (November): 951–92.

– and DAVID J. DANELSKI, eds. (1969). *Comparative Judicial Behavior: Cross-Cultural Studies in Political Decision-Making in the East and West.* New York: Oxford University Press.

STROUSE, JAMES C. and RICHARD P. CLAUDE (1976). "Empirical Comparative Rights Research: Some Preliminary Tests of Development Hypotheses", in Claude (1976), pp. 51–68.

TATE, C. NEAL (1977). "Martial Law and Decision-Making in the Philippine Supreme Court: An Empirical Analysis", in Stephen MacKinnon, ed., *Selected Papers in Asian Studies,* 2, Tempe, Arizona: Western Conference of the Association for Asian Studies.

– (1974). "The Philippine Supreme Court and Martial Law: Constitutional and Institutional Performance." Paper presented to the annual meeting of the Western Conference of the Association for Asian Studies, Tempe, Arizona.

TAYLOR, CHARLES LEWIS and MICHAEL HUDSON (1972). *World Handbook of Political and Social Indicators,* 2nd ed. New Haven: Yale University Press.

WAHLKE, JOHN C. and ALEX N. DRAGNICH (1971). *Government and Politics: An Introduction to Political Science.* New York: Random House.

CHAPTER 2

ALTERNATIVE CONCEPTUAL FRAMEWORKS IN COMPARATIVE CROSS-NATIONAL LEGAL AND JUDICIAL RESEARCH

JOHN R. SCHMIDHAUSER
UNIVERSITY OF SOUTHERN CALIFORNIA

It is the purpose of this chapter to initiate empirical examination and scientific testing of two alternative conceptual frameworks related to the determinants of the organization, purposes and personnel of the court systems and legal professions of selected developed and underdeveloped nations. Of necessity, this entails reassessment of some fundamental assumptions about the nature and purposes of judicial institutions and legal professions. The basic distinction embodies conflicting assumptions about law as conflict resolution and law as instrumentality of power.

The law as conflict resolution approach is perhaps best exemplified by Max Weber and Emile Durkheim, two of the greatest European theorists. They made unique and highly significant contributions to the analysis of those characteristics of social and political systems which may contribute to the stability or continuity of specific component institutions or total national systems. Their theoretical contributions and the special attention which they focused upon legal professionals and judicial institutions provide an excellent foundation for the development of rigorous cross-national or intra-national comparison of such personnel and institutions. National judicial systems and legal professions were deemed by both Durkheim and Weber to be system-stabilizing institutions of very special importance. Both underscored the conflict resolution function of law. Both, in somewhat different fashion, emphasized that law was the monopoly of the politically organized nation state. These and related assumptions about the system-stabilizing functions of law have become part of what is called the "received tradition" in many traditional law training programs throughout the world. Conversely, critics of the "law as conflict resolution" approach have posited alternative conceptual frameworks and historical evidence to argue that law often functions as the instrumentality of the powerful. The polar opposite of the conflict resolution and system-stabilizing perspective is that of many revolutionary leaders who treat the judicial system and legal profession associated with the regime they seek to overthrow as essential components of an entire system which is deemed corrupt, unfair, and authoritarian.

The contradiction inherent in these two characterizations of the attributes and nature of judicial systems and legal professions deserves serious consideration and critical analysis. It is important to describe the essential characteristics of two conceptual models of judicial systems and legal professions which embody the conflict in basic assumptions between law as conflict resolution and law as instrumentality of power. It is not the purpose of this inquiry to endorse one or the other of these models, but it is essential to map the components of each in order to provide alternative conceptual frameworks for comparative cross-national analysis. These contrasting perspectives are identified and distinguished in order to provide the conceptual bases for subsequent determination of the extent to which any particular national judicial system and legal profession conforms more closely to one or the other alternative model.

Much of the conventional literature on comparative cross-national judicial and legal systems is devoid of explicit macro-theoretical frameworks. Max Weber's contributions comprises, of course, one of the major exceptions. His conceptualization of an "ideal " legal system as one creating the optimum conditions for the achievement of capitalism may be viewed as a polar opposite of a dependency theory-based conception of judicial institutions and legal professions. In the latter, law and its institutions and personnel are frequently conceptualized as instrumentalities of dominant capitalistic nations (often referred to as center or core nations). But unlike Weber or Durkheim, dependency theory conceptions of law, such as Tigar and Levy's *Law and the Rise of Capitalism,* generally emphasize law's partisan role rather than its impartiality and its conflict resolution function (1977). Some dependency theorists concentrate upon economic relationships and tend to minimize law, judicial institutions, and legal personnel. Immanuel Wallerstein's extensive contributions on his World Economic System model is illustrative of this tendency (e.g., Wallerstein, 1979). Those dependency theorists who do recognize the significance of law have often done so very parsimoniously (Galtung, 1971) or have limited their analysis to a single nation (Anderson, 1974a and b).

It is one of the purposes of this exploratory investigation to integrate law and dependency theory conceptions more thoroughly than most dependency theorists have undertaken. Assuming, for the moment, the validity of Wigmore's generalization that "the rise and perpetuation of a legal system is dependent on the development and survival of a highly trained professional class" (1928: 1129), a broad array of historical evidence supports the notion that such a highly trained lawyer professional class was rather intimately related to the dominant forces which accomplished the transformation from the political patchwork characteristic of baronial independence under feudalism to national centralization under absolute monarchy and the transformation from single nation-state dynastic military conflict to a capitalistic world economic system.

Thus, in relation to the first transformation, Braudel summed up the evidence as follows:

> ... the more one thinks about it, the more convinced one becomes of the striking similarities, transcending words, terminology and political appearances between East and West ... Experts in Roman law and learned interpreters of the Koran formed a single vast army, working in the East as in the West to enhance the prerogative of princes. It would be rash and inaccurate to attribute the progress made by monarchy entirely to the zeal, calculations and denotions of these men. All monarchies remained charismatic. And there was always the economy. Nevertheless, this army of lawyers, whether eminent or modest, was fighting on the side of the large state. It detested and strove to destroy all that stood in the way of state expansion (Braudel, 1972: 683–85).

De Tocqueville made essentially the same argument regarding Germany (1955: 222–223) and Anderson similarly associated an elite lawyer class with English centralization and absolutism (1974a and b).

In his analysis of "the natural history of legal counsel", Dietrich Rueschemeyer emphasized two major factors contributing to the historic growth of legal professions – the bureaucratization of political rule and the development of a market economy (1973: 3). Both developments often resulted in the identification of key elements of the legal professions of particular nations with dominant political forces. Thus the bureaucratization of political rule was generally associated with the national centralization sought by absolute monarchs. Where absolutism persisted, efforts at establishing the independence and autonomy of legal professionals were frequently inhibited. Eisenstadt's investigation of absolutist empires underscored this. As he put it, "... the rulers' general objectives in the legal field were to minimize the legal autonomy of traditional groups and strata (e.g., the aristocracy and the patriciate) and to advance the development of more complex and differentiated legal institutions and activities. At the same time, the rulers wished to maintain control over these institutions and to keep them, as far as possible, from autonomous growth" (1963: 137). Rueschemeyer concluded that the emergence and development of a market economy and the resultant growth of commercial trade brought even greater reliance upon law and the work of legal professionals. The more transportation and commercial activity expanded the greater was the necessity for the development of trans-national modes of establishing stable economic and political relations and reliable agreements which generally involved the skill and inventiveness of the legal professional. The work of lawyers was crucial to the emergence and expansion of what Wallerstein characterized as the World Capitalist Economy (1979), despite the fact that many contemporary dependency theorists, including Wallerstein, give far less consideration to legal penetration than to economic penetration.

Although many contributors to modern debates over the nature of law and its relationship to capitalism and political power accept neo-Weberian or neo-Marxian positions, other analysts eschew both Weber and Marx. The challenging treatment of the development of the Western legal tradition by Harold J. Berman is perhaps the outstanding contemporary example of this approach. Central to Harold Berman's excellent analysis of law and revolution is the argument that "legal institutions in the West developed continuously over generations and centuries, with each generation consciously building on the work of previous generations ..." Berman cited as exceptions "certain periods of revolutionary change ..." But, he continued, "Even the great national revolutions of the past – the Russian Revolution of 1917, the French and American Revolutions of 1789 and 1776, the English Revolution of 1640, the German Reformation of 1517 – eventually made peace with the legal tradition that they or some of their leaders set out to destroy ..." (1983: 5). If one accepts these generalizations as characteristic of the development of Western law, it may be argued with countervailing plausibility that the apparently stable experience of Western law is not characteristic of non-Western law because concomitant stable development of many non-Western legal systems was effectively ended by military conquest and/or economic and cultural penetration and domination, commonly described as some form of colonialism. Berman's approach, discussed in his earlier works as well as his 1983 analysis (e.g., Berman, 1974), is, of course, contradicted in part by some of the neo-Weberian and neo-Marxist scholars he rejects in his concluding chapter in *Law and Revolution* (see, for example, for the former, Trubek, 1972, and for the latter, Anderson, 1974a and b).

The one group of modern scholars devoting considerable attention to the relationship of law and war are contemporary anthropologists (e.g., Bohannan, 1967). But for most, emphasis upon the conflict related behavior and disputes of primitive people or groups in underdeveloped nations far overshadowed the often close relationship of law and conquest among modern, technologically advanced nations. Bernard S. Cohn's analysis of law and change in north India is illustrative. He traced the transition in the manner in which the high caste Thakurs in Dobhi Taluka utilized law and legal institutions before and after British rule. He indicated that prior to British conquest, the Thakurs were not only high caste, but constituted the ruling class in the villages in the region. Law and legal institutions were instrumentalities of their governing role and, consequently, Thakurs valued dispute settlement procedures as useful to the maintenance of their political and economic ascendancy. Thus the prolongation of litigation was not sought in legal conflicts among high caste Thakurs and a tradition of paternalism was maintained in Thakur legal relations with lower caste Indians such as Chamars. All lower caste Indians were servants to the Thakurs, relegated to a position "little better than slaves" (Cohn, 1967). Thakurs stressed mediation in order to keep lower caste servants productive. Thakur emphasis upon the dispute settlement aspects of law during the era of their political independence in the kingdom of the Raja of Benaras was thus closely related to their overall political and economic goals as rulers.

When British imperialism extended to Benaras after the end of the 18th century, Thakur utilization of law and legal institutions changed dramatically. Law was no longer the instrumentality of Thakur political dominance. Ultimately, the British were constrained to develop a new legal system which would maintain stability. The British had initially tried to support the position of the Thakurs as the dominant caste in relation to lower castes by maintaining Thakurs as landlords while diminishing their political and military roles. The change in the position of the Thakurs brought about a dramatic change in the manner in which they utilized law. Because British law did not take into account caste differences and because Thakurs were no longer politically responsible for maintaining the stability of the kingdom aftter 1795, Thakurs systematically began using the courts to continue disputes rather than to settle them. In a manner similar to some contemporary American corporate litigants, the Thakurs often continued litigation until an economically weaker opponent, either Thakur or lower caste, was economically ruined. As Cohn described it, "there is apparently no quicker way of driving an opponent into bankruptcy than to embroil him in a lawsuit . . ." (1967: 154). The model for members of the previous ruling class was law as an economic weapon rather than as a means of limiting controversy. Cohn summed up the situation as follows:

> A wealthy Thakur who went to court looked forward to not just one quick case, but to a series of cases, appeals, adjournments, and counter appeals, through which a poorer competitor could be ruined. Since British procedure and justice appeared capricious to the Indians, someone with a bad case was as prone to go to court as someone with a good case. The standard was not the justice of his case, but his ability to outlast his opponents. It became a mark of pride among the Thakurs to outwit an opponent through the use of the courts and law, and the prestige of a family was tied to its success as a litigant and its ability to ruin its competitors in court . . ." (1967: 158–159).

But such an anthropological emphasis upon changes in the attitudes and behavior of the conquered towards law imposed by an imperialistic nation often ignores the concomitant legal purposes of the imperialistic nation itself. Cohn's work provides one of a few exceptions in the anthropological literature. Although Cohn's investigation was primarily devoted to analysis of changes in the law-related attitudes and behaviour of the Thakurs, he did recognize and report, albeit briefly, on the underlying legal goal of the conquerors, noting especially, that by 1795, Great Britain's East India Company extended its legal as well as administrative structure to Benares in order to insure "the full and regular collection of the land revenue . . ." (1967: 153).

Interestingly enough, an older generation of investigators, the analysts of late 19th and early 20th century imperialism, generally devoted far more attention to the impact of military conquest and economic penetration upon law than contemporary neo-Weberians, neo-Marxians, or "neutral" advocates such as Berman.

For example, among the contributors to comparative law in the late 19th and early 20th century, James Bryce provided an interesting perspective on the relationship of military conquest and legal development in his *Studies in History and Jurisprudence.* In it, Bryce wrote about ancient Roman and modern English law at a time when the British Empire seemed dominant. The introduction of the common law to India as a necessary and desirable part of British colonialism was the central assumption of his book. The tone of total superiority and self-confidence which characterizes Bryce's introductory comments provide a rather striking contrast to later 20th century analyses of the relationship of law to dependency theory or to related world economic systemic conceptions. Contemporary investigations of the interaction of law and societal attributes generally omit military conquest and political power as key influences upon the development of law. For Bryce it is a central, albeit occasionally understated factor. Thus he first referred to India as representing "the phenomena of contact between the *law of the conqueror and that of the conquered* on the largest scale and in the most instructive form."[2] Bryce treated the claimed superiority of the English common law as a gift to be bestowed upon the peoples of uncivilized nations. He summed up this approach as follows:

> . . . What the English have done in India is being done or will have to be done, though nowhere else on so vast a scale, by the other great nations which have undertaken the task of ruling and of bestowing what are called the blessings of civilization upon the backward races. Russia, France, Germany, and now the United States also, all see this task before them . . . (1901: 90–97).

Bryce's specific appraisal of the characteristics of Hindu and Moslem law (the latter was invariably referred to as "Musulman law") reflected the same strong British colonial orientation. After critical comments about such issues as the absence or weakness of Indian commercial law and the primitiveness and severity of punishment for crimes, Bryce stated that,

> . . . The conquerors have given their law to the conquered. When the conquered had a law of their own which this legislation has effaced, the law of the conquerors was better. Where they had one too imperfect to suffice for a growing civilization, the law of the conquerors was inevitable . . . (1901: 108).

Similarly, concerning the substantial codification of English law in India, Bryce wrote that

> . . . the work of throwing English law into the codified form in which it is now applied in India to Europeans and natives alike has been done entirely by Englishmen. In this respect also the more advanced civilization has shown its dominant creative force . . . (1901: 117).

Bryce concluded that legal systems based upon religion, although traditionally resistant, may rapidly collapse. Once again viewing European colonialism as inevitably victorious, he predicted the dominance of European law. The relationship of "European nations to those less advanced races over whom they are assuming dominion, and *all of whom will before long own some European master* . . ."[3] was predicted to be one of European legal cultural ascendancy (1901: 120–121).

The fundamental issue for Bryce was whether Roman law, exemplified in the civil law nations, or English common law would "prevail" throughout the world. Yet while Bryce emphasized the competitiveness of these "rival" systems of law, he acknowledged the possibility "that they may draw nearer". He suggested that,

> . . . The more any department of law lies within the domain of economic interest, the more do the rules that belong to it tend to become the same in all countries . . . (1901: 121–123).

James Bryce's chapter on the extension of Roman and English law "throughout the world" may properly be viewed in the 1980s as an unusually clear example of 19th century imperialistic pretentiousness. But it also contained a fairly complete summary of the findings of scholars of comparative law concerning the relationship of military conquest to the development of law in ancient Rome and in British India. Analyses such as Bryce's drew directly upon the work of a variety of investigators such as Sir Henry Maine. This whole body of historical inquiry is generally ignored by contemporary American commentators who treat "political jurisprudence" as a uniquely American approach and imply that issues like the role of military conquest and political power were largely ignored before the 1960s. Becker, for example, described contemporary investigations of the relationship of societal complexity to legal development as "explorations into a new area" (1970: 109) despite the fact that major controversies over issues of this sort had occured during the 19th century when Sir Henry Maine's hypotheses were subjected to searching intellectual scrutiny (Randall: 1918: 209–213). Among modern American scholars, this question has often been treated in the context of the relationship of societal complexity to the evolution of legal institutions. The contemporary contributions of Miller and Schwartz (1964) and Stuart Nagel (1962) are thus heirs to studies of the nineteenth and early twentieth century investigators. John H. Wigmore and his collaborators and students represent an intellectual bridge between the older group of investigators and the modern, but generally conventional, advocates of a "family of nations" mode of classifying national or regional legal systems (Kocourek and Wigmore, 1915, and 1918; Wigmore, 1928 and David and Brierly, 1978).

Neither the older generation nor newer generation of comparative judicial and legal scholars have definitely established the validity of either a law as conflict resolution basis or a law as instrumentality of power foundation for modern judicial systems and elites. But their research findings suggested sufficient contradictions to make desirable a systemic empirical investigation of the extent to which one or the other of these conceptions are most closely approximated in the judicial systems and legal professions of the nations of the world.

The key essentials of the law as conflict resolution conceptual framework comprise a modified version of Max Weber's ideal legal system. Conversely, the significant portions of the law as instrumentality of power framework consist of modifications of dependency theory and world economic system assumptions which give considerably greater emphasis upon law than dependency theorists such as Wallerstein. These conceptual frameworks are designed to integrate all major aspects of national judicial systems and legal professions, thus recognizing the linkage between basic assumptions about law and justice and the structure, procedures, and characteristics of the personnel of judiciaries and legal professions.[4] An excellent example of a 19th century attempt at such integration is provided by Weber in his classification of legal systems under three broad categories of governmental authority – traditional, charismatic, and legal. The elements of Weber's linkage are summarized in Table 2.1.

In order to clearly describe, distinguish, and evaluate the two conceptual frameworks, the key attributes of each of the major components of the frameworks, the rationales for these components, and some of their primary indicators are compared.

The first of these components embodies the nature of the foundation or basis of judicial authority. As noted in Table 2.1, central to Max

TABLE 2.1 Weber's Conception of the Relationship of Political Structure and Legal System[5]

	Types of domination (governmental authority)		
	Traditional	*Charismatic*	*Legal*
Obedience owed to	*Individuals* designated under traditional particularistic custom	*Individuals* considered to be extraordinary and/or endowed with special powers	*Enacted rules* made in accordance with objective universal standards
Law is legitimated by its	*Origin* in custom and tradition	*Origin* derivative from each particular charismatic leader	*Origin* in objective process determined itself by legal or constitutional standards
Nature of the judicial process and the manner in which judicial decisions are justified is	*Empirical-Traditional.* Case by case decision-making but precedent *may* or *may not* be invoked. Particularistic. Justified by custom or tradition	*Case Oriented but based on Revelation.* Particularistic and often idiosyncratic. Justified by revelation	*Independent and Universalistic.* Cases decided by formal rules and abstract principles and justified by the independence and universality of the decision-making process
Structure of the administration of law is	*Patrimonial.* Staff recruited through traditional modes, generally ascriptive. Duties allocated by discretion of master	*Structured Administration* Often ad hoc selection of staff on charismatic qualifications, with undifferentiated tasks	*Bureaucratic* Highly organized administration of law by well-trained professionals with a universally delimited jurisdiction.
Degree of discretion of ruler(s)	High	High	Low
Predictability of rules governing economic life	Low	Low	High

Weber's model is the assumption that law originates independent of non-objective factors. Thus, in neo-Weberian ideal legal systems the characteristics of judicial systems and legal professions are not determined by economic political and social forces. Instead, they are determined by impartial internal professional considerations. Conversely, a modified dependency theory-oriented conceptual framework assumes that the atributes of judicial systems and legal professions are determined directly or indirectly by economic and social forces, often described in terms of the needs of the world capitalist economy or its countervailing world socialist system.

Secondly, a neo-Weberian model, of necessity, would embody the assumption that judicial systems evolved or were created to incorporate and perpetuate dispute settlement peacefully on the basis of fair, objective and predictable principles and procedures. The obverse, based upon modified dependency theory assumptions, is that dispute settlement is often a secondary matter, while the underlying purpose of judicial systems and legal professions is to meet the needs of and defend the principles of the world capitalist economy (or its world socialist antithesis).

A third component concerns internal procedures and practices. Neo-Weberian judicial systems and legal professions presumably develop and utilize modes of procedure and decision-making which are independent of external institutional influences such as political parties, interest groups, the political branches of government, and religious organizations. In contrast, a countervailing dependency theory oriented conception would treat internal modes of procedure and decision-making as part of an overall governmental system designed to maintain and rationalize legally the world capitalistic economy or its world socialist counterpart.

Fourthly, a neo-Weberian approach to judicial decision-making posits objectivity and the absence of non-legal ideological influences, while a dependency based approach assumes that legal objectivity would be superceded by pro-world capitalistic (or world socialistic) ideological considerations.

The fifth component involves contradictory notions about the neutral or protagonistic roles of law. The neo-Weberian framework accepts the concept of law as a neutral arbiter of individual relations between equals. A dependency related framework views law as the protector of interests and institutions considered essential to the optimum functioning of the world capitalist economy or its counterpart, the world socialist economy.

Legal safeguards for contract and property rights *and* for non-economic personal liberties (human rights) are considered essential as the sixth component of the neo-Weberian conceptual framework. The countervailing dependency theory-based framework posits that while legal safeguards for contracts and property are essential for a world capitalistic system, non-economic safeguards are often considered expendable when the bourgeoisie has achieved effective control of a nation (Tigar and Levy: 1977).

The predictability and rationality considered vitally important as the seventh component of a neo-Weberian framework, may, as a matter of experience, be included in the countervailing conceptual framework. Tigar and Levy note, for example, that some absolute monarchs or other non-representative rulers have stressed legal predictability and rationality in order to encourage commerce and to gain the allegiance of the bourgeoisie (Tiger and Levy: 1977). But for the latter such predictability and rationality is not considered to be essential.

Consequently, it is not surprising that the eighth component of the neo-Weberian conceptual framework logically holds that judges and elite legal professionals are trained and socialized to develop goals of predictability and rationality. Conversely, such judicial and legal elites are trained and socialized to maintain and develop the world capitalist economy or its world socialist alternative in the dependency-based framework.

Max Weber had placed his major emphasis upon the relationship of the attributes of legal systems to capitalism. Thus, his original model did not deal meaningfully with the concept of a socialist legal system. While the October Revolution of 1917 occured before Weber's death, Weber did not alter his model legal system. One could infer that a socialist legal system represented a systemic failure because such a system, by its very nature and doctrinal emphases would obviously not create optimum conditions for the functioning of a capitalistic system. A neo-Weberian model is predicated upon an assumption of relative equality between the judicial systems and legal professions of all nations. Like Wilbert Moore's argument that "the world . . . is a singular system" because professionals in all nations generally have similar educational, economic, and ideological characteristics (1966), a neo-Weberian would assume legal and judicial commitment to the professional and bureaucratic standards basic to the eight components of the entire conceptual framework regardless of nation or ideology. Instead of Weber's original linkage of his ideal legal system with the creation of optimum conditions for capitalistic development, a neo-Weberian ideal legal system presumably would create optimum conditions for modernization. Indicators of modernization have generally been identified as rising levels of production and consumption, urbanization, the emergence of a money rather than a barter economy, the development and application of science and technology, advances in education, secularization, and the development of social, administrative, and political institutions based upon merit and evaluated performance rather than kinship or other ascriptive criteria (Beaver:1975). Although one may assume that a neo-Weberian would be inclined to identify capitalism as more conducive to modernization than socialism, many investigators of modernization reject or minimize such a relationship. Presumably, under a neo-Weberian conceptual framework an advanced socialist legal system might fulfill many of the requirements of such a framework as would an advanced capitalistic legal system. But the underlying assumptions basic to each conceptual approach suggest that if each system were constructed in accordance with its most divergent elements, quite striking differences would be manifested. The neo-Weberian approach would resemble an ideal conception of legal and judicial objectivity and fair play while its counterpart would represent a model of law as instrumentality of power. The striking differences between the models are made more clear by detailed examination of the rationale for and strongest indicators of the key components of each. The neo-Weberian relationships in Table 2.2 thus resemble a

TABLE 2.2 Attributes of the neo-Weberian conceptual model[6]

Components of the model	*Description-rationale*	*Strongest indicator*
(1) Nature of the foundation or basis of judicial authority	The Judicial system must be protected from short term political change and external influences in order to insure its objectivity and independence	Judicial institutions based upon constitutional rather than ordinary statutory authority
(2) Nature of the relationship between major branches of government	The Judicial system must be independent of other branches of government or external influences	Constitutionally required functional separation
(3) Nature of the tenure of justices and judges	Judicial independence and objectivity is assured when judicial tenure is guaranteed	Constitutionally protected tenure for life
(4) Inviolability of judicial salaries	Judicial independence is again safeguarded when salaries are inviolate	Constitutional prohibition on reduction of judicial salaries

TABLE 2.2 (continued)[6]

Components of the model	*Description-rationale*	*Strongest indicator*
(5) Nature of judicial selection standards	High standards are essential to insure professionally sound and objective decision-making	Highest quality professional training non-ascriptive standards
(6) Nature of the institutional procedures	Predictable institutional procedures are necessary to insure objectivity and impartiality in decision-making	Formal rules, universalistic criteria, and independence
(7) Nature of jurisdiction	Jurisdictional authority should be broad to provide the judiciary with significant governmental authority	Major jurisdiction provided in the constitution as well as statutes
(8) Judicial review	On matters of highest constitutional import, the highest appellate courts must exercise sufficient authority to determine the fundamental interpretation of that constitution	Full establishment and acceptance of judicial review
(9) Compliance with judicial decisions and orders	The judicial system cannot exercise full authority unless other appropriate branches of government enforce its orders and decisions and uphold its authority	Full enforcement of and compliance with judicial decisions and orders
(10) Regime stability	The judicial system is highly unlikely to retain its independence and objectivity in periods of serious political unrest	Fundamental political change by peaceful constitutional change
(11) Distributive justice	The judicial system is highly unlikely to administer justice objectively and independently in an unjust, class-stratified society	High standards and fair practices in economic, social, and political sectors
(12) Probity	The judicial system cannot maintain its independence and objectivity in a society characterized by bribery, nepotism, and conflicts of interest	Prohibition of bribery, nepotism, and conflicts of interest

TABLE 2.3 Attributes of the dependency-based conceptual model[7]

Components of the model	*Description-rationale*	*Strongest indicators*
(1) Origin of organization and purpose of the judicial and legal systems of nations	The genesis of the structure, purposes, and characteristics of judicial and legal systems is found in the requirements of the world capitalist economy (or its antithesis, the world socialist economy).	Core nations develop their judicial and legal systems independent of external influences, but in periphery and semi-periphery nations and territories, the judicial and legal systems are replaced or modified in accordance with core nation demands, world economy, and/or needs.
(2) Purposes of the judicial and legal system	A major purpose of each national judicial and legal system is the creation of conditions highly conducive to the operation of a capitalist world economy (or a socialist world economy).	The judiciaries and legal professions of core nations and of those periphery and semi-periphery nations and territories which are responsive to the legal needs of the capitalist world economy are heavily oriented toward providing legitimacy to the capitalist or socialist world economy and the heaviest emphasis in law is upon commercial and property related issues (or the goals of a socialist society). They are secular rather than religious oriented.
(3) The characteristics of judicial and legal personnel	The capitalist world economy requires that judges and lawyers be cosmopolitan and be part of an international community of legal professionals who maintain and protect the operation of the capitalist world economy or its socialist counterpart and, especially in underdeveloped nations, have more in common with the world economy of legal professionals than with their own countrymen.	In core nations and capitalist or socialist world economy oriented periphery and semi-periphery nations and territories, the highest ranking judges and most influential lawyers are products of a few influential schools, and constitute a world community of elite legal professionals whose work greatly facilitates the goals of the capitalist (or socialist) world economy.

framework for judicial and legal independence and objectivity, while the dependency-based relationships in Table 2.3 reject such objectives to stress power and expediency. Such frameworks may, indeed, caricature the real world of comparative legal and judicial systems where the differences between systems are often by no means as strikingly distinct. Thus while socialist legal systems would not be likely to fulfill the requirements of judicial independence detailed for neo-Weberian systems in Table 1, it is also unlikely that most capitalistic legal systems would meet the criteria for distributive justice. Conversely, capitalistic legal systems may, in actual doctrinal situations, develop doctrinal rationales which are expedient, economically and politically. The frameworks obviously are not descriptions of juridical and legal reality, but are designed to provide bases for systematic comparative cross-national investigation.

Just as Tables 2.2 and 2.3 are designed to provide characteristics of the key attributes of the two conceptual frameworks in terms of the logic of each of their internal organizations, so do Figures 2.1 and 2.2 provide preliminary conceptualizations of the relationship of each national judicial system and legal profession to other such systems and legal professions. These concepts each suggest that the legal systems are, in judicial and legal doctrinal, theoretical, and ideological terms, not only designed differently, but are counterparts of competitive world economic systems. This underlying competitiveness is made more explicit in the dependency-based preliminary conception, but is also implicit in the neo-Weberian preliminary conception. In this respect, the distinctions between the two conceptual models resemble but are, of course, not identical to the dimensions between socialist and capitalistic legal systems which are, on occasion, discussed candidly in scholarly critiques and polemical treatises such as V.A. Tumanov's *Contemporary Bourgeois Legal Thought.* Tumanov suggested that

> ... the bulk of the great political issues of the day, around which the ideological conflict between differing socio-political systems, social classes, states, and political parties revolves, all bear a clearly-defined legal aspect and often turn out to be problems of law.
>
> ... The criticism of bourgeois legal theory is something more than participation in a scientific controversy. It is part of the global conflict of two ideologies – the communist ideology and bourgeois ideology – a conflict that reflects the historical process of the transition from capitalism to socialism ... (1974: 8 and 11)

The notion that there is competitiveness between the legal systems of capitalism and socialism is one of a number of propositions about the nature of national judicial systems and legal professions which may be tested empirically. It is, of course, related to the more fundamental assumption that law and legal institutions were developed to provide objective institutionalized dispute resolution. If world economic and political systems consciously employ law, judicial institutions, and legal personnel as instrumentalities for the development and perpetuation of political, economic, and social objectives, law presumably would be classified as comprising attributes identified with the dependency theory-based conceptual framework. Perhaps a more compelling issue involves the reasons why law would be invoked as an instrumentality of power under certain circumstances or utilized as an institution for objective dispute resolution under differing circumstances. The

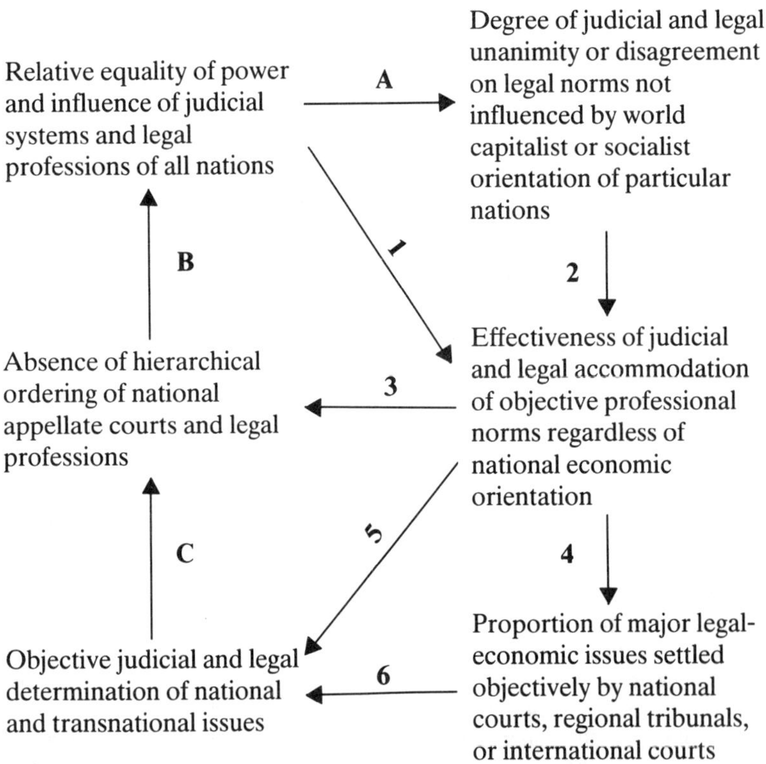

FIGURE 2.1 A preliminary conception of the judicial systemic and legal professional properties of a neo-Weberian world system of legal institutions

examination of such rationales is very important because a number of overarching conceptual examinations of legal systems explicitly or implicitly are based upon assumptions which have not been tested by means of detailed investigation of *negative* as well as *positive* evidence. One of the most sweeping of these conceptual examinations involves the often-stated distinction between "Western" and non-Western law.

Harold J. Berman's monumental analysis of the formation of the Western legal tradition quite appropriately rejects the tendency of many legal historians to exaggerate the distinctively national characteristics of law in Western civilization and to minimize the common feature of law in all "Western" legal systems such as English, French, Italian, Polish, Hungarian, and Russian (1983: 538–540). But

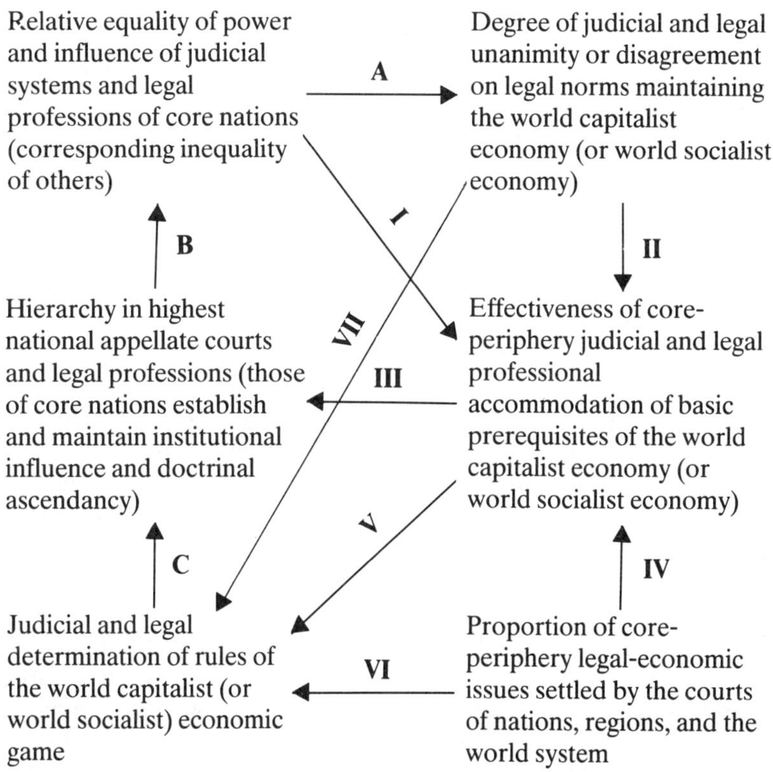

FIGURE 2.2 A preliminary conception of the judicial system and legal professional properties of a dependency based world system[8]

Berman's own criticism of these vestiges of "the exaggerated nationalism of the nineteenth century" (1983: 538) is equally applicable to those who explicitly or implicitly claim or suggest that the elements of law which are associated with peaceful dispute settlement, objectivity, and positive attributes of legal professionalism, and non-ascriptive selection of judicial and legal elites are largely associated with the Western tradition of law.

A close examination of the negative as well as positive evidence in an historic era identified by Berman as seminal to the development of this tradition suggests that within the West itself there are rather contradictory tendencies. The uses of law and religion by William the Conqueror illustrate the abundance of negative evidence as well as positive evidence.

An examination of the uses of law by William the Conqueror is especially suggestive of the need for investigation of non-legal sources as well as standard legal histories in the longitudinal analysis of legal elites and institutions in the context of neo-Weberian and dependency theory-based conceptional frameworks. Most legal historians emphasize the positive legal contributions of William the Conqueror. These include his support for and maintenance of the Truce of God as Duke of Normandy. Special legal historical emphasis has been placed upon William's preservation of Anglo-Saxon legal and judicial institutions after the Battle of Hastings and the conquest of England in the aftermath of 1066. Notable among the legal institutions and offices maintained in England were the office of sheriff and the traditional local shire and hundred judiciaries. Perhaps the greatest innovation which had a lasting impact upon England's long range contribution to the Western legal tradition was King William's policy of sending members of his own court, his *curia regis,* as itinerant justices to conduct important local trials in order to establish and maintain a law "common to the realm". His contributions also included some uses of trial by jury (Douglas, 1964: 273–309). William's contributions to the church and to specific traditions of authority such as the Truce of God (in Normandy, but *not* England), the authority of the Pope, and to specific monasteries and bishoprics are similarly often cited as part of the Conqueror's benefactions and authoritative support of religion. Combined with his own military and ducal and monarchical authority, William's support for law and religion has sometimes been viewed in the context of his era as enlightened and generous, providing reinforcement to important institutions in dangerous and unstable times. Presumably, there is some evidence for such a benign portrait.

But one has the impression that contemporary Anglo-Saxons may have had a considerably different view. The important point, however, is not whether William was beloved by those he conquered, but whether his uses of law and religion may be classified properly as meeting or not fulfilling the criteria of either a neo-Weberian model or a dependency theory-based model. A summary of those uses provides an interesting counterpoint to conventional historical evaluations.

Whether or not his origins as the bastard son of Duke Robert I of Normandy and the daughter of a tanner contributed to William's unusual emphasis upon the major institutions capable of bestowing and reinforcing legitimacy is a challenging psycho-historical issue. But it is clear that Duke William devoted a great deal of attention to law and religion as well as to the ducal and later, monarchical sources of legitimacy. His benefactions to the church and especially to those prelates and religious centers in Normandy, and later in England, which enhanced his military and political power and authority must be viewed in the context of an era in which the distinction between religious and secular authority was not very precise. Law similarly was closely related to both ecclesiastical and secular political authority. Thus, it is not surprising that William's most significant modern biographer, David C. Douglas, indicated that it would be rash to consider "such transactions simply as benefactions . . . or simply gifts" (1964: 114).

For example, in the period 1047–1066, Duke William not only tied the rising Norman aristocracy in his duchy to his leadership, but he assumed practical leadership of most institutions of the church. William's benefactions and secular and religious leadership of the Norman church helped gain him papal support against Harold of England and ultimately to provide a limited basis to attempt to make his attack on Harold resemble a crusade. At Hastings, Duke William marched under a papal banner and wore "consecrated relics around his neck". As Douglas put it, William's appeal for volunteers in the attack against the Anglo-Saxon king was made "in terms whereby a crude promise of plunder was buttressed by higher considerations of moral right" (1964: 188–189).

After defeating Harold at Hastings, Duke William constantly employed the forms related to legitimacy whether based upon the traditions of the predecessor Anglo-Saxon monarchy, Anglo-Saxon law, or papal or Norman church tradition. For example, despite the fact that the papal authorities wished to diminish secular political influence in church affairs, William increased such influence in the Anglo-

Norman kingdom and assumed the role of "priest-king" (Douglas, 1964: 256–7).

King William demonstrated a remarkable talent for plundering England and bestowing most of its lands upon himself and his largely Norman military and ecclesiastical aristocracy by invoking the established Anglo-Saxon legal forms and procedures to give the swift transition a sense of legitimacy. As his biographer put it

> ... A declared respect for legal precedent was thus paradoxically made to pervade the whole process whereby within a short space of twenty years a new nobility was given to England and this in part explains William's success in effecting so great a redistribution of land without provoking irreparable disorder ... (Douglas, 1964: 272).

In the period 1066 to 1086, only 8% of the land of England remained in the possession of the old Anglo-Saxon nobility or local leaders. King William himself took 20%, nearly 25% went to largely Norman church leaders (who in turn owed William feudal obligations including knights for military service), and nearly 50% went to his Norman leaders and to some Breton and Flemish supporters. A quarter of England was given to eleven men. William and his two half brothers owned nearly half of the land of England by 1086 (1964: 266–9).

By using Anglo-Saxon legal institutions and offices, William impoverished many Anglo-Saxons virtually destroying the old Anglo-Saxon nobility and reducing many Anglo-Saxon freemen to indentured servitude. The Anglo-Saxon legal office of sheriff was maintained, but the Norman aristocracy took it over virtually completely within a few years. William made the sheriff a royal agent and as such his new Norman appointees exercised the broad administrative and judicial powers that had been associated with the old Anglo-Saxon office. Thus, sheriffs collected royal revenue, executed royal justice, and controlled the traditional local shire and hundred judiciaries. Many Norman sheriffs enriched themselves by using the courts to seize property. Indeed there were instances involving the taking of church and monastery property where some sheriffs were brought to trial under William's authority (Douglas, 1964:298). But the use of Anglo-Saxon legal institutions to plunder Anglo-Saxons was the generally applied policy. New Norman legal penalties combined with Norman use of old Anglo-Saxon legal forms ultimately resulted in policies which were so brutal and avaricious that they represented regional genocide. The expulsion of approximately five hundred families for the creation of King William's New Forest in Hampshire was accompanied by brutal penalties for poaching thus depriving the dispossessed of a common source of food. Killing the King's deer was punishable by death; poaching rabbits or wild boar by blinding. In the twenty years after Hastings, it has been estimated that fully twenty percent of the Anglo-Saxon population was killed or starved to death (Howarth, 1977: 198). Biographer Douglas had, of course, underscored King William's leadership qualities, but he summed up his overview by writing simply that "William was stained with blood. But his avarice was almost equally repulsive" (1964: 377).

In balance, the uses of law and religion as instrumentalities to lend legitimacy to the plundering of Anglo-Saxon England, to the reduction to lower status of vast numbers of its people, and to the brutal reduction of its population by killing and starvation, clearly suggest that the regime of William the Conqueror belongs largely in the category of the dependency theory conceptual framework. Law was generally invoked as an instrumentality of power. Many of the institutions and forms of Anglo-Saxon justice were preserved, but standards of objectivitiy and fair play were often not maintained. The judicial and legal elite which was imposed by King William was obviously not chosen on the basis of professional training or merit, but ascriptively. This elite was also obviously not independent of the dominant political, religious, and social forces of the era. The uses of law as an instrument of power in the period of the Norman Conquest can not, of course, provide the basis for a total rejection of the conventional interpretation of law as dispute settlement. Nor can the invocation of law and religion by William to legitimize the plundering of Anglo-Saxon England be invoked to dismiss all the subsequent positive interpretations of the meaning and significance of the Western legal tradition. The evidence from the Norman Conquest does, however, provide the basis for challenging the often one-sided conventional interpretation of law, legal elites, and courts as impartial dispute settlement institutions.

That the era seminal to the development of the English common law was largely characterized by use of law as an instrument of power, does not mean that the entire evolution of that common law, one of the two major components of the Western legal tradition was characterized by use of law as an instrument of power, but it does suggest several challenging investigative propositions. What, if any, differences between Western and non-Western legal traditions can be found with respect to fulfillment or non-fulfillment of the standards for a neo-Weberian or a countervailing dependency-based model of law? For example, did a follower of Mohamed, such as Suliman the Magnificent, adhere to the neo-Weberian criteria with more fidelity than the Western William the Conqueror? Rigorous assessment of all major periods of significant change, Western or non-Western, whether characterized by conquest or revolution, can provide longitudinal evidence. Similarly, has legal imperialism been a characteristic dimension of the relationship of core and periphery nations in the nineteenth and twentieth centuries? What are the attributes of such imperialism as manifested by adherence to or rejection of neo-Weberian or dependence-based characteristics of the judicial systems and legal professions of the approximately 150 nation states in the mid-1980s? Are distinctions between world capitalistic or world socialist political and economic systems more significant in classifying legal systems than the classifications utilized in conventional "families of law" analyses? These are some of the most compelling issues awaiting comparative cross-national investigation of national judicial and legal systems.

NOTES

1. For example, is "judicial review" as ordained in the contemporary constitutions of Japan, West Germany or Italy conceptually equivalent to the American model? For a definitive analysis of the necessity for such a shift in emphasis see John C. Wahlke, "Policy Demands and System Support in Gerhard Loewenberg, ed., *Modern Parliaments* (New York: Atherton, 1971), pp. 141–171. Gerhard Loewenberg, assessing the empirical problems raised by the functional approach in comparative legislative research, states flatly that "unless the functional requisites of political systems are defined in operational terms which are equivalent cross-nationally, the concept cannot be used in comparative research . . ." In the same analysis, he also observed that ". . . whether any set of functions is performed in all political systems is itself an empirical question, which has hardly been raised, let alone answered . . ." Gerhard Loewenberg, "Comparative Legislative Research," in Samuel C. Patterson and John C. Wahlke, (ed.) *Comparative Legislative Behavior: Frontiers of Research* (New York: Wiley Interscience, 172), p. 11.

2. Italics added.

3. Italics added.

4. While these conceptual frameworks are either derivative of or related to the contributions of Weber, Durkheim, Wallerstein and others, strict conformity to their models or systems is not sought in this preliminary investigation.

5. This is a modified version of Table II, "Administration, Law and Economic Regulation under the Pure Types of Domination," in David M. Trubek, "Max Weber on Law and the Rise of Capitalism," *1972 University of Wisconsin Law Review*, p. 735.

6. Table 2.1 is reproduced from John R. Schmidhauser and Larry L. Berg, "Toward an Understanding of Mediterranean Legal Culture in the Contemporary World Capitalist Economy" in Carl I. Pinkele and Adamantia Pollis (eds.), *The Contemporary Mediterranean World* (New York: Praeger, 1983), p. 335; reproduced with the permission of the publisher and editors.

7. Table 2.2 is reproduced from Schmidhauser and Berg, *op. cit.,* p. 338, with the permission of the publisher and editors.

8. Figure 2.2 is reproduced from Schmidhauser and Berg, *op. cit.,* p. 342, with the permission of the publisher and editors.

References

ANDERSON, P. (1974a) *From Antiquity to Feudalism.* London: New Left Books.
— (1974b) *Lineages of the Absolutist State.* London: New Left Books.
BEAVER, STEVEN E. (1975) *Demographic Transition Theory Reinterpreted.* Lexington, Massachusetts: Lexington Books.
BECKER, T. L. (1970) *Comparative Judicial Politics: The Political Functioning of Courts.* Chicago: Rand McNally.
BERMAN, HAROLD J. (1974) *The Interaction of Law and Religion.* New York.
— (1983) *Law and Revolution: the Formation of the Western Legal Tradition.* Cambridge: Harvard University Press.
BRAUDEL, F. (1972) *The Mediterranean and the Mediterranean World in the Age of Philip II.* New York: Harper and Row.
BRYCE, J. (1901) *Studies in History and Jurisprudence.* London: Oxford University Press.
COHN, BERNARD S. (1967) "Some Notes on Law and Change in North India" in Paul Bohannan (ed.) *Law and Warfare: Studies in the Anthropology of Conflict."* Garden City: Natural History Press.
DAVID, R. and J. E. C. BRIERLY (1978) *Major Legal Systems in the World Today: An Introduction to the Comparative Study of the Law.* London: Stevens and Sons, Ltd.
DOUGLAS, D. C. (1964) *William the Conqueror: The Norman Impact upon England.* Berkeley: University of California Press.
DURKHEIM, E. (1958) *Professional Ethics and Civic Morals.* Glencoe: The Free Press.
EISENSTADT, S. N. (1963) *The Political Systems of Empires.* New York: Free Press.
GALTUNG, J. (1971) "A Structural Theory of Imperialism". *Journal of Peace Research* **8.**
HOWARTH, D. (1981). *1066 The Year of the Conquest.* New York: Penguin Books.
KOCOUREK, A. and J. H. WIGMORE (1915) *Primitive and Ancient Legal Institutions.* Boston: Little, Brown and Company.
— (1918) *Formative Influences of Legal Development.* Boston: Little, Brown and Company.
LOEWENBERG, G. 1971) "The Influence of Parliamentary Behavior on Regime Stability." *Comparative Politics* **3.**
MAINE, H. (1963) *Ancient Law.* London: Murray and Boston: Beacon Press.
MOORE, WILBERT E. (1966) "Global Sociology: The World as a Singular System." *American Journal of Sociology* **72.**
NAGEL, S. S. (1962) "Culture Patterns and Judicial Systems." *Vanderbilt Law Review* **16.**
PARSONS, T. (1960) "Durkheim's Contribution to the Theory of Integration of Social Systems" in Kurt H. Wolff (ed.), *Emile Durkheim, 1858–1917.* Columbus: Ohio University Press.

PEDERSEN, M. N. (1972) "Lawyers in Politics: The Danish Folketing and United States Legislatures" in S. C. Patterson and J. C. Wahlke (eds.) *Comparative Legislative Behavior: Frontiers of Research.* New York: Wiley-Interscience.

PREZEWORSKI, A. and H. TEUNE (1970) *The Logic of Comparative Social Inquiry.* New York: Wiley-Interscience.

RANDALL, H. J. (1918) "Law and Geography" in A. Kocourek and J. H. Wigmore, *Formative Influences of Legal Development.* Boston: Little, Brown and Company.

RUESCHEMEYER, D. (1973) *Lawyers and Their Society.* Cambridge: Harvard University Press.

SCHMIDHAUSER, JOHN R. (1982). "The Circulation of Judicial Elites: A Comparative and Longitudinal Perspective" in Mosche M. Czudnowski (ed.) *Does Who Govern Matter?* De Kalb: Northern Illinois University Press.

SCHMIDHAUSER, J. R., and L. L. BERG (1983) "Toward an Understanding of Mediterranean Legal Culture in the Contemporary World Capitalist Economy" in Carl F. Pinkele and Adamantia Pollis (eds.), *The Contemporary Mediterranean World.* New York: Praeger.

SCHWARTZ, R. P. and J. C. MILLER (1964) "Legal Evolution and Societal Complexity." *American Journal of Sociology* **70.**

TIGAR, M. E. and M. R. LEVY (1977) *Law and the Rise of Capitalism.* New York: Monthly Review Press.

DE TOCQUEVILLE, A. (1955) *The Old Regime and the French Revolution.* Garden City, N.Y.: Doubleday.

TRUBEK, D. M. (1972) "Max Weber on Law and the Rise of Capitalism." *University of Wisconsin Law Review 1972.*

TUMANOV, V. A. (1974) *Contemporary Bourgeois Legal Thought: A Marxist Evaluation of the Basic Concepts.* Moscow, USSR: Progress Publishers.

WALLERSTEIN, I. (1979) *The Capitalist World-Economy.* Cambridge: Cambridge University Press.

WEBER, M. (1947) *The Theory of Social and Economic Organization.* Glencoe: The Free Press.

WIGMORE, J. H. (1928) *A Panorama of the World's Legal Systems.* Washington: Washington Law Book Company.

PART II

SINGLE NATION ANALYSES: MAPPING THE BASES FOR SCIENTIFIC INVESTIGATION

Introduction

The need to provide empirical data upon which meaningful conceptually equivalent comparative cross-national analysis must be based is one fundamentally important reason for the portion of this volume devoted to single nation analysis. But the five chapters devoted to the investigation of the judicial systems, decision-making behavior, and doctrinal and political characteristics of Canada, Great Britain, India, Israel, and the Weimar Republic contribute far more than vital information. The authors address themselves seriously and frequently provocatively to issues related to the manner in which comparative judicial politics may be investigated. In Chapter 3, Professor Edward McWhinney provides an insightful appraisal of the "reception" of judicial review in Canadian law which comprises not only a (predominant) English common law component, but a constitutionally guaranteed French civil law component as well. A third important factor is, of course, the influence of the American institution of judicial review. His examination of the transformation of Canadian legal elite values and preferences regarding judicial review are instructive. Professor Henry W. Ehrmann, in chapter 4, describes the significant role played by judges who were products of the Imperial German Empire in undermining the democratic institutions of the Weimar Republic. His contribution is a significant addition to the comparative literature on what Otto Kirchheimer called "political justice".

Professor Martin Edelman's contribution, Chapter 5, delineates the significance of change in the highest appellate court of a new nation, the Supreme Court of Israel. The analysis of a non-partisan judicial institution in a young society beset by external enemies and occasionally racked by partisan and religious internal divisions is of intrinsic interest. Yet Professor Edelman has judiciously applied criteria of cross-national significance where pertinent. Drawing upon comparative cross-national literature rarely applied by judicial analysts, Professor George H. Gadbois employed Samuel Huntington's concept of institutionalization as the basis for an analysis of the Supreme Court of India. Here again the changing position of a highly influential Supreme Court in an occasionally turbulent young democracy is of great interest. Gadbois' application of the institutionalization approach provides the foundation for the development of conceptually equivalent judicial institutionalization criteria. Finally, in Chapter 7, Burton Atkins proposed an approach designed to comparatively assess the structuring of trial court outputs utilizing the British High court, a tribunal of general civil jurisdiction, as the setting for a preliminary test of his research design.

CHAPTER 3

JUDICIAL REVIEW IN A FEDERAL AND PLURAL SOCIETY: THE SUPREME COURT OF CANADA

EDWARD McWHINNEY, Q.C.
SIMON FRASER UNIVERSITY

Historical precursors of judicial review of the constitution in Canada: the Imperial (British) element

The popularity of judicial review as a constitutional institution is a post-World War II phenomenon, in Canada not less than in other countries. The influence of American constitutional thinking on judicial review, at that time, owed a very great deal to the political predominance of the United States at a time when many countries were engaged in constitution-making in the period of national rebuilding and reconstruction of the social and economic order following on military defeat or military occupation. Direct and overt American influences in West Germany and in Japan were to be expected, granted the American physical presence as the main Occupation power in the crucial formative years for the new constitutional system. They were less likely, perhaps, in the case of France with the hesitant steps under the Fourth Republic to a system of constitutional review through the institution of a standing legislative committee, gathering momentum under the Fifth Republic towards an independent, autonomous council.

What is often overlooked is that there was also a large-scale, if indirect, export of American constitutional ideas, after World War II, to countries that were neither occupied nor liberated by American arms. This latter process of peaceful "reception" of American constitutional ideas came about through the intellectual prestige of the US example in the immediate post-war years. It was a legal "reception" that also was immensely aided by the wave of Fulbright scholars and related graduate fellowship-holders who came to study at the major American Law Schools after World War II, much as in the "Dark Ages" scholars from Northern Europe had flocked to the North Italian universities in search of the new Enlightenment. It involved, in the cases of many countries, old and new, such a massive "reception" of American constitutional legal learning and legal ideas and thought-ways that it often displaced pre-existing local stereotypes and models.

In the case of Canada, the main influence and emphasis of legal studies up to World War II had been British, the English Common Law having been implanted by original settlement, conquest, and territorial expansion; though the French Civil Law had been conserved and guaranteed for the French-speaking enclave of Quebec through fundamental English-French political compromises reached after the final French military defeat at Quebec in 1759, the Treaty of Paris of 1763 and the Quebec Act of 1774 being the earliest and most notable of such political compromises. While students from French-Canada, understandably enough, directed their graduate studies in Law to European French universities and research centres, those from English-Canada preferred the universities in Great Britain. However, the widespread shift in the location of graduate legal education, supervening after World War II, from Great Britain to the United States, meant a certain "Americanization" of constitutional attitudes, supplementing and extending tendencies already there through the inherent logic of a federal constitutional system. We may thus speak, in the case of Canada, of an "original" English Common Law constitutional strain through the fact of British colonisation and conquest in the seventeenth and eighteenth century; a politically tolerated and constitutionally protected, but geographically regionalized or localized, French Civil Law strain; and a latter-day, "received" American constitutional element.

English Common Law constitutional thinking had always denied the concept of a judicially-based control of constitutionality as an alien, "American" legal idea; though, paradoxically, the American concept itself owes much of its historical inspiration to the seventeenth century English constitutional battles directed by the English Common Law judges and their Parliamentary allies against Royal Prerogative powers. Sir Edward Coke's early-seventeenth century rebuke to King James I and his legal advisers, that is rightly celebrated by British-trained

Common Lawyers is, in its way, as much an assertion of a judicial authority to override "unconstitutional" acts of the other arms of government as Chief Justice Marshall's lecture delivered two centuries later, to President Jefferson in *Marbury v. Madison,* on the obligations of Presidential executive restraint in regard to the other, coordinate arms of government. As it happens, the English Common Law judiciary in Great Britain itself, from the late nineteenth century onwards as British society moved increasingly towards acceptance of social democratic ideas, mounted its own continuing and often successful guerilla war of delaying action against collectivist ideas in legislation, parallelling in kind, if not in degree and intensity and certainly not in constitutional-legal expression (for it was all done through the guise of Common Law construction of statute law), the last-ditch struggle on behalf of economic *laissez-faire* maintained by the conservative majority on the United States Supreme Court up to the "Court Revolution" of 1937. All this raises, of course, some larger questions concerning the relation of judges to the social and economic values of the essentially middle-class, *bourgeois* groups from which they have tended to spring, such considerations lying beyond the scope of the present study. For present purposes, this form of what we might call English Common Law *indirect* judicial review was supplemented, historically, in the case of the countries of the old ninteenth century British colonial Empire, and of the later British Commonwealth (and still later un-prefixed Commonwealth) of independent, self-governing nations which succeeded to it in the early twentieth century, by the role of the Privy Council – the highest Imperial and Commonwealth tribunal, sitting in London – as guardian of the uniformity of colonial law and its compatibility with Imperial, British law. Applying Austinian, pyramidal concepts of the hierarchical subordination of colonial to Imperial, British law, the Privy Council also exercised a "watchdog" role over colonial constitutions and colonial constitutional law, in so far as the colonial constitutional charters were formally enacted as, and derived their formal legal authority from, statutes of the Imperial, British Parliament in London. When those colonies that had graduated, from the 1920s and 1930s onwards, to the legal status of independent Commonwealth countries, began to abolish – on the argument that it was an anachronistic vestige of their earlier colonial status – all jurisdiction of the Privy Council in relation to their national constitutions and their national laws – as Canada did in 1949 – the habit and practice of judicial review of the constitution remained, nevertheless, in those erstwhile colonies as a form of acquired custom, justified pragmatically and experientially if need be long after its original *raison d'être* and justification as an instrument of Empire had been forgotten or conveniently overlooked.

But judicial review, British Privy Council-model, differed in basic legal technique and method and what we might call, broadly, constitutional "style", from judicial review, American-model. It was, first of all, much less open and avowed as to its own creative, policy-making, "legislative" opportunities. It was also more inclined to insist on proper observance of procedural forms and on the existence of an adequate jurisdictional base or "interest" as a condition prerequisite to any constitutional ruling. It was always much closer to Justice Felix Frankfurter's respect for procedural etiquette, for example, than to the judicial free-wheeling of liberal activists like Frankfurter's colleagues, Justices Hugo Black and William O. Douglas. And the judges of the Privy Council, in comparison to their American Supreme Court colleages, consciously sought, and for the most part succeeded in maintaining, collegiality in their decision-making and also a substantial degree of judicial anonymity from public or professional criticism of their decisions.

The French, Civil Law element: impact of Quebec's "Quiet Revolution"

While the meeting of the two streams – British and American – of constitutional law, after World War II, has had important consequences for judicially-based constitutional review in Canada, by comparison the French Civil Law-based constitutional heritage has never been pervasive *qua* legal technique or legal process. The "French" constitutional influence has tended to operate, more directly, upon substantive legal values, and often through the political rather than the strictly constitution-legal processes. Such political-constitutional influences have been accentuated, in recent years, as a consequence of the "Quiet Revolution" in Quebec from the opening of the 1960s onwards. As French-Canadian latter-day nationalism mounted within Quebec, it found its political outlet in demands for maintenance and extension of the "French fact" within Quebec – of the French language and culture, of course, but also, and more importantly, in commerce and industry and labour within the Province of Quebec, hitherto controlled by a very small, English-speaking, Anglo-Saxon, monied élite. But the "Quiet Revolution" also sought self-determination in the larger, pan-Canadian context, basing demands – until the vanguard French nationalist elements later shifted direction to goals of outright succession or separation of Quebec from English-Canada – for recognition of a species of "special" or "particular" constitutional status within Canadian federalism, involving, at the institutional level, among other things an equating of direct French Quebec representation on the highest federal court, the Supreme Court of Canada, with that of all the nine other, English-speaking Provinces combined. This particular Quebec constitutional demand – equality of representation on the federal Supreme Court – bespoke a sophisticated, latter-day post-Legal Realist conclusion (not yet fully recognized in English-Canadian legal circles), of the extent to which, in a federal system in which the courts exercise constitutional review, the constitutional judiciary may become the ultimate political arbiter of the federal system and its constitutional divisions and allocations of law-making competence. In fact, such Quebec political awareness owed less to constitutional legal theory, and still less to any reception of modern American thinking on judicial review, than to one of those great switches or changes in appellate judicial philosophy that seem to occur from time to time within any court system, and that coincided, this time, in Canada more or less with the abolition of the appeal from Canadian courts to the Imperial Privy Council, in 1949. The Privy Council, as an alien, British (and quite often, in terms of its dominant judicial personalities, Scottish) tribunal, had a certain remoteness from the exigent here-and-now of Canadian political life and hence from early Quebec Government disputes with the then largely "Anglo-Saxon" -dominated federal government in Ottawa. Aided by somewhat casual historical events such as the presence on the Boards of the Privy Council summoned to decide Canadian cases in the late nineteenth century and the first decades of the twentieth century, of key personalities like the philosopher-judge Lord Watson, and the philosopher-turned-political-activist (and sometime Minister of War in the Asquith Government), Lord Haldane, who happened to hold liberal-pluralist philosophical and political ideas, the Privy Council tended to favour Provincial (States') Rights and hence the curtailment of federal governmental legislative intervention in social and economic matters, long after *laissez-faire* ideas had ceased to prevail at the ballot boxes in the federal elections held throughout Canada.

When the Canadian Supreme Court became final appellate tribunal in its own right, after 1949, it was a period when Keynesian economic planning ideas were dominant in governmental decision-making; and when the federal government arena, (rather than a plethora of different Provincial Governmental arenas), was the logical place in which to choose to bring such economic ideas into operation in political-governmental terms. The Supreme Court of Canada, with its judges wholly selected and appointed by the federal executive, uniformly favoured the federal government and the expansion of federal executive and legislative power in federal-provincial inter-governmental constitutional conflicts that happened to reach the Court. In addition, as a court of general appeal – for the private law, in addition to its public and constitutional law responsibilities – the Supreme Court of Canada had final appellate jurisdiction over the Quebec Civil Law; though with only a third of the Court's members being selected from Quebec, the awkward possibility always existed of decisions on appeals on the Quebec Civil Code being rendered by a Court two-thirds of whose members would be totally un-lettered in the Quebec Civil Law. The political inconveniences of this were perhaps more notional than real, as English Common Law judges could normally be expected to exercise political common-sense and hence self-restraint in Quebec Civil Law cases, and thus wisely to exercise self-restraint and defer to the views of their Quebec Civil Law colleagues on the Court, in deciding such cases. The failure, however, of the political arm of government directly concerned – the Canadian federal executive – to make appropriate legislative changes in the federal Supreme Court's jurisdiction so as to confer final appellate jurisdiction over the Quebec Civil Code to Quebec courts, in a matter that was surely of marginal importance only to the larger, national or pan-Canadian polity, suggests a failure in problem-solving capacity of the Canadian federal political élite and in the ability to make constitutional changes while they are still timely and before the political situation has become out-of-hand. The accompanying failure to address oneself to the larger problem of the federal Supreme Court's political role in exercising judicial review of the constitution in a plural federal society that has suddenly become politically self-conscious as to its bicultural, bi-national character, becomes politically understandable (if not excusable), in this same light.

"Reception" of American constitutional ideas on judicial review

The "reception" of American constitutional ideas began in the 1920s, when Canadian law school graduates first began to choose the Harvard

Law School as a centre for graduate legal education, in place of the erstwhile obligatory trek to Great Britain and its Inns of Court and its ancient universities. (The fact that Mr Justice Ivan Rand, perhaps the greatest of the Canadian Supreme Court judges, graduated from the Harvard Law School in its undergraduate, LL.B. programme, just before World War I, can be explained as a special case, Rand's home province, New Brunswick, not having any Law School at that time). After 1945, the opting for US Law Schools as the preferred choice for Canadian law graduates to perfect their legal skills, became the rule, with other US Law Schools like Yale, Columbia, Virginia, Michigan, and Berkeley beginning to emerge in their own intellectual right and to challenge Harvard's primacy. The massive switch, after 1945, from Great Britain to the United States, meant that Canadian Law graduates, and the professors who taught them in Canada, increasingly adopted US patterns of judicial reasoning and judicial opinion-writing, and also US models of Court organization and professional structure, in place of British ones. The late 1940s and 1950s happened to be a particularly attractive period in US legal education – one of intellectual confidence in one's professional skills, and also of a certain long-range optimism as to the ability to resolve community social and economic conflicts, rationally and equitably, by legal means and application of legal processes and ideas. The US Supreme Court of that same period was, perhaps, at the summit of its political popularity and prestige, as a result of the changes in judicial personnel and the introduction of a new, liberal activist group of jurists who were committed, in substantial degree, to ideas of sociological jurisprudence and of social control through law. The US "great debate" of the 1950s over the opportunities, and also the prudent limits, of judicial policy-making and of judicial activism in pursuit of community change, carried on among the judges appointed by President Roosevelt after the "Court Revolution" of 1937, was widely studied in Canada: and it is not surprising that the US Supreme Court, in its turn, was increasingly cited in Canadian Law Schools as a role model for the Canadian Supreme Court in its new status of final appellate tribunal for Canada in its own right, since the final abolition of the appeal to the Privy Council in 1949. Although, as late as 1953, the Chief Justice of Canada, Patrick Kerwin, could peremptorily dismiss counsel's attempt to cite US Supreme Court decisions before him, on the score that they were irrelevant to the adjudication of Canadian constitutional cases since founded on another and totally different constitutional system, the jurisprudence of the Canadian Supreme Court throughout the decade of the 1950s – what might be categorized, without exaggeration, as the "Golden Age" of the Court's constitutional decision-making – shews the unmistakeable imprint of US constitutional ideas. The vehicle for this American "reception" is the opinions of Mr. Justice Ivan Rand, already referred to. In stylistic terms and his gift for graceful and laconic literary expression, Rand resembles Mr. Justice Holmes; in substantive ideas on the reach of constitutional liberties, perhaps he resembles even more Mr. Justice Brandeis. Rand does not, however, refer, in his opinions, to either of these two US judges, whose views (in common with those of Learned Hand and Felix Frankfurter) he knew at first hand from his Harvard days; and indeed Rand does not acknowledge any US case law in reaching his majority or specially concurring opinions in the major civil liberties decisions of the 1950s. After Chief Justice Kerwin's earlier stern admonition against trying to invoke US authority, it might have been politically counter-productive and fatal to building judicial majorities in what were, often, close (5-to-4) decisions, to try to do so, in terms. It is an historical irony, however, that it was not until a decade after Rand's retirement from the Supreme Court that the first of the modern US-trained Canadian jurists, Justice (later Chief Justice) Laskin, was appointed to the Court; though the trend, once started, has continued thereafter. Paradoxically, Laskin seems to have been appointed, then, not so much for his particular philosophical approach to constitutional law – strongly favouring federal government authority in federal-State (Provincial) inter-governmental conflicts and the "centralizing" of governmental decision-making on social and economic matters, along the lines of the "Roosevelt Court" in the US after 1937, which Laskin had studied, at the time, as a graduate student at Harvard. Laskin's policy preferences were well enough known in the Law Schools, since amply evidenced in his academic writings over the years. But Prime Minister Trudeau, who made the initial appointment and then the subsequent promotion to Chief Justice, never seemed to take an interest in judicial "policies" as factors in judicial appointments, until belatedly, at the very end of his career as Prime Minister; and other considerations than "policy", for example, the recognition of the rising role of the Universities in constitutional development, and the very welcome (and long overdue) desire to widen the hitherto rather narrow ethno-cultural base for appointment of judges at the federal level, probably determined the choice of Laskin. There has been little attempt, until very recently, to lobby the federal government in favour of, or against, particular judicial candidates; though the first woman was appointed to the Canadian

Supreme Court shortly after the first woman was appointed to the US Supreme Court, and women's activist groups in Canada borrowed from the US experience to mount, for the first time, a sophisticated lobbying campaign in favour of their own, ultimately successful candidate. Supreme Court judges in Canada, with only occasional exceptions, over the years, like Rand, have remained unknown to the general public, and un-debated in public fora; and so it is not surprising that the judicial appointment process should remain anonymous too. The fact that the federal government, (and effectively the federal Prime Minister), conserves a constitutional monopoly over the appointment of Judges to the Supreme Court and all other federal courts, with absolutely no legal obligation to consult anyone as to the choices made, has helped to keep the appointing process an arcane one up to the present; though the enactment of the new, constitutionally entrenched, federal Charter of Rights in 1982, can be expected to bring new political pressures on the Court and, ultimately, on the selection and appointment of judges to the Court, as the great social and economic tension-issues of the day begin to arrive before the Court for the first time.

Contemporary dilemmas of judicial review on the Canadian Supreme Court

The Canadian experience with judicial review of the constitution since Canada's dispensing, in 1949, with the appellate review of the old Imperial Privy Council ("juridical decolonisation"), and since Quebec's "Quiet Revolution" of the post-1960 era ("juridical self-determination", within Canadian federalism) has some major implications for constitutional review in general, viewed here in terms of comparative constitutional legal science.

First, it may be suggested that judicial review of the constitution operates with especial difficulty when it is conjoined to a *general* appellate jurisdiction, comprising (as it does in Canada), review of the private law (in Canada, both the English Common Law and also the Quebec Civil Law) in addition to constitutional law proper. The demands in range and character of judicial expertise will normally be so great that judicial credibility, in technical and also political terms, can be maintained only with great difficulty. Judicial specialization, in the form of a special constitutional tribunal or jurisdiction, would seem desirable – either *de jure* as in West Germany, or *de facto* as in the

United States since the passage of the reforms of the US federal Judiciary Act of 1925.

Second, the general strains on the integrity of the judicial process and on its public acceptance are increased very markedly in the case of a plural society – whether plural-lingual, plural ethnic-cultural, or both. Indeed, there may be reason to doubt whether great political *causes célèbres* going to the basic premises *(Grundnorm)* of such a plural society can be effectively resolved by judicial arbitrament alone. Should such political problems more sensibly be left to other institutions of community problem-solving, – executive or legislative, -– or to constituent power itself, with the courts applying an enlarged concept of "political questions" to immunize themselves from the need to adjudicate in such cases? It may be suggested, on the empirical record since Quebec's "Quiet Revolution", that the Canadian Supreme Court has been neither very effective nor politically particularly helpful in resolving French-English conflicts within Canadian federalism, and that the Court might, with advantage, have applied judicial self-restraint by denying jurisdiction and leaving such inherently "political questions" to the executive-legislative arenas of government for political arbitrament.

Third, the public acceptance of judicial review – its legitimacy in political as well as constitutional terms, in an era of participatory democracy – would seem to require involvement of the other, coordinate, popularly elected institutions of community policy-making in the judicial selection or appointing process. This could imply, for example, direct election of the constitutional judges by the federal legislature, as in West Germany; or else confirmation or ratification of executive nomination of the judges by the federal legislature, as with the United States Senate's power of rejection of Supreme Court candidates. If the constitutional judges do not have that extra constitutional mandate flowing from direct involvement of the legislative arm of government in their selection, then it would seem prudent for the judges to eschew judicial activism and to exercise some jurisdictional self-restraint as to venturing into judicial legislation on political *causes célèbres,* (where angels and legislative majorities might normally choose not to tread). The Court's own jurisprudence, dramatically relaxing the requirements as to standing-to-sue and the minimum constitutional "interest" necessary for raising an issue before the Court, has hardly helped the Court in reaching such a politically prudent self-denying ordinance.

In sum, the constitutional "patriation" project of 1980–82 which, with the enactment of the Constitution Act, 1982, eliminated the last – by this time purely vestigial and symbolic – legal ties between Canada and Great Britain, a full half century after the Statute of Westminster of 1931 and Canada's attainment of full juridical sovereignty and independence, added to the Supreme Court's responsibilities and political problems, without doing anything to resolve the institutional dilemmas, already referred to, as to the judges' role in constitutional policy-making. For the Constitution Act, 1982, added to the Constitutional system, for the first time, an "entrenched" Bill of Rights, somewhat longer and more "bureaucratic" in language than the US and other major Western models but covering much the same range of older, classical liberal, political and civil rights. The anticipated flood of new civil rights litigation – just beginning to arrive at the Supreme Court's doors three years after the enactment of the Constitution Act, 1982 – will undoubtedly transform the Court's jurisdiction, very quickly, into that of a specialist, public law or constitutional law tribunal, from the sheer weight and number of the civil rights cases coming to the Court from now on. Yet the existing judges of the Supreme Court were, in the past and even up to the present, invariably appointed as "generalists", without specialist constitutional training or experience, and through purely informal selection processes that emphasized their political "neutrality" and their technical, rather than "policy", orientation in law. The issue of institutional reform, involving the Supreme Court and including the processes of judicial appointment, had been raised by Quebec, but was hardly discussed in the period 1980–82, because the pressures of political compromise on other issues in the "patriation" reform project effectively precluded any consideration of the concomitant necessary restructuring of federal institutions. It is clear, however, that new challenges to traditional English Common Law constitutional conceptions of judicial independence and freedom from institutional responsibility before counter-vailing executive-legislative authority, can hardly be avoided as the first major cases on the great social and economic conflicts of contemporary Canadian life arrive before the Court, under the Court's presently rather relaxed views on standing-to-sue and the constitutional "interest" necessary to invoke its jurisdiction which – very much more than modern US Supreme Court jurisprudence – reflect Dicey's late-nineteenth cedntury English Common Law ideal of encouraging every citizen to have his day in Court on any issue of constitutional-governmental power.

References

BEAUDOIN, G. A. (1982) *Le partage des pouvoirs.* Ottawa: Editions de L'Université d'Ottawa. (2nd edition).

– (ed.) (1981) *Mécanismes pour une nouvelle Constitution.* Ottawa: Editions de l'Université d'Ottawa.

DION, L. (1980) *Le Québec et le Canada. Les voies de l'avenir.* Montreal: Les Editions Quebecor.

HOGG, P. W. (1977) *Constitutional Law of Canada.* Toronto: Carswell.

LEDERMAN, W. R. (1981) *Continuing Canadian Constitutional Dilemmas.* Toronto: Butterworths.

McWHINNEY, E. (1982) *Canada and the Constitution.* Toronto: University of Toronto Press.

– (1981) *Constitution.Making.* Toronto: University of Toronto Press.

– (1969) *Judicial Review in the English-speaking World.* Toronto: University of Toronto Press. (4th edition).

McWHINNEY, E. (1979) *Quebec and the Constitution.* Toronto: University of Toronto Press.

RUSSELL, P. H. (1982) *Leading Constitutional Decisions.* Ottawa: Carleton University Press. (3rd edition).

SMILEY, D. V. (1980) *Canada in Question. Federalism in the Eighties.* Toronto: McGraw-Hill Ryerson. (3rd edition).

CHAPTER 4

JUDICIAL ACTIVISM IN A DIVIDED SOCIETY: THE RULE OF LAW IN THE WEIMAR REPUBLIC

HENRY W. EHRMANN
UNIVERSITY OF CALIFORNIA AT SAN DIEGO AND DARTMOUTH COLLEGE

The Weimar Republic, the first German experiment with democratic institutions, perished almost half a century ago. Yet the discussion about the factors that contributed to its demise and about the conclusions to be drawn from it, continues and not only in the Federal Republic where "Bonn" and "Weimar" are still compared and confronted. Since the early 1920s the role which the German judiciary played in the weakening of democratic institutions has often been described. Forty years later a German historian (Bracher, 1966) acknowledges that the fundamentally anti-democratic beliefs of a majority of judges provided an unbroken transition to the Nazi regime. During the years of Weimar, both the friends and the foes of the republic acknowledged the existence of an all-pervasive crisis of confidence *(Vertrauenskrise)* between the judiciary and broad sectors of the public.[1] Then as now the responsibility for the deep chasm has been attributed above all else to the obvious partiality of the courts in treating the political right and left in prosecutions arising out of revolutionary or counter-revolutionary plots or uprisings, the assassinations or the libeling of political leaders. The abrasive partisanship of many judges turned such trials into manifestations of "political justice" which Kirchheimer (1969) has defined as the "utilization of judicial proceedings for political ends". The trials shook public confidence in a republic obviously unable to defend itself against its enemies and to protect its supporters. The bench did little to prevent defendants and their attorneys from turning courtroom proceedings into effective political propaganda. Yet in 1926, hence during a period of temporary normalization, the then Chief Justice, Walter Simons, asserted in a much-quoted speech that the courts deciding civil and administrative matters were distrusted at least as much as the criminal courts.[2]

The Rule of Law – Transformed

The sapping of the *Rechtsstaat* – that German version of the rule of law – resulted from a changed attitude of the judges concerning their own role. During the days of the authoritarian German Empire the strictest positivism, the narrowest possible interpretation of legislation and executive rulings had been prevalent. Such a style of judicial decision-making satisfied the desire for certainty and security of the social groups with which the judges identified. But when the "Legislative Power" (to use Locke's term) had shifted to a fully representative institution, its output was viewed by the judiciary in a critical spirit. The search for literal meaning was discarded and an ever wider judicial discretion was exercised. I do not wish to suggest that in the tribulations which Weimar Germany had to face the judiciary could be expected to adhere to its traditional ways of decision-making. But in quieter times the great historians of English law have sketched the preconditions of permissible judicial discretion:

> "Discretion" is not of necessity "the law of tyrants", and yet we may say with the great Romanist of our own day that formalism is the twin-born sister of liberty. As time goes on there is always a larger room for discretion in the law of procedure; but *discretionary powers can only be safely entrusted to judges whose impartiality is above suspicion and whose every act is exposed to public and professional criticism.* (Pollock and Maitland, 1898:563 emphasis added)[3].

German judges had switched quite suddenly to the exercise of judicial discretion; they did so at a time when their behavior inside and outside the courtrooms gave rise to justified doubts in their impartiality and when they rejected public criticism as objectionable vagaries of the democratic market place. Hence forms and substance of judicial law-making under Weimar failed rather than served the premises of the rule of law; indeed it contributed substantially to its breakdown.

Almost from the beginning of the republic and increasingly so as each of the subsequent crises destroyed whatever political and social consensus might have existed, parliament was unable to fulfill its legislative functions. During certain periods an actual paralysis of legislative determination hid behind an apparent plethora of rule-making. Vaguely worded statutes concealed uncertain and frequently contradictory value formulation and expressed the raw input of interest groups. A lack of parliamentary confidence in the appropriateness of its own rules resulted in the frequent granting of indeterminate exceptions. The elected representatives extended thereby an invitation to the experts, be they judges or administrators, to determine the concrete meaning of all legislation. Unavoidably, the latter lost the generality and predictability, imminent in the rule of law.[4] Few if any modern democracies are free from such a muddling of roles. What made the situation in Weimar Germany pernicious was that an anti-republican judiciary took a position of outright hostility to a parliament which became progressively more impotent. The inflation of 1920–23 and the depression beginning in 1929 were only the most dramatic phases of a continuing development. Executive rule-making, whether based on the generalities of Article 48 ("Restitution of public order and law") or empowered explicitly by a Reichstag lacking a workable majority moved into the foreground even though, as a one-time Minister of Justice admitted (Radbruch, 1951:175), sometimes neither a true emergency nor the enabling law justified the decrees or ordinances. The extent of such practices emboldened a presiding justice of the Reichsgericht to declare (Lobe, 1925) that the *Rechtsstaat* had perished and that the definition and defense of the rights and duties of citizens had fallen to the judiciary.

The foremost technique which the judiciary resorted to in order to exercise an amount of discretion never practised during the Wilhelmine era was the wide use of the so-called "general clauses" *(Generalklauseln)*. These clauses had been incorporated at the turn of the century into the civil and occasionally also the criminal law (e.g. Articles 138, 157, 242, and 826 of the Civil and Article 54 of the Criminal Code); they all prescribed, with slight variations, the application of open-ended standards of good faith, good morals, public morality, etc., when viewing the interests involved in the settlement of legal disputes. These provisions had been available before 1918, but only in the 1920s did they, in the words of a foreign observer (Dawson, 1968: 415), begin "to blanket the legal order . . . In more and more sweeping terms (the standard of good faith) was described as a universal principle, pervading and qualifying all legal rules". "Having formerly been the stepchildren of the law, they [the general clauses] now became its darlings." (Neumann, 1957: 57).

Sweeping changes were acknowledged by a Supreme Court justice and one-time president of the national judges association writing in 1926:

> He who has lived, as a jurist, through the legal developments of the last three decades, knows which fundamental transformation has taken place in judicial decision-making. Instead of a logical and abstract way of thinking one conceives of law as something biological . . . one understands that right and equity are problems not amenable to (logical?) solution . . . And these have not been timid suggestions, but a real turning away from formalistic and mathematical concepts of the law. (Reicherl, quoted from Fraenkel, 1973: 111-112.)

The author's reference to a development reaching through three decades must be evaluated as a historical fabrication, at least as far as court decisions were concerned. In the first thirty volumes of published Reichsgericht decisions the "good faith" article (Article 242) was hardly ever mentioned. Only after 1919 did it become a core reference for a great variety of decisions.

It is true that before the war the so-called free-law school, a movement developed by liberal attorneys and a few professors of law outside the mainstream had pleaded for replacing the rule formalism of the German courts by the forcefulness and creativity of the common law judges. In his often sweeping and idealistic formulations Ernst Fuchs, the principal spokesman of the school, had insisted that evolving economic needs and above all the consensus of "reasonable and decent citizens" should be the judges' lodestar.[5] Under the monarchy the German judiciary had turned a deaf ear to such pleadings; its reactions to them were rather those of scornful contempt. But in the republic, when the consensus, invoked by Fuchs, was almost totally destroyed and the judges felt threatened by the "economic needs" of the society surrounding them, they adopted the methods of free interpretation.

The "general clauses" provided the means of introducing judge-made standards, described by court decisions as expressing the sense of justice prevalent in the national community or simply as corresponding to the judges' own feelings *(Rechtsgefuhl)* about what the law ought to be beyond the narrowly conceived edict of the legislature.[6] Policy-oriented considerations, based on barely hidden value preferences took the place of legal rationality. Since parliament could no longer be trusted or was actually unable to accomplish the proper balancing of interests, the courts took this task upon themselves in reaching their decisions in single cases. This means that judicial decisions became almost indistinguishable from administrative orders, again to the detriment of the rule of law, for which this distinction is essential. Moreover, while at least in principle, administrative discretion is exercised within the framework and subject to the control of the law under which the courts operate, the freewheeling decisions of the Weimar courts infringed upon the very system of positive law.[7]

COURTS AND CURRENCY CRISIS

It was with the help of the good faith clause that the Reichsgericht sought to master the legal consequences of the major economic catastrophy in post-war Germany, the run-away inflation. After some hesitations the court did so almost with brutality and fully conscious that it was arrogating to itself a role properly belonging to parliament.[8] For some years the judges had altered conditions of private contracts, affected by the currency devaluation, by applying to the mutual obligations the widely recognized principle of *rebus sic stantibus*. But for debts arising out of money loans, whether or not secured by a mortgage, previous legislation had prescribed that mark equalled mark and seemed therefore to preclude judicial relief when a debtor, at the height of the inflation, could discharge his debt by paying a pittance. In the fall of 1923, shortly after the stabilization of the mark, the Reichsgericht stepped in, declaring that the previous legislation violated the good faith principle and that in all cases brought before them the courts would have to "revalorize" debts according to the circumstances of the individual case.

Because of the inactivity of the legislator and its failure to protect assets widely held by the middle classes, the court's decision was not entirely unexpected. But the enormous consequences the decision would have was recognized immediately. More drastically than before, law was dissolved into individual court decisions depending on judicial discretion. Whether government and industry would be able to bear the massive re-evaluation of old mark-debts which the decision foreshadowed was doubtful. The just-achieved stabilization of the currency might be jeopardized. When rumors circulated that the government considered legislation to prohibit the re-evaluation envisaged by the court, one of the Reichsgericht's Senate Presidents, also the chairman of the Association of Supreme Court Justices voiced his, and presumably his brethren's protest in a scathing public declaration:

> When the highest court of the Reich, after careful consideration of the arguments for and against has come to such a decision (on the re-evaluation) it can expect that the government will not set aside the view taken by the court by fiat *(Machtspruch)* of the legislator.

The chosen term *Machtspruch* obviously sought to liken legislation by the republican government to the ukasses of the absolute rulers of the past. If the government wanted to muster its might *(Macht),* the declaration continued, the judiciary could be counted upon as defending the right *(Recht).* In somewhat veiled terms the statement concluded that if legislation was to violate the standards of good faith, the courts might refuse to apply it as an unconstitutional confiscation of property or as a discriminatory tax.[9]

Just after the Hitler *putsch* in Munich, the communist uprising in Hamburg, left-wing episodes in Thuringia and Saxony, the government felt too weak to rebuke the threatening judges with all the vehemence it had envisaged at first and which might have clarified what the republic expected from its judiciary. The duel ended in something of a stand-off. The Supreme Court refrained from annulling compromise legislation; a divided legislature and an unstable government never pursued any major reform which might have invited the outright censure of the high court.

Judicial review

When the spokesman for the Supreme Court justices uttered the threat that the court might invalidate a law, he touched upon one of the most controversial questions of public law under Weimar: the problem of judicial review. During the course of the nineteenth century the very concept of the German *Rechtsstaat* came to be identified with the denial of judicial review of formally correct legislation. After the German Empire was installed there was universal agreement that promulgation by the monarch bestowed final validity on any law. No court ever questioned its constitutionality. Where equality before the law was specifically guaranteed, as in the Prussian constitution of 1850, this did not bind the legislator to any controllable standards, but was considered an order addressed to the bureaucracy in charge of administering the law; hence, equality after, rather than before, the law!

In the Constituent Assembly at Weimar conflicting viewpoints concerning the future relationship between parliament and judiciary left the question unresolved. A left-socialist (USPD) suggestion to entrust a parliamentary committee with the scrutiny of certain judicial decisions was rejected out of hand. The proposal by a liberal member, Ablass (DDP), to submit upon request by one hundred members of parliament the decision on the constitutionality of any law to the newly-formed *Staatsgerichtshof,* was also voted down.[10] The adopted wording of Article 102 ("judges are independent and are subject only to the law") amounted, in the opinion of some writers, to a deliberate non-decision on the problem.

The Reichsgericht did not wait long to depart from the tradition which had prevailed under the monarchy in matters of judicial review. As early as 1921 it observed in an off-hand remark (a typical *obiter dictum)* that the Reichsgericht in the past had "constantly" granted to "the courts" such a right, a remark which a prominent professor of public law characterized as a "fairy tale". The fact that the particular decision could have been reached without such a pronouncement was quite significant: the court obviously wished to announce that it reserved itself the role to act as a political arbiter between different political and social forces and their conflicting claims. After some uncertain wording in intervening decisions the Court, in a widely discussed decision of 1925, came out unequivocally in favor of judicial review. It argued that since the constitution did not specifically deny the right to the judiciary nor had entrusted it to anybody else, it was the right as well as the duty of *all* courts to scrutinize the constitutionality of legislation.[11]

The new course taken by the Reichsgericht was enthusiastically acclaimed by a majority of constitutional lawyers. They greeted it as a vindication of beliefs which they had expressed since (but never before) the establishment of the Republic as the very fulfillment of the *Rechtsstaat.* For Von Hippel judicial review was a check on the "absolutism of an abstract majority" in parliament and the vindication of a *true* constitution expressing the will of the people and not that of the parties. Von Biederstein in an address as rector of a major university spoke about "the struggle of the law against legislation *(das Recht gegen die Gesetze)".*[12]

The significance of the turnabout by the Reichsgericht cannot be measured by the frequency of cases in which federal legislation has actually been invalidated. It seems that the Reichsgericht itself never had any occasion to do so. However the specialized federal courts and some state supreme courts referred repeatedly to the recognition of a right to judicial review as established law. To what extent lower courts made use of the right to which the Supreme Court had entitled all of them, seems not to have been ascertained. Decisions by the Berlin Labor Court which refused to apply a provision of the new law on procedures in labor courts, because in the court's opinion it violated "unwritten constitutional law" were overturned on appeal. But it must not be forgotten that after *Marbury vs. Madison* more than half a century elapsed before another federal statute was invalidated in *Dred Scott vs. Sanford.* The foremost reason for the sparing use of the newly discovered right, at least by the Reichsgericht, was the inability or unwillingness of parliament to legislate forcefully. Between 1925 and 1933, and with only a two-year interruption, the government was controlled by right-wing parties. Moreover much (and after 1930 most) rule-making took the form of executive decrees which had always been considered subject to judicial control. The earlier opposition of the judiciary to the exercise of emergency powers had all but ceased when the presidential decrees bore the signature of the new President of the Republic, von Hindenburg.

Carl Schmitt in his discussion of the judiciary as guardian of the constitution (1931: 14–23) maintained that compared to the United States practice, the rights claimed by the Reichsgericht were modest and merely accessory.[13] Nonetheless when the social democrats re-entered a coalition government in 1928, they were concerned that hostile courts might use the powers which the Reichsgericht had extended to them to void reform legislation. The government therefore introduced a bill concentrating the right of constitutional review in a special *Staatsgerichtshof* (not unlike the Constitutional Court of the present Federal Republic). The bill disappeared in the turmoil of the ensuing years but not before having been criticized sharply by the journal of the liberal jurists, *Die Justiz,* by the trade unions and their legal advisors. They pointed out that minority rights, supposedly to be protected by judicial review, were secured by the constitution through political rather than juridical means. What was to be feared, they argued, (Neumann, 1929) was that in view of the ways in which the courts were interpreting the Weimar constitution, the formal recognition of judicial review by any, even a specially appointed, court would not alone hamper future reform legislation. It would also damage rather than promote the principles of the rule of law in a democracy. Under the given circumstances it would increase the politization of the judicial process and thereby further aggravate the existing crisis of confidence.

The Weimar Bill of Rights

The prolonged uncertainties of the legislature had been preceded by the ambiguities of the constitution of 1919. It was equally true that the origin of the Weimar Constitution coincided with the second high point of the bourgeois era and also "the Germany of 1919, which was then still viewed as the strongest fortress of continental socialism . . . sought through its basic rights (laid down in Part II of the constitution) to open the door for a new social order." (Kirchheimer, 1969: 71–72).[14] Whether and how these rights were to be implemented could determine the nature of the German republic. But parliament, too weak to legislate effectively, was also incapable of providing the implementation of the constitution and of lifting thereby the existing equivocation.

The interpretation, however, of the "Basic Rights and Duties of Germans" offered excellent opportunities for judicial activism to an assertive judiciary, anxious to throw its weight into the political balance. In fact, the greater the obstacles for the normal functioning of republican institutions according to the rules laid down in the first part of the constitution, the more emphasis was put on Part II. The very same year the Reichsgericht enthroned the principle of judicial review, it idealized Part II as a "shrine" *(Heiligtum)* of the German people. Even more ecstatic than the justices were constitutional lawyers such as Rudolf Smend, Erich Kaufmann, Carl Schmitt and others.[15] By 1927 more than one hundred decisions of the Reichsgericht had touched upon one or the other of the basic rights. The wording of the constitutionally granted basic rights was as broad as that of the general principles of the codes; it therefore left equally wide and possibly even wider possibilities for discretionary interpretation and the dispensing of substantive justice – as the judges understood it.

Only a few of the politically most relevant interpretations can be discussed here.

The wording of Article 153 guaranteeing private property and describing its possible limitations seemed to give the legislator more leeway for restricting property rights than other European constitutions. But decisions of the Reichsgericht first proceeded to enlarge the concept of protected property in line with the doctrine of a respected professor of civil law so as to include the total assets of persons and corporations. They then limited the conditions under which the state can take over property without indemnification more strictly than had been the rule under the laws of the nineteenth century. Expropriation entitling to compensation included any interference with property rights, also those introduced in the public interest by general legislation.[16] Proposed anti-trust legislation, control of cartels and the projected reform of the coal and steel industries were therefore abandoned. From year to year the Court obliterated more completely the distinctions which the text of the constitution had drawn.

Whereas previously the principle of equality before the law, now guaranteed by Article 109, had served merely as a defense against administrative arbitrariness, it now became the yardstick for evaluating the appropriateness of legislation. As such it was used increasingly, though not always consistently, to discourage or limit changes of the economic and social status quo. Special interest groups invoked, most of the time successfully, the principle of equality against attempts to alleviate existing injustices in the distribution of resources.[17]

The constitution had combined the freedom of association (Article 159) with the attribution of a special role to the organizations of capital and labor in the field of social and economic legislation (Article 165 whose wording betrayed another compromise between different traditions of social thought). In their interpretation of these articles the courts did not limit themselves to largely negative interventions as they did in regard to the defense of property rights and of equality. Instead the regular as well as the labor courts used the text of the constitution, subsequent legislation on collective bargaining and shop stewards and the civil code provisions on unlawful acts, to develop their own concept of industrial relations. Their construction of an existing plant-community involved a sharing by the workers of the "common" risks of the enterprise. Industrial conflicts were, in the main, viewed as a pathology. Not only secondary, but eventually all strikes whose strictly economic character could not be demonstrated were considered unlawful and possibly exposing the unions to damage suits.[18]

Viewing what had become of the constitutional promises, Otto Kirchheimer concluded sadly during the declining years of the republic (1969: 60)

> Thus the basic rights of the German people have on the whole not achieved the functions which basic rights should fulfill . . . Rather they have, through their opalescent ambiguity, significantly intensified that serious lack of

> political decision-making capacity which marks the agony of our contemporary political life. They have not provided the democratic state with that clear programmatic support which it and its organs needed more than ever before.

Of course, it was not the judiciary alone which caused such agony. But aided and abetted by representative scholarship the courts construed constitutional provisions, legislation and contracts in ways which frequently eviscerated the intent of constitution-makers, the legislator and the groups called upon to participate in rule-making. The courts therefore had a share in inhibiting reforms which might have lent vitality to the new institutions.

The estrangement between the judiciary and the public was aggravated by the fact that the trade unions, and probably workers in general, were out of sympathy with the new activist stance of the courts. In 1911, at a time when socialists viewed the efforts of the free law school rather favorably, because greater judicial discretion might bring progressive ideas into a reactionary legal system, Max Weber had warned (1956: vol. II, 512):

> It is moreover not certain that the classes which today enjoy only negative privileges, particularly the working class, can expect from an informal administration of the law those gains which the ideology of jurists attribute to it.

Instinctively workers distrusted and rejected as "rubbery", and of dubious value to them, the general principles of the codes giving much leeway to a judiciary which the workers considered hostile to their own interests. They believed to be better served by judicial formalism, especially after post-war legislation had granted them what Weber would have recognized as "positive privileges." The broad discretion used by the courts for interpreting the new labor legislation was resented as a threat even when a court decision favored the labor side. What the judges considered a new jurisprudence of equity was merely wantonness in the eyes of the workers and their spokesmen.

Whether or not this was a Lassallean legacy, the German working class had a fundamentally positive attitude towards the law as an institution, an attitude not shared by either the French or the British labor movement. But this was only an additional reason for feeling antagonistic toward judges whose administration of the law amounted, in the worker's eyes, to little more than a manifestation of "class justice". In his speech, the president of the Reichsgericht had acknowledged that this image of the courts' output was accredited widely and not easy to dispel.

The judges of the republic

The composition of the judiciary did not inspire general confidence. The transition from monarchy to republic had taken place without a change in judicial personnel. The first Minister of Justice of the Weimar regime, a social democrat, had threatened to resign if the immovability of judges would be tampered with. Accordingly, the constitution guaranteed the independence of judges and their life-time tenure in classical terms. This meant that the courts were settled with most of the judges and that had served under the monarchy; only attrition and retirement, the latter provided for solely by legislation, would create vacancies.

The judges that served under the Empire came almost without exception from the moderately well-off middle-classes. The ultra-nationalist fraternities to which they belonged during their student years, the reserve officer corps which they joined thereafter did not only shape their political orientation but also steered their professional career. In Prussia the chief justices and court presidents attained their high posts after having been previously, and usually for many years, prosecuting attorneys and under the direct control of the governments of the monarchy. In the somewhat sweeping characterization of Franz Neumann (1957: 45):

> The judge of this period exhibited all the characteristics of the class of his origin: resentment against the manual worker (especially when he was organized and well paid), reverence toward throne and pulpit, and, at the same time, complete indifference toward financial capitalism and monopoly capitalism. The judges represented the alliance between crown, army, bureaucracy, landlord and bourgeoisie.[19]

Military defeat and the fall of the monarchy, political disorder and the ravages which inflation inflicted especially on the class to which the judges belonged, plunged many of them into a grave psychological and intellectual crisis. Its consequences were for some a protracted mental reserve, for others an unforgiving hostility towards the republic.[20] Such feelings were not relieved by the fact that compared with its pre-war status, visibility and weight of the judiciary were enhanced in the republic. To have left behind the anonymity and caution of positivist and mechanistic jurisprudence, to have assumed the role of policy makers (even if mostly by barring policies), and to have presented themselves publicly as champions of citizens' rights against governmental regulation gave the judges an importance they did not have under the monarchy when they were outranked both politically and socially by the high bureaucracy.[21]

Those who joined the judiciary and the corps of prosecuting attorneys under the republic had mostly, though not exclusively, the same background as their older colleagues. Liberal jurists found the atmosphere in the courts and in the meetings of the judges' associations uncongenial. They considered their chances for a successful career generally unpromising since the staff of most Ministries of Justice, federal and state, which decided on appointments and promotions, was among the most conservative of the bureaucracies. The socialization of the future judges and prosecutors in the law schools and during their internship was about the same as it had always been, except for the teachings of a few professors at a few universities. If there were no longer reserve officers around, most fraternities were as exclusive, chauvinistic and reactionary as they had ever been.[22]

This resulted in political alignments and an ambiance on which some light was shed by a remark in the previously quoted speech by Dr. Walter Simons, the President of the Reichsgericht, a jurist considered more liberal and more "republican" than many of his colleagues. He stated that "in principle" *(an sich)* there were no "external" obstacles to a social democrat becoming a judge. "Internally" however such obstacles existed, presumably because of the social democrats' alleged commitment to an ideology of class struggle.[23] (The judge referred to a party which from the beginning of the republic until 1932 furnished the largest group in parliament!) At the same period another judge, himself a member of the small "Republican Judges' Federation" estimated (without indicating the source for his estimate) that five percent of the judges were loyal to the republic, fifteen percent were reactionary and the remainder "undecided". It is fair to assume that the latter shared with the reactionaries that "sceptical attitude towards the present state" which, as Dr. Simons admitted, could be detected in quite a few decisions. The Republican Judges's Association had reportedly 400 members as against 12,000 members in the "politically neutral" German Judges' Association.

To alter the existing situation, a group of prominent social democrats, generally known for extreme moderation, recommended at the party congress of 1925, hence at a moment when the republic seemed consolidated, that one should follow the example of the early

Third Republic in France and suspend the immovability of judges for a few months in order to purge the judiciary of unreliable elements.

The more the judges' partisanship was criticized in the press and in parliament, the more they and their spokesmen rebuked such criticism as unwarranted attacks on their integrity and professional honor. Under the monarchy the presumed neutrality of the judiciary had been described as an "existential deception" *(Lebensluge)*. Under the republic the fiction of a judiciary "above politics" was maintained, undoubtedly by some in good faith. But when courts tried, as they frequently did, to manipulate evidence so as to be able to ignore the political motives of right-wing defendants, neither good faith nor objectivity could be pleaded. In the words of the foremost students of the dissolution of the republic:

> One-sided political trials generated hatreds in those that had been treated unjustly, and in those that had been favored, cynicism and sceptical contempt for the judiciary. (Bracher 1966: 10–11).

The point has been made (Unger, 1976: 216ff) that the decline of legality in the Weimar Republic is but a prime example, a "concentrated setting", of trends that are at work in most if not all liberal democracies of our age. The decline of parliament and, partly as a consequence, the transformation of judicial adjudication into an ad-hoc balancing of contending interests without precise and predictable standards deprive, according to Unger, in many political systems the law of the generality, neutrality and autonomy which are essential for a working rule of law. But if this be the case, should not then the Weimar experience be a warning that, unless such developments are reversed, democracy cannot survive?

Conclusion

These parallels are misleading. It has been the point of this article that it was the deep crisis of confidence, "a state of war between people and judiciary"[25] which contributed to the downfall of the republic. In a society lacking in consensus, judges will always have difficulties in assuming their institutional role of first defining and then applying community values in concrete cases and on specific issues (Kirchheimer, 1961: 215). The German judges forfeited this role altogether when the most vocal among them, and a majority of those officiating in political trials, allied themselves or at least sympathized openly with one of the sides contending for political legitimacy. The exercise of broad discretion and unfettered judicial law-making, the claims to control the substance of the legislative output by applying unsubstantiated values, the restrictive interpretation of the constitution in the interest of some power group, in brief judicial activism, might be subject to criticism everywhere. In Germany such activism was destructive of legality because of the court's partiality.

"One of the most fundamental social interests", Benjamin Cardozo has written (1921: 112) "is that law shall be uniform and impartial. There must be nothing in its action that savors of prejudice or favor or even arbitrary whim of fitfulness". This test the Weimar judges failed in troubled times.

NOTES

1. The most impressive description of the crisis of confidence is provided by Schiffer, 1928. The author, a one-time Federal Minister of Justice, belonged to the moderate Democratic Party. He attempts to give a carefully balanced picture sometimes leaning over backwards in his defense of the courts. Just for this reason, the evidence he presents on judicial partiality is all the more devastating.

2. Simon's speech, published originally in 1926, is quoted here from Ramm (ed.) 1968: 100–107.

3. For many examples see Dessauer, 1928. The present article owes much information to this prescient and excellently informed essay.

4. See Unger, 1976. Professor Unger's discussion of the rule of law concept has been very valuable for the argument of this article, even though in the end I disagree with him about the significance of the Weimar experience.

5. For a summary and analysis of Ernest Fuchs' writings, see Hempl, 1978: 74ff. An early and balanced account of the goals of the Free Law school was presented by Kantorowicz, 1906. In the United States Professor Kantorowicz became best known for his criticism of the American realists, 1933–34, dealing in part with the problem of judicial discretion.

6. For a forceful justification of the new juridical style, see Isay, 1929. In concluding the author leaves it to the "tact" of the judge whether in a given case the difference between a legal norm and his inner feelings is so blatant that he must invalidate the norm.

7. For many telling examples see Dessauer, 1928. For an excellent theoretically oriented discussion, partly based on Dessauer's findings, see Unger, 1976: 189. Also Neumann's discussion, (1957: 54) remains highly valuable even though his emphasis on "monocapitalism" as a somewhat simplistic explanation for judicial behavior, was revised in Neumann's later writings.

8. The best account of legal developments accompanying the currency crisis is Dason, 1968: 465–475. Some of the most important decisions by the Reichsgericht concerning the impact of the inflation are translated together with a pertinent documentation, in von Mehren and Gordley, 1977: 1078–1095.

9. The "Manifesto" by the judges was published in Juristische Wochenschrift January 8, 1924. For a full documentation of the episode, see Hempl. 1978: 93–100.

10. This means that the USPD took the position which, for a short time, the French Revolution attempted to enact. The proposal submitted by Ablass corresponds to the practice the Fifth Republic introduced by constitutional amendment in 1976.

11. The landmark decisions of the Reichsgericht and the reactions they provoked are summarized in Anschutz, 1933: 370–375. Anschutz, author of the leading commentary on the Weimar constitution, remained one of the few constitutional lawyers critical of judicial review.

12. For von Hippel's statement, see Anschutz and Thomas, 1932: vol. 2, 556. For Marschall von Bieberstein, see Sontheimer, 1962: 92–93.

13. In part the author misunderstood aspects of the US practice. But it is also well known that Professor Schmitt wished to reserve the function of the guardian of the constitution not to the courts but to the president.

14. In his article, published originally in 1930, the author suggests that the Weimar basic rights did not amount to a compromise but rather attempted to fuse a variety of value systems.

15. I am not discussing here the question whether and to which extent this new emphasis was tantamount to a return to natural law concepts. Neither of the authors mentioned in the text nor any court decision I know of referred explicitly to natural law, possibly because this would have been too drastic a departure from the previously predominant positivism.

16. On the judicial and administrative treatment of property rights see Kirchheimer, 1969: 56–57 and especially the same author's first book, 1930.

17. For the controversies and their significance, see the excellent and judicious account in Anschutz, 1933: 505–527, 703–721. On the political significance of the debate on Part II of the constitution, see also Meinck, 1978.

18. The emerging doctrines on labor law and industrial relations, principally as developed by the Federal Labor Court, were criticized magisterially by Potthoff and Kahn Freund in articles reprinted in Ramm (ed.), 1966.

19. Bracher, who does not share Neumann's Marxist views, draws a similar picture, 1966: 10–12.

20. Fraenkel, writing in 1927 in an article reprinted in Ramm (ed.) 1968: 88–101, gives a realistic account of what he calls the mental crisis of the German judiciary after the First World War.

21. Many of the procedural reforms, discussed by Dessauer, 1928, had in fact enhanced the position of the judges in both civil and criminal matters. Further reforms

introduced by the conservative governments of the early 1930s strengthened this trend.

22. The similar analysis by Dahrendorf, 1964: vol. 3, 259–274, includes developments since the Second World War.

23. The episode is explained more fully in Schiffer, 1928: 53. After the social democrats had re-entered a coalition cabinet in 1928, Dr. Simons embarassed them by an ostentatious resignation from his post as Chief Justice.

24. See also the same author's more complete analysis, 1955: 192–198.

25. Words used in a statement by Professor Radbruch upon assuming the office of the Federal Minister of Justice, see Schiffer, 1928: 15.

References

ANSCHÜTZ, G. (1933) *Die Verfassung des Deutschen Reiches vom 11. August 1919.* 14th ed. Berlin: Stilke.

— and R. THOMAS (1932) *Handbuch des Deutschen Staatsrechts,* vol. II. Tübingen: Mohr.

BRACHER, K. D. (1955) *Die Auflösung der Weimarer Republik.* Villingen: Ring Verlag.

— (1966) *In Hannover, H. and E., Politische Justiz, 1918–1933.* Frankfurt: Fischer.

CARDOZO, B. (1921) *The Nature of the Judicial Process.* New Haven: Yale University Press.

DAWSON, J. P. (1968) *The Oracles of Law.* Ann Arbor: University of Michigan Press.

DAHRENDORF, R. (1964) "The education of an elite; law faculties and the German upper class," in *Transactions of the Fifth World Congress of Sociology,* vol. 3. Louvain: International Sociological Association.

DESSAUER, F. (1928) *Recht, Richtertum und Ministerialbürokratie.* Mannheim: Bensheimer.

FRAENKEL, E. (1973) *Reformismus und Pluralismus.* Hamburg: Hoffmann & Campe.

HEMPEL, N. (1978) *Richterleitbilder in der Weimarer Republik.* Frankfurt: Lang.

ISAY, H. (1929) *Rechtsnorm und Entscheidung.* Berlin: Vahlen.

KANTOROWICZ, H. (1906) *Der Kampf un die Rechtswissenschaft.* Heidelberg: Winter.

— (1933–34), "Some Rationalism about Realism," *Yale Law Journal,* **42:** 1240–53.

KIRCHHEIMER, O. (1930) *Die Grenzen der Enteignung. Ein Beitrag zur Entwicklungsgeschichte des Enteignungsinstituts und zur Auslegung des Art. 153 der Weimarer Verfassung.* Berlin: de Gruyter.

— (1961) *Political Justice.* Princeton: Princeton University Press.

— (1969) *Politics, Law and Social Change. Selected Essays.* F. S. Burin & K. Shell (ed.) New York: Columbia University Press.

LOBE, D. (1925) "Der Untergang des Rechtsstaats," *Deutsche Juristenzeitung.* **111** (Heft 1): 16–21.

MEINCK, J. (1978) *Weimarer Staatslehre. Eine Studie zum Problem der Kontinuität im Staatsrechtlichen Denken in Deutschland 1928–1936.* Frankfurt and New York: Campus Verlag.

NEUMANN, F. (1929) "Gegen ein Gesetz über die Nachprüfung der Verfassungsmässigkeit von Reichsgesetzer, "*Die Gesellschaft* **12:** 517–36.

NEUMANN, F. (1957) *The Democratic and the Authoritarian State.* New York: Free Press.

POLLOCK, F. and F. W. MAITLAND (1898) *The History of English Law before the time of Edward I.* 2nd ed. Cambridge: Cambridge University Press.
RADBRUCH, G. (1951) *Der Innere Weg. Aufriss meines Lebens.* Stuttgart: Koehler.
— (ed.) (1966) *Arbeitsrecht und Politik. Quellentexte 1918–1933.* Neuwied & Berlin; Luchterhand.
RAMM, T. (ed.) (1968) *Hugo Sinzheimer und Ernst Fraenkel, Die Justiz in der Weimarer Republi. Eine Chronik.* Neuwied & Berlin: Luchterhand.
SCHIFFER, E. (1928) *Die Deutsche Justiz.* Berlin: O. Heymann
SCHMITT, C. (1931) *Der Hüter der Verfassung.* 24th ed. Tübingen: Mohr.
SONTHEIMER, K. (1962) *Antidemokratisches Denken in der Weimarer Republik.* München: Nymphenburger Verlag.
UNGER, R. M. (1976) *Law in Modern Society.* New York: Free Press.
VON MEHREN, A. T. and J. R. GORDLEY (1977) *The Civil Law System.* Boston: Little, Brown.
WEBER, M. (1956) *Wirtschaft und Gesellschaft.* Vol. II. Tübingen: Mohr.

CHAPTER 5

THE CHANGING ROLE OF THE ISRAELI SUPREME COURT

MARTIN EDELMAN
STATE UNIVERSITY OF NEW YORK AT ALBANY

In the course of the 35 years of Israel's statehood, its Supreme Court has come to play an increasingly important political role. In 1948 it functioned very much like the House of Lords in the British system; its impact on the political process was on the margins rather than at the center. Now however the Israeli Supreme Court is beginning to exercise power akin to that of its American counterpart.

In its 1982–83 Term, the Court dealt with such issues as the religious-secular dispute involving the archeological dig at the City of David; the Government's limited supension of publication of an East Jerusalem (Arab) newspaper; the continued validity of the 1948 eviction of the Arab residents of Ikrit; and the right of Reform rabbis to perform marriages in Israel. When the Supreme Court decided these and similar issues it was obviously directly affecting public policy. Yet unlike its American counterpart, the Israeli Supreme Court is functioning as an important policy-maker in the absence of a written constitution. How the Supreme Court came to play this role tells us much about the nature of Israeli society as well as judicial statecraft.

I

Professor R. Taylor Cole (1974) has suggested a set of variables for assessing the political impact of constitutional courts. Professor Cole's schema permits a cross-cultural comparison that does not distort our understanding of the distinct features of the Israeli Supreme Court.

1. THE PRESENT ISRAELI "CONSTITUTION"

To this day, Israel functions without a formal written constitution. The Israeli leadership began with the belief that every modern state ought to have a written constitution. In addition they were seeking to comply with the terms of the UN Resolution which had called for the establishment of a Jewish state in Palestine.[1] Following Independence, the Provisional Government of Israel (14 May 1948–10 March 1949) called for an election of a Constituent Assembly to adopt a written constitution.

The attempt to adopt a written constitution foundered on the division between religious and secular parties about the role of Jewish religious law in the new State. That issue could not be resolved without doing irreparable harm to the much-needed consensus of all elements in the community. (Edelman, 1980a: 145–147). Moreover, many Israeli leaders – most notably Prime Minister David Ben Gurion – saw political advantages in a constitutionally unrestricted supreme parliament. The move for a formal written constitution was tabled. (Edelman, 1980b; Klein, 1971: 378, 382; Likhovski, 1971).

Because the Constituent Assembly was more representative than the Provisional Government, it was decided that the newly elected body would function as the supreme governing agency. Therefore the Constituent Assembly assumed the functions of a parliament; it became the First Knesset (Transition Act, 1949). Israel's constitutional arrangements are in large measure a product of the decisions of the Provisional Government and the 1949 Transition Law. Because of the stability of those institutional arrangements, it is possible to describe the country's "operative" constitution: Israel is a secular republic, with a theoretically supreme parliament (the Knesset), a powerful cabinet, (the Government) a largely ceremonial president and an independent civil judiciary.

2. THE ISRAELI POLITICAL CULTURE

The key political institutions of Israel, however, are not the formal governmental agencies but the political parties. Israel is a highly politicized society. The reasons for this go back to the Zionist Movement where most existing parties had their origins. They were voluntary associations formed to help bring the Jewish State into existence. Each Zionist group sought to influence the course of events not only by direct political action in Palestine and within the World Zionist Organization but also by establishing a network of institutions reflecting its own ideology. Since the establishment of the State, the extra-governmental element of Israeli parties has been reduced; it has not been eliminated. Most parties still provide their members with a variety of ancillary services – youth movements, health insurance, recreation and vacation facilities. And some party institutions – like the kibbutzim – are still all-enveloping. Furthermore, the creation of government agencies did not entirely displace the parties; many Israeli bureaucracies show excessive partisanship. Professor Benjamin Azkin's (1955: 509) statement is still accurate: political parties in Israel "occupy a more prominent place and exercise a more pervasive influence than in any other state, with the exception of some one-party states."

Moreover until May, 1977, Israeli politics was dominated by the Labor Party and its predecessor, Mapai. For the first 29 years of statehood, and indeed throughout most of the Mandate period (1918–1948), the Jewish community in Palestine was led by socialists. While the Mapai-Labor leadership were more pragmatic than doctrinaire, while they were never completely able to enact their party program, they were ideologically disposed to a state-run society. By design, the "House of Labor"[2] permeated all aspects of Israeli society (Medding, 1972; Perlmutter, 1970). The current Likud-led Government is seeking to change this pattern into a more liberal, market-oriented society. For the present, however, Israel remains a society thoroughly permeated by freely competing political parties.

In this political culture, overt partisan considerations are an inseparable element in the workings of the Knesset and the Government. Party discipline is exceptionally strong; the Knesset Member is expected to carry out faithfully the party's program as defined by its leadership bureau. The centralized, hierarchical nature of Israeli political parties all but insures a majority for a Government proposal. Despite the multi-party system, and despite the failure of any party list ever to obtain a parliamentary majority, decisions reached by the Government are rarely overturned by the Knesset. (Weiss and Brichta, 1969-70). As a result, Israelis expect that public policies emanating from these institutions will reflect the partisan concerns of the ruling coalition.

3. THE ISRAELI CIVIL COURT SYSTEM

With a keen awareness of their highly politicized society, the Israelis have taken great pains to insulate the judiciary from the political environment. The Judges Law (5713–1953) states that "A judge in judicial matters, is subject to no authority other than that of the law." The primary institutions of the civil court system are the Magistrates' Courts, the District Courts, and the Supreme Court.[3] In addition to the usual concern for the quality of the judges, both the composition of the Nominations Committee,[4] and the formal qualifications for judicial office (Baker, 1968: 204–206) bespeak an overriding desire to avoid any taint of partisanship.[5] Once appointed, the judges, of the Supreme and inferior courts, hold their offices until attaining the mandatory retirement age of 70.[6] Thus there was a decision early in the institution-building years of the State to protect the judges on the civil courts from outside influence. It was plainly a deliberate choice in a policy where virtually everything else was allotted on the basis of party affiliation.

This same concern has meant that judicial behavior is circumscribed by a series of informal norms designed to insure political neutrality and to project that image. The most obvious is the most rigidly observed: civil judges do not engage in politics. Individuals who find that prohibition is too constraining invariably resign their judicial appointments.[7] When in 1983 Prime Minister Begin convinced Supreme Court Justice Menachem Elon to stand as the Likud-backed candidate for President of Israel, the Justice publicly announced his decision not to participate in court cases during the brief period preceding the presidential election.[8] Justice Elon lost the election, and resumed his normal judicial duties, but even this did not satisfy all Israelis: "According to every accepted public test, and according to the sentence which Justice Elon imposed on himself during the campaign period, someone who has been proposed for such a high office by overtly political bodies should not serve on the Supreme Court." *(Ha'aretz:* 15 March 1983). As a result of deliberate political decisions and continuous judicial behavior patterns, the Israelis have succeeded in keeping their civil judiciary fully independent.

4. PUBLIC SUPPORT FOR THE CIVIL COURTS

The support for the civil courts in Israel, and hence their power and authority, is rooted in the public's respect for the "rule of law." From this perspective, law is seen as something quite distinct from politics. In politics, values and principles are perceived as instrumental tools for achieving certain results. Law is perceived as flowing from an impartial, objective analysis of principles. Law and politics are seen as distinct methods of conflict resolution. (Wechsler: 1959, 14–15). Functioning, observable judicial independence has meant that respect for the civil courts has become deeply implanted in the Israeli political culture. Although no survey data is available, all the indirect evidence supports this conclusion. Judges are frequently selected to perform tasks which are required to be non-partisan in both appearance and reality. They serve as presiding officers on a variety of special committees and tribunals such as the National Insurance Tribunal and Rent Tribunal. By law, a Justice of the Supreme Court, chosen by members of that Court, chairs the Elections Committee which supervises the fairness of Israeli elections.

Perhaps the best indication of the public's perception of the Supreme Court is the structure of the Israeli Commissions of Inquiry. They are created to investigate matters of current and vital public importance which require clarification. The most famous Inquiries were the Agranat (1974) and Kahan (1983) Commissions (named for the Presidents of the Supreme Court who chaired them). The Agranat Commission investigated the Government's actions before and during the 1973 Yom Kippur War. Largely as a result of its finding, Prime Minister Golda Meir and Defense Minister Moshe Dayan felt compelled to resign. The Kahan Commission investigated the Phalangist massacre of Palestinian civilians at the Shattila and Sabra refugee camps in Beirut. As a result of its finding that he did not exercise proper care (that he bore indirect responsibility), Defense Minister Ariel Sharon was forced to resign from that position.

The President of the Supreme Court appoints all the members of a Commission Inquiry and a sitting Supreme Court Justice must chair the Committee. Peter Elman (1971: 405) explained why these politically important bodies are dominated by the non-partisan judiciary:

> In view of the nature of a Commission of Inquiry, its tasks and functions, which call for public confidence, as far as humanly possible, *in its neutrality and freedom from party pressures and considerations,* it is very necessary that its members should be of the highest integrity and reputation and therefore proper that the power of nomination should reside in *the traditional repository of independent, objective and impartial decision.* [Italics added]

Precisely because of the rampant partisanship of their society, Israelis see the utility of independent, objective and impartial decision-making. Because the civil judiciary are seen as the institutional repository of non-partisan judgment, authority has flowed to their courts. That authority gives the Israeli civil judiciary, particularly the Supreme Court, considerable political power.

5. THE JURISDICTION OF THE ISRAELI SUPREME COURT

The Israeli Supreme Court has both appellate and original jurisdiction. As an appellate court, its jurisdiction includes civil, criminal, administrative, fiscal matters. The Supreme Court hears appeals from the District Court and such other institutions as the labor courts, workers' compensation boards and rent tribunals. As a court of first instance, the Supreme Court sits as the High Court of Justice. In this capacity it deals with matters in which it may be necessary to grant relief in "the interest of justice" and which are not within the jurisdiction of any other court or tribunal. In both its appellate and general equity capacities, the Supreme Court can consider matters within the jurisdiction of the various religious court systems only with regard to the jurisdiction of those court systems to resolve a particular matter.[9] In all its functions, the Supreme Court is the final, authoritative interpreter of the law of the State of Israel. (Courts Law, 5717–1957; Judges Law, 5713–1953).

6. ACCESS TO THE SUPREME COURT

The Israeli citizen has direct easy access to the civil court system. In 1979, a total of 671,313 matters were entered in these courts: 182,369 civil; 488,944 criminal (all types); 243,486 criminal (excluding minor traffic offenses). Of these, 4368 were entered in the Supreme Court. (Judicial Statistics, 1979: 5). In the 23-year period from 1956 to 1979, the number of matters entered on the Supreme Court's docket

TABLE 5.1 Supreme Court cases, entered, 1956, 1979

Type of matter	*Year* 1956	1979	*% increase*
Civil	313	1,990	635
Criminal	285	1,478	518
High Court of Justice	203	900	433
Total	801	4,368	545

(Government Yearbook, 5718–1957, 328; Judicial Statistics, 1979, 5)

increased by a staggering 533% while the population of Israel increased by 209%.

The growth in the Court's workload has accounted for the growth in the size of the Court itself. Cases are still usually heard by a panel of three Justices; only the more important issues are heard by a larger, uneven number of Justices (Courts Law, 5717–1957). But the larger case load noted above has required a gradual increase in the number of Justices. In the 35 years of statehood, the Supreme Court has gradually increased from 6 to 12 members.

No point of access to the Supreme Court is more important than its function as the High Court of Justice. In the exercise of its broad equity jurisdiction, the High Court is now receiving more than four times as many petitions as it did 23 years ago. In the highly centralized governmental system of Israel, and one that is highly politicized, the potential for arbitrary action by public officials is obvious. The High Court of Justice, by emphasizing the rights of citizens and other residents who have come into conflict with governmental agencies, has enhanced the judiciary's reputation for fairness and objectivity. That reputation has encouraged still more petitions to the High Court of Justice.

7. THE TREND OF SUPREME COURT DECISIONS: THE COURT AS POLICY-MAKER

In all its activities, the Court has extended its authority as policy-maker. As Jeffrey M. Albert (1969) noted:

> Yet despite the non-existence of a written constitution or bill of rights . . . the Supreme Court has begun to assert a significant constitutional function. In a number of important cases it has asserted the right to read legislation in the light of supra-statutory principles which are said to exist independently of the legislative authority . . . Rights to hearing and cross-examination have been required in statutory proceedings that did not provide such safeguards, and administrative discretion to deny licenses, to determine election lists, to register companies, and to censor newspapers has been substantially whittled down. When statutory language is equally susceptible to either of two readings, resort to a superstatutory standard is simply a technique of deducting the legislature's intent which does not involve wide use of the Court's creative power. But where a court adds requirements to a statutory scheme, as the Israeli court has done in the hearing and cross-examination cases, or when it bends language away from its ordinary meaning to conform to some superstatutory norm, as it has done in the administrative discretion cases, it has taken upon itself a much more significant function. [Citations omitted].

While the Israeli Supreme Court could use these means to extend its authority, there were obvious limits so long as it could not invalidate governmental actions for being unconstitutional. In the guise of "interpreting" legislative intent, the Court was bound by subsequent Knesset clarification. When the Court added procedural protections – whether by filling in "lacunae" or by transforming words into terms of art within the legal craft – it faced essentially the same limitations. For it must be remembered that in the classic debate between James I and Chief Justice Coke *(Fuller's Case;* 1607) about whether law was to be read by "natural" reason or only through the "artificial reason and judgment of law,"[10] the political sovereign won in the court of history (Dicey, 1885; McWhinney, 1969). The English judges *(Kruse v. Johnson,* 1898) may say "Parliament never intended to give authority to make such rules; they are unreasonable and ultra-vires." The Israeli Justices *(Altagar v. Mayor,* 1966) may say, "The Legislator well knows of the existence of the rules of natural justice." But in each country such rulings of the courts will prevail only so long as the political sovereign (the parliament) acquiesces.

In Israel, the authority of the Court, and its care in imposing only the most basic, most widely accepted values of natural justice has precluded Knesset reversal.[11] The Knesset's non-interference with the Court's judgments has been based on the perception of the Justices as neutral, impartial guardians of "the law." And this tradition of legislative respect for the judiciary had the practical political effect of adding still further to the Court's prestige and authority. Yet the Justices and commentators were well aware of the fragile political and legal base of the Court's actions.[12]

II

Because of the rampant partisanship within the political system of Israel, the demand for a written constitution had not died with the 1949 Constituent Assembly decision to transform itself into the First Knesset. A written constitution, by its very nature, would regularize procedures and define governmental powers. It would help ensure that the Government of the day would not simply act as it pleased. Moreover, a written constitution would undoubtedly contain a bill of rights articulating those fundamental human concerns which were to be beyond governmental authority in most circumstances. The support for a written constitution therefore transcended party interests; it was rooted in a concern for democracy itself.

Thus try as he might, Prime Minister Ben Gurion had not been able to kill the idea that a democratic Israel needed a written constitution. Towards the end of 1949 Ben Gurion's cabinet voted to postpone idefinitely the drafting of a constitution. Yet the Knesset's Constitution Law and Justice Committee continued to consider the issue. They were unable to resolve the matter, but it was too important to die in committee. The issue was referred to the full plenum where it was debated at great length. Ultimately, a compromise resolution was passed. On 13 June 1950, the Knesset agreed that a constitution would be built up, chapter by chapter, upon the enactment of Basic Laws *(Divrei Ha Knesset,* 1950).

Six Basic Laws – The Knesset (1958); Israel Land Administration (1960); The President (1964); The Government (1968); The State Economy (1976); The Armed Forces (1976) – were later enacted. But their relationship to other laws enacted by the theoretically supreme Knesset was unsettled. Israeli scholars frequently discussed the operative nature of Israel's "piecemeal constitution." (Rubinstein, 1967, Likhavski, 1968). In *Bergman v. Minister of Finance* (1969)[13] the Supreme Court forced the issue of Israel's constitution back onto its overt political agenda.

Dr. Aharon Bergman brought an action before the Supreme Court, sitting as the High Court of Justice, to block the implementation of the (Campaign) Financing Law of 1969. Dr. Bergman's complaint was that the law unfairly discriminated against new political parties because it provided governmental funds only for those parties represented in the outgoing Knesset. Specifically, he argued that the Financing Law violated the equality required by section 4 of The Basic Law: The Knesset.[14] Moreover, that section expressly provided that its provisions "shall not be varied save by a majority of the Members of the Knesset." In 1959, the Knesset had entrenched that provision still further.[15] Because the Financing Law had passed its first reading in the Knesset by a vote of 24 to 2 (a majority of the plenum would consist of not less than 61 votes), Dr. Bergman also argued that it plainly could not be viewed as an amendment to section 4 of the Basic Law: The Knesset.

In his opinion for all five Justices who participated in the case, Justice Landau agreed that the Financing Law was in conflict with the equality required by section 4 of the Basic Law: The Knesset. The absolute denial of funds to a new list constituted a major violation of equal opportunity in the democratic electoral process. Justice Landau acknowledged the absence of any provision in Israel's law which expressly authorized the Court to construe statutes in terms of the natural justice principle of the equality of all before the law. "Nevertheless, this principle that is nowhere inscribed breathes the breath of life into our whole constitutional system." *(Bergman v. Minister of Finance,* 1969: 562–3). It was therefore right and just, Justice Landau argued, for the High Court to use it in interpreting the law. On this basis the Supreme Court declared an Act of the Knesset void for violating a Basic Law. In a state without a formal written constitution, its highest court had declared an Act of the "sovereign" parliament unconstitutional.

The Court's opinion was a skillful amalgam of the conventional and the radical. It purported to be doing nothing more than using the principle of natural justice to interpret a "borderline case," "open to two interpretations." As noted above, this had become familiar Israeli judicial practice. Actually, without so much as a single comment, the Court had decided the case on novel grounds. It had applied its natural justice approach to a Basic Law and then used its interpretation to block the implementation of the subsequently enacted Financing Law.

Normally, Israeli courts adhere to the principle of *lex posterior derogat priori.* If the Knesset was the sovereign legal authority in Israel, each Knesset had the same unlimited authority as its predecessors. The duly enacted Financing Law, precisely because it was posterior in time, should have prevailed over any conflicting interpretation of an earlier law. Plainly, the Supreme Court had acted on the unarticulated premise that section 4 of the Basic Law had constitutional status and as such was superior to ordinary law.

The Court's silence left important theoretical issues unaddressed. Why were Basic Laws – which had been enacted by the same procedure as all other statutes – to be regarded as fundamental? Was their special status derived from their designation as Basic Laws? Was it derived from their lineage – the early debates about a constitution and the chapter by chapter compromise? Perhaps these questions gave the *Bergman* decision on "constitutional" dimension it did not warrant. Perhaps the key to that opinion was simply the fact that an entrenched provision had not been observed. If so, what gave one Knesset the authority to entrench provisions and thereby limit the freedom of action of its theoretically equal successors? The Justices had not attempted to resolve these issues.

As it stood, the *Bergman* opinion meant that the political leadership could only surmise the premises on which the Supreme Court Justices had operated. Yet to deal with the consequences of the *Bergman* decision – to replace the Financing Law held invalid – the Israeli political elite had to enter into serious discussion about the nature of a constitution for their policy.

Events proved that the *Bergman* decision was indeed a landmark case. It provided the catalyst for Israel accepting the principle that it ought to be governed within the parameters set by a written constitution authoritatively interpreted by its highest court. That theoretical consensus has not led to concrete action: Israel still functions with its same "piecemeal" constitution. Yet the agreement on principle has further enhanced the authority and hence the power of the Supreme Court. A series of events in the political arena indicates the transformation.

Two days before the High Court had rendered its decision in the *Bergman* case, the Minister of Justice had indicated that the time was approaching when the Knesset should complete the Israeli constitutional structure through its chapter by chapter approach. He indicated that his ministry was drafting Basic Laws on the Judiciary, on Human Rights, and on Legislation. Significantly, the Minister indicated that the completed constitution would not be superior, paramount law. The Ministry was acting on the premise that the Knesset, like the British Parliament, was the sovereign legal authority in Israel (Klein, 1969).

The Knesset too was operating on that theory. True, they amended the Financing Law to comply with the *Bergman* decision. Ignoring the decision was not possible in Israel. And the major Israeli political parties were simply unwilling to enter the forthcoming election campaign without public funds. Nor were politicians willing to re-enact the original law by the requisite majority specified by section 4 of the Basic Law: The Knesset; that would have made the major parties vulnerable to the charge that they favored playing with a stacked deck. So within two weeks of the *Bergman* decision the Knesset found a formula for providing campaign funds for new election lists as well as the established parties. Thus the Knesset once again complied with a Supreme Court's ruling.

Yet at the same time that the law was amended to bring itself into compliance with *Bergman,* the Knesset pointedly enacted a law by a 68–8 majority reasserting its *own* legal authority: "For the purpose of removing doubt it is hereby laid down that the provisions contained in Knesset Election Laws are from the date of their coming into effect valid for every legal proceeding and for every matter and purpose." (Elections (Ratification of Validity of Laws) Law, 5729–1969).

But within six years most members of the Israeli political and legal elites had changed their minds. In December 1975, the Government finally introduced the draft Basic Law: Legislation. It frankly acknowledged that it was proposing a "fundamental change." The "important innovation" related to the status of Basic Laws. Under the proposal, all Basic Laws were to be treated as superior to other Knesset legislation. The Supreme Court sitting as a special Constitutional Court, was to be authorized to nullify laws which conflicted with Basic Laws (draft Basic Law: Legislation, 1975, Introduction.).[16] After six years of study and much comment from Israeli and foreign experts, the Government had reversed its position. (Edelman, 1980b: 175).

While there were a number of factors involved in the Government's change of position (Edelman, 1980b: 175–176), none was more important than *Bergman* itself. That decision meant that the existence of a legally sovereign Knesset, unfettered by judicial review, was no longer an unquestioned truism. As Attorney General (now Justice) Shamgar (1974) noted, "That case pointed out that in the absence of some contrary legislative provision, the Supreme Court and perhaps every court of the country is bound to decide the question of the legality or validity of laws." It had become doubtful whether the legal *status quo* really safeguarded the continued acceptance of the principle of parliamentary sovereignty. "The developments accentuated by the *Bergman* case," the Attorney General maintained, "cast doubt on parliamentary supremacy and accelerated the readiness for legislative intervention in order to create more exact definitions." (Shamgar, 1974: 474).

In point of fact, the Government's draft would have resolved most of the remaining questions concerning the Israeli constitution and the Supreme Court's authority to interpret it.

The question – much discussed in the scholarly literature (Nimmer, 1970: 1227–1238; Rubenstein, 1968: 202-208; Likhovski, 1968) – about whether the Knesset could legitimately enact constitutional provisions was answered with a clear affirmative. The proposed Basic Law: Legislation explicitly authorized the Knesset to enact Basic Laws (draft Basic Law: Legislation, 1975: Chapter I, section 1). The source of that authority, however, was not discussed either in the text of the draft or in the official explanatory notes. The logical paradox created by giving one parliament the power to control the actions of its theoretically equal successors remained.[17] But less than theoretically ideal resolutions are frequent occurrences when constitutions are established.[18] Moreover, because Knesset enactment of Basic Laws had become the established Israeli practice, investing the parliament with continuing constituent power was certainly an acceptable resolution.[19]

The proposed Basic Law: Legislation also resolved the ambiguous status of the six existing Basic Laws. The *Bergman* decision had involved an entrenched provision of the Basic Law: The Knesset. Therefore some Israeli scholars (Likhovski, 1971: 90–103) had argued that *only* such entrenched provisions were to be regarded as superior to ordinary statutes. Other scholars (Rubinstein, 1968: 206–208) had argued that only fundamental provisions within the Basic Laws were to be given constitutional status. The proposed Basic Law: Legislation explicitly conferred constitutional status on all provisions of all six prior Basic Laws as well as future Basic Laws.

The Governmental draft recognized the great status of the Supreme Court and sought to utilize it in constitutional matters. Under the proposal, the basic mechanism for applying the higher law embodied in the Basic Laws was to be vested in the Supreme Court functioning as a Constitutional Court. The Constitutional Court was to consist of a panel of at least seven Justices selected by the President of the Supreme Court. Only the Constitutional Court was authorized to rule on the question of a law's constitutional validity. A legal provision declared unconstitutional was to be null and void. (Draft Basic Law: Legislation, 1975: Chapter I, section 12 and accompanying notes). In short, under the proposal, the Israeli Supreme Court, sitting as the Constitutional Court, was to be explicitly authorized to exercise judicial review like its American counterpart.

It was precisely on that point that most of the objections to the Government's proposal were focused. After the Draft was introduced by the Minister of Justice, the first to attack it was another leading figure of the Labor Party, the Speaker of the Knesset. In a letter to all Members of the Knesset, he criticized the proposal as an unwise denigration of parliament's legal sovereignty. The Speaker maintained that if the Draft were adopted, a group of non-elected judges would function as the Supreme Legislator instead of the 120 Members elected by – and politically responsible to – the people. According to the Speaker, the proposal would eliminate the distinction between law and politics and would lead to the eventual politicization of the Supreme Court itself. (*Jerusalem Post* International Edition, 23 June 1976.) And in a special symposium arranged by the Speaker and held in the Knesset building, Supreme Court Justice Haim Cohn also asserted that the proposal would assign an essentially political non-judicial function upon the Court.

Despite such opposition, the bill proceeded through the legislative process with strong support. Even the change in Government in May 1977 from a Labor-led coalition to a Likud-led Cabinet did not affect this support. Thus by May, 1978 even Justice Cohn perceived further opposition to be futile; he expected that the draft Basic Law: Legislation would soon be promulgated. (Edelman, 1980b: 176–177).

That expectation has not materialized. The reasons do *not* concern the substance of the proposed Basic Law: Legislation. The support which developed during the last fifteen years remains. Rather, concern is now focused on the substantive provisions of the draft Basic Law on Human and Civil Rights. Sections of that proposal have become controversial in the extreme. The Israelis cannot envision a written constitution without a bill of rights. In fact, much of the impetus behind the drive for a written constitution is linked to the demand for a formal bill of rights. The Israelis are unwilling to adopt a written constitution (as envisioned by the proposed Basic Law: Legislation) until they are assured that a bill of rights would shortly be added to the existing Basic Laws. (Edelman, 1980b: 178–179).

Thirty-five years of statehood, therefore, have not removed all the obstacles to a written constitution. In light of *Bergman* and the consensus surrounding the draft Basic Law: Legislation, however, the ability of the Supreme Court to continue as an important policy-maker is assured. Nor have the justices been hesitant in exercising their power. The Justices are deciding matters which the first generation of Israeli leaders believed to be within the exclusive purview of the elected branches of government.

The Supreme Court's impact on national policy is well illustrated by the way it intervened in the ongoing debate about settlement policies in Judea and Samaria (the West Bank). Acting in its capacity as the High Court of Justice, it ordered the Government to dismantle Elon Moreh within 30 days. That settlement had been established on land seized from 17 Arabs. The Government of Prime Minister Begin had given specific approval to the project. The Israeli Defense Forces had seized the land. The Chief of Staff had testified that the settlement would enhance Israel's military position in the Administered Territories. Moreover, the project was also in accord with the West Bank settlement policies of the Cabinet majority. Nonetheless the Justices who heard the case had looked behind the national security argument and found it wanting (*Elon Moreh* case, 1979). The Court's decision was obeyed by the Government.

Thus the prescient comment that Tocqueville (1835: I, 290) made a century and a half ago is now equally applicable to Israel: scarcely any political controversy arises that does not find its way, in some form, into the courts. The ensuing decisions in Israel, as in the United States, have important consequences.

III

In sum, in the highly politicized democracy that is Israel, authority has flowed towards its premier non-partisan institution – the Supreme Court built upon the tradition of respect for the "rule of law." The Justices began by insisting upon their role as interpreters – not creators – of law. Gradually the Justices began to use principles of natural justice to help them interpret the meaning of the Legislator. By carefully using that indirect form of judicial review only when abiding, consensual values were present, the Justices were not accused of abusing their discretion. They were not seen as using their positions to advance a special cause; they were perceived as the protectors of fundamental values. When at last, in *Bergman,* the Justices openly exercised judicial review, it became the occasion to confirm, rather than deny, their place in the political system. The boldness of the Justices' recent actions indicates that they well understand their stronger position.

NOTES

1. The Resolution on the Future Government of Palestine (The Partition Resolution) called for a constituent assembly in both the proposed Jewish and Arab states in order to draft written constitutions embodying protection for basic human rights. (U.N. General Assembly, Resolution 181, November 29, 1947; Part I, B. 10.)

2. This refers to the entire range of groups within the socialist-labor camp. They are now all politically identified with the Labor Alignment.

3. There are currently 106 Magistrates, 85 District Court Judges, and 12 Justices of the Supreme Court. (There are also 18 Traffic Court Judges and 19 Judges of the Civil Domestic Courts).

4. The Nominations Committee is chaired by the Minister of Justice, contains one other Minister selected by the Government, the President of the Supreme Court and two other Justices elected by the members of that Court, two Members of the Knesset selected by secret ballot (to mitigate the effects of party discipline), and two practising advocates elected by the Chamber of Advocates. The Nominations Committee decisions are by a majority vote and its selections are binding on the President of Israel who makes the actual appointments. (Judges Law, 5713–1953: section 5.)

5. The entire range of issues and the factors affecting the outcome are evident in the extended Knesset debate. *(Divrei Ha Knesset,* 1950: 2331–2450) (in Hebrew).

6. There is a Disciplinary Committee to insure proper behavior during this life tenure. (Baker, 1968: 206–207).

7. The most prominent recent example is the long term mayor of Be-er Sheba, Eliyahawu Nawi. He was a District Court judge before he resigned to become the Labor Party candidate for that municipal office.

8. Israeli Presidents are elected by a secret vote of the Knesset. Five members of the parties supporting Mr. Begin's Government took advantage of that opportunity to help elect the Labor candidate, Haim Herzog. This latest use of the secret ballot to negate party control emphasizes the importance of the secret ballot procedure in the nominations process discussed in note 4.

9. The religious courts of the 12 religions recognized by the State deal with divorce, alimony and certain other matters of personal status. (Edelman: 1980a).

10. "Then the king said that he thought the law was founded upon reason, and that he and others had reason as well as the judges. To which it was answered by me that true it was that God had endowed his majesty with excellent science and great endowments of nature; but his majesty was not learned in the laws of his realm of England, and causes which concern the life or inheritance or goods or fortunes of his subjects are not to be decided by natural reason, but by the artificial reason and judgment of law – which law is an act which requires long study and experience, before that a man can attain to the cognizance of it – and that the law was the golden metwand and measure to try the causes of the subjects, and which protect his majesty in safety and peace. With which the king was greatly offended, and said that then he should be under the law – which was treason to affirm, as he said. To whom I said that Bracton saith quod rex non debet esse sub homine, sed sub Deo et lege. (That the kings ought not to be under man, but under God and the law)." (*Fuller's Case,* 1607: 64).

11. The Knesset has indeed reversed Supreme Court interpretations which were not based on fundamental principles of natural justice, particularly on matters of major political concern to the coalition. Note, for example, the Knesset debates and actions on Supreme Court decisions touching upon the question of "Who is a Jew" in the State of Israel. (Kraines, 1976).

12. "The question is not one of interpretation, but of the supremacy of the Knesset and the finality of its determination in a law duly passed by it . . . the Knesset is supreme in the enactment of laws . . . Every law or part of a law which is passed by the Knesset must be enforced . . . the court can only interpret the law and can question neither its validity nor its contents." *Basul v. Minister of the Interior,* 19 P.D. (I) 337, 379 (1968) as translated by P. Elman, Comment, 4 *Is. L. Rev.* 567 (1969).

13. The English Translation, by Peter Elman is used for all quotations in this article. (Elman, 1969b).

14. "The Knesset shall be elected by general, country-wide direct, *equal,* secret and proportional elections . . ." [Emphasis added].

15. "The Majority required by this law for a change of sections 4, 44 or 45 shall be required for decisions of the Knesset plenary at *every stage* of law-making except on

a motion for the Knesset agenda. In this section "change" means both an express or an implied change." (Basic Law: The Knesset, section 46).

16. There is no official English Translation of this draft Basic Law. I have relied upon the translation of Rabbi Judah Kogen. I wish to thank him for his gracious assistance with the difficult task of translating technical, legal Hebrew.

17. From a theoretically logical perspective, the people should enact all constitutional provisions; in a democracy, the people are the ultimate source of all authority. Resort to the inherent constitutent power of the people would also enhance the significance and authority of the Basic Laws.

18. For example, the Constitution of the United States of America, the oldest current written constitution, was adopted by procedures which by-passed the provisions of the then existing Articles of Confederation. Hans Kelsen (1967: 194–221) maintained that the validity of the final norm in a national legal order cannot be derived from a still higher legal norm; it is invariably a political act whose validity depends upon its acceptance and effectiveness.

19. Investing the Knesset with continuing constitutional power, however, might enable a temporary parliamentary majority to entrench its particular policy objectives in the Basic Law. To guard against that potential abuse of power and to enhance the authority of all future Basic Laws, the proposal provided that all such laws must henceforth be enacted, at all stages of Knesset decision-making, by a majority of the full plenium. Ordinary laws require only a majority of those present and voting (and absentions are not counted). The Knesset could further entrench a provision by requiring a still larger majority. And under the proposal, there could be no implicit repeal or amendment of a Basic Law (draft Basic Law: Legislation, 1975: Chapter I, section 5 and accompanying notes).

References

(a) Cases

Altagar v. Mayor (1966). *Piskei Din* **(I)** 20: 29–33.
Bergman v. Minister of Finance (1969). *Piskei Din* **(I)** 23: 693–705.
The Elon Moreh Case (1979): Dwikat et al. v. The Government of Israel. *Piskei Din* **(I)** 34: 1–17.
Fuller's Case (1607). *Coke's Reports* **12:** 64.
Kruse v. Johnson (1898) *Queen's Bench* **2:** 91–100.

(b) Knesset Debates (in Hebrew).

Divrei Haknesset (1950) vol. 5: 1745.
Divrei Haknesset (1950) vol. 14: 2331–2450.

(c) Articles

AZKIN, B. (1955) "The Role of Parties in Israeli Democracy", *Journal of Politics* **17** (November): 507–545.
COLE, R. T. (1974) "The Political Impact of Constitutional Courts", *Notre Dame Lawyer* **49** (June): 953–1050.
EDELMAN, M. (1980a) "The Rabbinical Courts in the Evolving Political Culture of Israel", *Middle Eastern Studies* **16** (October): 145–166.

– (1980b) "Politics and the Constitution in Israel", *Statsvetenskaplig Tidskrift (The Swedish Journal of Political Science)* **3:** 171–181.
ELMAN, P. (1969a) "Comment", *Israel Law Review* **4** (October): 565–568.
ELMAN, P. (1969b) "Bergman v. Minister of Finance" (Translation), *Israel Law Review* **4** (October): 559–569.
– (1970) "The Commissions of Inquiry Law, 1968", *Israel Law Review* **6** (July): 396–416.
Ha'aretz (independent Hebrew language newspaper) "Editorial – 15 March 1983": 8.
Jerusalem Post International Edition (independent English language newspaper) 23 June 1976: 1.
KLEIN, C. (1969) "Comment", *Israel Law Review* **4** (October): 569–575.
– (1971) "A New Era in Israel's Constitutional Law", *Israel Law Review* **6** (July 376–397.
LIKHOVSKI, E. (1968) "The Courts and the Legislative Supremacy of the Knesset", *Israel Law Review* **3** (July) 345–367.
NIMMER, M. (1970) "The Uses of Judicial Review in Israel's Quest for a Constitution", *Columbia Law Review* **70** (June 1217–1260.
RUBINSTEIN, A. (1967) "Israel's Piecemeal Constitution", *Scripta Hierosolymitana* **16:** 201–215.
WECHSLER, H. (1959) "Toward Neutral Principles of Constitutional Law", *Harvard Law Review* (November): 1–35.
WEISS, S. and A. BRICHTA (1969/70) "Private Members" Bills in Israel's Parliament – The Knesset", *Parliamentary Affairs* **23** (Winter) 21–33.

(d) Books

BAKER, H. E. (1968) *The Legal System of Israel.* Jerusalem: Israel Universities Press.
DICEY, A. V. (1885) *Introduction to the Law of the Constitution.* London: Macmillan.
KELSEN, H. (1967) *The Pure Theory of Law.* Berkeley: The University of California Press.
LIKHOVSKI, E. (1971) *Israel's Parliament: The Law of the Knesset.* London: Oxford University Press.
MCWINNEY, E. (1969) *Judicial Review.* Toronto: University of Toronto Press.
MEDDING, P. (1972) *Mapai in Israel.* Cambridge: Cambridge University Press.
PERLMUTTER, A. (1970) *Anatomy of Political Institutionalization: The Case of Israel and Some Comparative Analysis.* Cambridge: Harvard University Center for International Affairs, Occasional Paper #23.

CHAPTER 6

THE INSTITUTIONALIZATION OF THE SUPREME COURT OF INDIA

GEORGE H. GADBOIS, Jr.
UNIVERSITY OF KENTUCKY

Institutionalization, "the process by which organizations and procedures acquire value and stability" (Huntington, 1968: 12), "is one of the grand themes in all of modern social science" (Polsby, 1968: 144–145). It was a concern of Aristotle, and in this century it has returned in different incarnations in the works of Sir Henry Maine, Max Weber, Emile Durkheim, and, of course, in Parkinson's Law. In the more recent past, the most influential contributor to the institutionalization literature has been Samuel P. Huntington, whose initial efforts at dealing with the concept appeared in 1965 in his seminal article "Political Development and Political Decay", and later became the centerpiece of his classic *Political Order in Changing Societies* (1968).

Students of judicial institutions are unlikely to be familiar with Huntington's conceptualization of institutionalization because, with one partial exception (Schmidhauser, 1973), specialists on courts have made no use of it. Proceeding on the assumption that there are neither persuasive theoretical nor empirical reasons why courts should not or could not be examined in terms of their level of institutionalization, this study will utilize Huntington's criteria in an effort to assess the strength of the Supreme Court of India. Huntington (1968: 12–24) spelled out four criteria for gauging institutionalization, conceiving each as a continuum: adaptability-rigidity, complexity-simplicity, autonomy-subordination, and coherence-disunity. The more adaptable, complex, autonomous and coherent an organization, the more highly institutionalized it is. The more institutionalized an organization is, the greater its amount of strength, viability, stability, capacity, and power.

It should be acknowledged that although Huntington's theory and concept of institutionalization have attracted much attention, not all of it has been favorable. Several critics have raised questions about whether the four components of institutionalization go together (Kesselman, 1970; Ben-Dor, 1974, 1975; Sigelman, 1979), i.e., whether one or more may decline while the others remain stable or even increase. The temptation to revamp Huntington's criteria has been resisted, and we will be content with assessing their adequacy for measuring the strength of courts as we go along and at the conclusion. But, while remaining faithful to his criteria, one must go beyond the operationalizations he offered for each of his components, in part because his are not uniformly clearcut, but more so because Huntington's major interest was the institutionalization of whole political systems, while ours is the capacity of the Supreme Court of India.

I. Adaptability-Rigidity

According to Huntington:

> The more adaptable an organization or procedure is, the more highly institutionalized it is; the less adaptable and more rigid it is, the lower its level of institutionalization. Adaptability is an acquired organizational characteristic. It is, in a rough sense, a function of environmental challenge and age. The more challenges that have arisen in its environment and the greater its age, the more adaptable it is. Rigidity is more characteristic of young organizations than of old ones. Old organizations and procedures, however, are not necessarily adaptable if they have existed in a static environment... So long as it is recognized that environments can differ in the challenges they pose to organizations, the adaptability of an organization can in a rough sense be measured by its age (1968: 13).

Thus adaptability deals with organizations enduring over time, overcoming challenges, surviving the disappearance of the first generation of its leaders, and surviving the loss of major original functions. Huntington suggests (1968: 12–17) that the adaptability of an organization can be measured in three ways: chronological age, generational age, and functional age.

CHRONOLOGICAL AGE

"The longer an institution or procedure has been in existence, the higher the level of institutionalization. The older an organization is, the more likely it is to continue to exist through any specified future time period" (Huntington, 1963: 13). Older institutions will have met and survived more challenges and will, therefore, be more apt to meet, adapt to, and survive other challenges in the future.

Although the Supreme Court began its life in 1950, the Court is a lineal descendant of illustrious forebears, and its ancestry can be traced back at least to 1862, when the High Courts of Bombay, Madras, and Calcutta began functioning. Thus, it can be said that the Supreme Court was not in all respects a new institution in 1950. The Court was not a radical departure from the past, and there were very few discontinuities in 1950 when the Court began functioning. Certainly the reader of the *Constituent Assembly Debates* (1946–50) would reach this conclusion, for the framers sought to build upon the judicial structures that had been functioning for nearly a century, and which were believed by the framers to have worked well. There was little support then, and little since, for any radical departure from what a century earlier was an alien system of administration of justice. Responding to charges by some that India's system of judicial administration was so British as to be unsuited to Indian conditions, the landmark *14th Report* of the Law Commission (1958, I: 24) reported that the élite opinion it surveyed revealed "with almost complete unanimity that the system which has prevailed in our country for nearly two centuries though British in its origin has grown and developed in Indian conditions and is now firmly rooted in the Indian soil".

The Supreme Court's jurisdiction is wider and its powers greater than predecessor institutions, but a large number of procedures and conventions from the past were inherited by the Court. The Court is a direct descendant of the Federal Court, which existed from 1937 to 1950. The latter was also a constitutional court, and, though it did not possess explicitly the power of judicial review which today's Supreme Court has, it had and rather robustly exercised the power to declare measures of the colonial executive *ultra vires* (Gadbois, 1964). Moreover, unlike most other Third World countries (Nwabueze, 1977), India held in 1950 an abundance of superbly trained and highly qualified indigenous lawyers and judges (most High Court judges were Indians on the eve of independence) capable of serving on the Supreme Court. Over the preceding century, High Court and, later, Federal Court judges, both Indian and English, had earned a reputation for independence, honesty and impartiality that became part of the institutional inheritance of the 1950 Court. Thus the Court inherited a great deal of legitimacy.

In other ways, too, the judicial system was well-rooted by 1950. The British had maintained a sharp distinction between the political and judicial institutions, with the result that the Supreme Court inherited also a large degree of autonomy. Most pre-1950 High Court and Federal Court judges were recruited from outside of the political arena. This convention was a very hard one by 1950 and has continued to the present. In sum, the Court did not have to start on square one in 1950, and is much older institution than the new name suggests.

GENERATIONAL AGE

"So long as an organization has its first set of leaders, so long as a procedure is still performed by those who first performed it, its adaptability is still in doubt" (Huntington, 1968: 14). Generational age, of course, is largely a function of chronological age. But there can be a gap between chronological age and generational age, and an organization may change leadership without changing generations of leadership. "One generation differs from another in terms of its formative experiences" (Huntington, 1968: 14–15), which would include background and socialization experience. It is unlikely there is another apex judicial tribunal in the world which has changed leadership more often than the Indian Supreme Court, for the current chief justice, Y. V. Chandrachud, is the sixteenth since 1950. This rapid succession of chiefs is a function of the working together of mandatory retirement at age 65 and the convention of the seniormost associate judge moving into the center chair when a vacancy occurs. The Court is an institution which has changed leadership often without a significant change in generations of leadership. Both the first chief justice and the present one share very similar socialization experiences. Both spent their entire adult careers in the law, i.e., spent their entire pre-Supreme Court careers first as High Court advocates, and later as High Court judges. Indeed, in terms of formative experiences, the leadership of the Court had been strikingly homogeneous. No chief had any noteworthy experience in public life except on a High Court. The explanation for this is only partly that there are constitutionally prescribed qualifications for judges. The Government constitutionally could appoint someone directly from the bar who had been overtly involved in active political life. The convention, however is to select associate judges from the High Courts, and chief justices from a category of one -- the seniormost associate judge of the Court.

There were two quasi-departures from this convention – the so-called "supersessions" in 1973 and 1977, but in both instances, the new chief was selected from the Supreme Court, and was not an outsider. Had Mohan Kumaramangalam been named chief justice in the early 1970s, as rumor had it for a while (Nayar, 1973: 16), this would have signaled a generational change, because although Kumaramangalam's background included lengthy experience as a High Court and Supreme Court advocate, and as Advocate-General of the State of Tamil Nadu, it included also years as a prominent member and a leading strategist of the Communist Party, and Kumaramangalam's political views would have clashed sharply with those of most of his colleagues on the bench. The supersessions, particularly the first one, were nonetheless major ruptures in terms of different procedures for determining Court leadership, and precipitated what can correctly be termed "succession crises". That the Court survived these crises is a sign of greater institutionalization.

FUNCTIONAL AGE

> An organization that has adapted itself to changes in its environment and has survived one or more changes in its principal functions is more highly institutionalized than one that has not. Functional adaptability, not functional specificity, is the true measure of a highly developed organization. Institutionalization makes the organization more than simply an instrument to achieve certain purposes. Instead, its leaders and members come to value it for its own sake, and it develops a life of its own quite apart from the specific functions it may perform at any given time. The organization triumphs over its function (Huntington, 1968: 15).

By these indices, the Court seems to be an adaptable organization. The Court has certainly survived a variety of environmental challenges, and can probably be said to have survived changes in its principal functions, although it could be argued that its principal functions have either not changed markedly, or if changed, have not been accompanied by the dropping of older tasks. Among the challenges the Court has survived include a period of authoritarian rule (the 1975–77 Emergency), Mrs Gandhi's famous election appeal *(Indira Nehru Gandhi,* 1976),[1] the 42nd Amendment of the Constitution (an institution-threatening enactment during the Emergency aimed at reducing the power of the Court), more than a dozen other court-curbing amendments, and the two supersessions. The list might also include three recent national elections. The Court was an election issue in 1971, and after Mrs Gandhi's massive victory her Government enacted several amendments aimed at reducing the Court's power. The Court's response to the latter is found in the landmark *Kesavananda* (1973) decision, where the Court ruled that constitutional amendments which altered the "basic structure" of the Constitution were unacceptable, and proceeded to declare unconstitutional parts of a recent amendment which had sought to reduce the scope of judicial review. The 1977 election was another type of challenge in that the Court had to adapt for the first time to a non-Congress Government, but the Court adjusted with remarkable ease to that change in environment. The return of Mrs Gandhi in 1980 was another environmental challenge, although the Court may not have perceived that change as such, for it greeted Mrs Gandhi with the bold *Minerva Mills* (1981) decision, by which it struck down as unconstitutional two of the major features of the 42nd Amendment, enacted just before Mrs Gandhi's first regime departed in 1977. Declared unconstitutional were the parts of the 42nd Amendment that accorded parliament unlimited power to amend the Constitution and denied the Court authority to review the constitutional validity of amendments. The main messages of *Minerva Mills* are that judicial review is a basic feature of the Constitution, and that the Court will not tolerate its diminution beyond limits it finds acceptable. But, at the same time, the Court adapted to Mrs Gandhi's return by quietly removing from its docket the litigation against her and her son which had been filed after her defeat in 1977 (Rudolph and Rudolph, 1981).

The Parliament-Executive would argue that many of the various amendments affecting the Court were made necessary by the Court's own inability or unwillingness to adapt to agrarian reform and other economic and social reform measures. It could be argued that the protracted battle over these matters, which by the time of *Golak Nath* [2] (1967) saw the issue of property rights joined with the much larger one of institutional hegemony, could have been avoided had the Court been willing to make use of the ideology the Constitution provided, i.e., the Directive Principles of State Policy. In 1978, the 44th Amendment did move the right to property from the Fundamental Rights to a less exalted place in the Constitution, but in the process, the Court did not lose what in Huntingtonian terms was one of its principal functions.

The most alarming and ominous adaptability problem the Court faces today is the problem of arrears (Dhavan, 1977: 112–127; 1978; 1980: 92–108). Although the Supreme Court decides a large number of cases each year, the backlog continues to mount. By the end of 1960, there were 2319 cases pending; by 1970, the figure had climbed to

7104, and by 1978, the number of eight years earlier had more than trebled to 23,092 (Dhavan, 1978: 43, 51). The backlog in 1985 is over 40,000 cases, and the situation seems uncontrollable. In recent years, the Court has been accepting for hearing six times as many cases as it decides each year. Only 40% of its time is spent in deciding cases listed for final disposal. The remaining 60% is spent in admitting or rejecting new litigation. The Court is almost literally sinking under the weight of these arrears. The problem is a complex one, raising questions ranging from why the demands on the Court have increased so dramatically, to internal questions of jurisdiction, procedure, finance, and management. Here we shall focus on jurisdiction and procedure, leaving finance and management for consideration in our discussion of complexity-simplicity, and coherence-disunity.

Unlike the Supreme Court of the United States, the Indian Court does not have full control over its docket. From Dhavan's figures (1978: 29; 1980: 90), it seems that approximately half of the cases that come to the Court come as a matter of right, or are sent up to the Court by the State High Courts on the ground that such cases involve substantial questions of law which need to be decided by the Supreme Court. The other half arrive by virtue of the Court's special leave jurisdiction, i.e., the Court exercises its discretion to accept these appeals. Since the majority of the cases in arrears are special leave cases, it is evident that the Court has contributed to the problems of arrears by accepting far more cases than it can handle. The Court has behaved as if it is anxious to preserve its wide jurisdiction, and has not adapted to the flood of applications by evolving doctrines whereby it will consider only cases which raise a substantial question of public importance which require the Court's consideration. The problem of arrears is in large measure a result of the inability of the Court to innovate from within and evolve new doctrine limiting access to the Court.

II. Complexity–Simplicity

> The more complicated an organization is, the more highly institutionalized it is. Complexity may involve both multiplication of organizational subunits, hierarchically and functionally, and differentiation of separate types of organization subunits. The greater the number and variety of subunits the greater the ability of the organization to secure and maintain the loyalties of its members. In addition, an organization which has many purposes is better able to adjust itself to the loss of any one purpose than an organization which has only one purpose (Huntington, 1968: 17–18).

Of Huntington's four criteria of institutionalization, this is the least applicable to judicial organizations, for courts almost everywhere are small organizations, and are not usually characterized by hierarchical and functional differentiation. We propose to resolve this problem by utilizing as an indicator of the growth of internal complexity the growth of resources assigned to the Court in terms of personnel, facilities and money. This index of organizational complexity was persuasively used by Polsby (1968) in his study of the institutionalization of the US House of Representatives. Moreover, while matters of personnel, facilities and finance were not explicitly mentioned by Huntington, they are certainly implicit, for each clearly has a bearing on the increasing complexity of an organization. We shall also devote some attention to the divisional bench system employed by the Court to the extent that it represents a type of functional differentiation. Finally, we will discuss the Court's extremely wide jurisdiction in connection with Huntington's point that the more purposes an organization has, the more complex it is.

Concerning the matters of personnel, facilities and finance, it is again Dhavan (1978: 61–81; 1980: 108–119) who has done the groundbreaking research. The Court began functioning in 1950 with a sanctioned strength of 8 judges. At the request of successive chief justices, judicial strength was increased to 11 in 1956, 14 in 1960, and 18 in 1978. Thus, the number of judges has more than doubled. The total staff of the Court has increased more than seven-fold, from 79 in 1950 to 582 in 1977. During the same period, the Court's budget increased seven-fold also, from Rs. 911,000 in 1950 to Rs. 6,511,000 in 1977.[3] The symmetry of these staff and budget figures is explained by the fact that salaries account for about 80 percent of the Court's budget. During the first decade, there was also a symmetrical relationship between the increases in the number of cases instituted and the number of judges on the Court to deal with them; there were about 200 new cases per judge in 1951, and 229 per judge in 1960. By the late 1960s, however, the number of new cases per judge rose to 537, and by 1977, when 14,501 new cases were filed, the workload had increased to 1,035 per judge (Dhavan, 1978). Thus, on a per-judge basis, there was a five-fold increase in caseload between 1951 and 1977. The 14,501 new cases filed in 1977 represent a nine-fold increase over the 1951 figure (1602). During these years, the number of judges increased from 8 to 14.

More significant *re* complexity (and efficiency) is the fact that the judges have no research staff and no law clerks in the American sense.

The Court acquired one photocopying machine only a few years ago, and its first electric typewriter in 1983. At the beginning of 1978, the largest single category of Court employee, comprising 25 percent of all staff, was the peon, followed closely in number by junior clerical staff. Dhavan (1978: 66–67) provides a breakdown of the Court's staff, and it would appear that only a small fraction of the Court's employees would be in a position to be of any real assistance to the judges in dealing with litigation or preparing judgments. Even the library staff does not perform research functions. The picture one gets is that of an institution virtually without modern machinery and highly trained and skilled staff, i.e., the antithesis of a modern institution.

The divisional bench system raises issues more pertinent to our discussion of coherence (below), but it merits brief mention here in the context of functional differentiation. Unlike the Supreme Court of the United States, the Indian Court almost never sits *en banc.* During the 1950s, there were usually three benches functioning simultaneously, one to handle civil appeals, another for criminal appeals, and a third to hear constitutional cases. With today's larger court, there are generally 5 to 7 benches functioning simultaneously. The functional differentiation continues, but apparently not to the extent of earlier years. How much functional specificity there is among benches is difficult to say, largely because no one has examined this matter carefully. We do know that the chief justice makes bench assignments, and that some judges participate far more frequently than others (Gadbois, 1980; 1982), but it is not clear why. Moreover, the membership of the benches does not remain stable for periods longer than about six weeks.

The jurisdiction of the Court is so broad that it could lose functions and purposes and still have plenty to do and significant roles to play. The Court, it must be stressed, is not just a constitutional court, but also a court of general appeal. Indeed, constitutional cases are but a small fraction of its output, although some of them (*Kesavananda* consumed 69 days of oral argument before the full Court) take up an inordinate amount of its time. The Court's jurisdiction includes an original jurisdiction to enforce the Fundamental Rights, appellate jurisdiction in civil, criminal and constitutional matters, a discretionary jurisdiction to grant special leave to appeal in civil and criminal matters, and an advisory jurisdiction. The Court is obviously a multifunctional one. For Huntington, an organization with multiple purposes is stronger than one with few. But, for the Court, its multiplicity of purposes is more of a curse than a blessing, for there is an obvious relationship between the problem of arrears and the Court's broad jurisdiction.

III. Autonomy-Subordination

Huntington's third measure of institutionalization is the extent to which organizations and procedures exist independently of other social groupings and methods of behavior (1968: 20). Highly institutionalized organizations are autonomous rather than subordinate, meaning that the stronger institutions will be more independent of other institutions and social forces, and will have developed a separate life of their own. Thus, autonomy would deal with the differentiation of the Court from other spheres, with how well insulated the Court is. Although Huntington had little to say about judicial organizations, he did observe that "A judiciary is independent to the extent that it adheres to distinctly judicial norms and to the extent that its perspectives and behavior are independent of those of other political institutions and social groupings" (1968: 20). Organizations which lack autonomy are, "in common parlance, said to be corrupt" (1968: 21). Moreover, in a highly institutionalized organization, there would be mechanisms that either slow down the entry of new types of individuals, or through process of socialization, impel changes in the attitudes and behavior of such individuals (1968: 21). Positions of leadership would normally only be achieved by those who have served an apprenticeship in less important filter positions. There would be a channeling of career opportunities in such an organization, and turnover would be relatively infrequent. Thus, autonomy deals largely with the establishment and maintenance of boundaries which differentiate one institution from another.

APPOINTMENT OF JUDGES

The process of appointing judges has a great deal to do with the autonomy of the Court, and with the establishment and maintenance of boundaries which differentiate the court from other institutions and social forces. The framers of the Constitution wanted an independent Court, and viewed the method of appointment as the most important decision they would reach affecting the Court's autonomy. An enormous amount of the time of the Constituent Assembly was spent discussing various appointment strategies, in search of a method which would maximize the insulation of the highest echelons of the judiciary from political patronage or control *(Constituent Assembly Debates,* 1946–50; Austin, 1966: 175–184; Dhavan and Jacob, 1978: 36–51). Ultimately, it was decided that Parliament would have no role (there would be no confirmation process), and that the President (Prime Minister and Cabinet) would appoint the judges but only after *consultation* with the chief justice *(Constitution of India,* 1950: Art. 124).

Available evidence points to the conclusion that at least until the 1970s, the chief justice had the preponderant voice in selecting his colleagues. In 1959, the Home Minister informed the Lok Sabha (lower house of Parliament) that "since 1950, 17 judges have been appointed to the Supreme Court and every one of those judges was nominated and recommended by the Chief Justice of India" (Gadbois, 1969: 222). In the early 1970s, however, this extraordinary power of the chief justice has been eroded by the intrusion of the political branches. According to one of the judges of that period, after H. R. Gokhale became Law Minister in 1971, he "started following a procedure which was hitherto unknown in the matter of appointments of Judges. He took upon himself the task of discussing with the Chief Justice or even trying to persuade him to recommend such Judges who were the nominees of the Government" (Nayar, 1973: 64). S. M. Sikri was chief justice at this time and, according to K. S. Hegde (Nayar, 1973: 31), who also was an associate judge at the time, Sikri once threatened to quit when the Government tried to force upon him an individual he found unacceptable. Upon learning of Sikri's strong objections, Mrs Gandhi withdrew the name. Sikri was also successful in resisting Government pressures to appoint V. R. Krishna Iyer, who some years earlier had served as a minister in the communist Government in the State of Kerala, but shortly after A. N. Ray, the beneficiary of the first supersession, replaced Sikri as chief in 1973, Krishna Iyer was elevated to the Supreme Court. Conversations with judges who served on the Court during the past decade lead to the conclusion that Chief Justices Ray and Beg, who led the Court from 1973–78, were either amenable to the Government playing a large role in the selection process, or were otherwise pervious. Y. V. Chandrachud, chief justice since 1978, has resisted Government nominees, sometimes successfully, sometimes not. Thus, the once hard boundary between the Court and the political leadership concerning the critical matter of who has the upper hand in staffing the Court has softened in recent years. The kind of extreme boundary maintenance represented by the convention of allowing chief justices to select their colleagues has been to some extent overcome by political forces, and chief justices now share their patronage powers with actors in rival institutions.

Although these recent changes in the appointment process – because that is the point at which political encroachment could be most damaging to the Court's autonomy – point to less differentiation of structure and a less rigid compartmentalization of law and politics, it is important to note that the types of individuals who have served on the Court in recent years are only marginally different from those appointed during the Court's formative years. The archetypal judge in the 1950s and 1960s (Gadbois, 1968–69: 317–336), and in the 1970s (Dhavan, 1977: 19–31; Dhavan and Jacob, 1978), was the product of a socially and economically advantaged family, was educated at one of the better Indian universities or in England, spent 20 years in private law practice before the High Court in his home state, had never participated openly in active politics, was appointed to the High Court before which he practised when he was 47, spent 10 years as a High Court judge by which time he was the chief justice or an otherwise very senior judge of that Court, and then was promoted to the Supreme Court when he was 57 years of age. They are, in short, a remarkably homogeneous lot, virtually all having shared the same socialization experience. Only two of the 76 judges who served from 1950–85 failed to undergo a period of High Court grooming preceding their appointment to the Supreme Court. So apprenticeship on a High Court has become one of the crucial rites of passage to the Supreme Court.

The Constitution (Article 124) sets forth certain threshold qualifications for Supreme Court justices – one must have either at least 5 years' experience as a High Court judge, or 10 as a High Court advocate, or be "in the opinion of the President, a distinguished jurist." All judges appointed to date have met one or both of the first two criteria, and no "distinguished jurist" (e.g., an eminent law professor who failed to meet one of the first two criteria) has been appointed. Of the three categories of the pool of potential recruits, by far the largest is the second, for among India's nearly 300,000 lawyers, several thousand must have 10 years' experience as a High Court advocate. The Executive would be within the boundaries of constitutional propriety if it began attempting to staff the Court with individuals not only without High Court bench experience, but from the ranks of those active in the type of politics preferred by the Government of the day, providing such individuals had the requisite High Court bar experience. That entry to the Court is closed except to senior High Court judges is just a convention, but a very strong one that the Executive must be reluctant to violate.

A court whose judges could be easily removed or whose judges were harrassed by threats of removal would lack autonomy. The constitutional and statutory machinery for the removal of Supreme Court judges is extremely cumbrous and complicated, making it very difficult for a judge to be removed. Judges enjoy a large measure of formal protection, and political retaliation against them is extremely difficult to accomplish. Formal removal proceeding have never been invoked against a Supreme Court judge.

Noteworthy also is the fact that the Supreme Court, more than any other major institution, survived the 1975–77 Emergency virtually unscathed. Leading political figures and members of Parliament were jailed, and 16 High Court judges were transferred to other High Courts during the Emergency, in most instances as a means of punishment for bold decisions disliked by the Government. Apart from functioning in an atmosphere of fear, the autonomy of Supreme Court judges was not perceptively reduced.

Because of the extraordinarily high rate of turnover of Supreme Court judges – to be discussed further in the next section – because of the coherence-reducing effect of the turnover, the matter of appointments poses a constant potential threat to the Court's autonomy. Fully 76 judges were appointed during the first 35 years, an average of more than two per year. Such rapid turnover obviously increases the number of opportunities the political leadership has to politicize the Court, and/or to make it a captive institution. An executive bent upon doing so could change the complexion of the Court within a very short period of time. During the 15-months from July 1971–October 1972, a highly charged period in that Mrs Gandhi had achieved a massive victory in the March 1971 national elections and in the 1972 state elections, had defeated Pakistan in the December 1971 war, and was riding at the crest of the Indira wave, no fewer than nine new judges were appointed to the Court, i.e., nearly three-quarters of the then strength of the Court. Later events (major decisions and the voting behavior of these judges) would demonstrate that although Mrs Gandhi had tried to appoint pro-Government judges at that time, she was not notably successful. But, the rapid turnover of judges remains a characteristic of the Court, and provides a constant wedge for the entrance of overtly political appointees. On the autonomy dimension, this turnover represents the Court's Achilles' heel. To the extent that the chief justice is able to have the preponderant or at least an important voice in the appointment of judges, he may be the key to protecting the Court's boundaries from attempted invasions by the political branches. This assumes, of course, that the chief himself is independent of the executive and not a servant of the regime. If the Government of the day could capture the chief justiceship, packing the Court would be made easier.

SALARIES AND PENSIONS

The level of judges' salaries and pensions have a bearing not only upon the Court's autonomy, but upon the quality of those it is able to attract to service on the Court. A poorly paid judge is more likely to succumb to various forms of bribery and unethical behavior than a well remunerated judge. If the salaries of judges lag too far behind those of the best legal talent in the country, the latter are less likely to accept Court appointments, and judgeships will be filled by lesser talents, which in turn will affect adversely the quality of the Court's output. Inadequate retirement pensions may tempt sitting judges to ingratiate themselves with those litigants who would be in a position to offer them attractive post-retirement employment.

Over a century ago, salaries of High Court judges were established at a level of Rs. 4000 per month. When the Federal Court of India was established in 1937, associate judge salaries were set at Rs. 5500 per month, and the chief justice's salary at Rs. 7000 per month. In 1950, however, the new Constitution fixed the salary of the chief justice of the Supreme Court at Rs. 5000 per month, and that of associate judges at Rs. 4000. Thus, today's Supreme Court judges receive the same salaries as their High Court predecessors of a full century earlier! But, of course, the actual situation is incalculably worse. Rs. 4000 in the 19th century was a handsome salary by any nation's standards. In contrast, given the ravages of inflation and taxation, today's Rs. 4000 (about $335) is probably worth no more than one-tenth, probably much less, of that figure a century earlier.

In comparison with the salaries of top office holders in other Indian government institutions, today's judicial salaries are not disproportionately less, and the salary reductions in 1950, effected in order to bring the post-colonial official salary structure more in line with Indian economic conditions, affected other high office holders as well. Since 1950, while the salaries of Supreme Court and High Court (Rs. 3500 for associate judges, Rs. 4000 for the chief justice) have remained constant, those of leading lawyers have increased enormously, and such lawyers are unwilling to accept High Court judgeships, where future Supreme Court judges are groomed.

According to Seervai (1978: 122), a Bombay High Court chief justice once stated publicly that 27 members of the bar who had been offered High Court judgeships had rejected the offer. As early as 1958, the Law Commission in its *14th Report* (I: 81) acknowledged the widespread belief that because of low salaries, the quality of the judiciary had been diluted, lesser talents were being recruited, resulting in a lowering of the overall quality of the higher judiciary.

Because of the practice of recruiting Supreme Court judges from the High Courts, as the quality of the latter declines, that of the former is diminished also. According to Seervai (1970: 31), attempts to persuade leading lawyers to accept Supreme Court judgeships "have failed largely because the terms and conditions of a judge's service hold no attraction for leading members of the Bar." As early as 1960, the Government acknowledged that Supreme Court judgeships offered to leading advocates had been turned down because of the salary level (Gadbois, 1969: 223). The full magnitude of this recruitment problem is not known, but on the basis of what information is available, the problem is very serious and the implications ominous. All who have addressed this matter in recent years are in agreement that the quality of the higher judiciary has declined. Yet, there is no evidence that salaries might soon be raised. The *80th Report* of the Law Commission (1979) which focussed on the method of appointment of judges, though emphasing that only persons "of the highest calibre" (99) be appointed to the Supreme Court, never addressed the issue of salaries.

The other side of the coin – the matter of pensions for judges who must retire at age 65 – is equally bleak. The actual pension figures of retired judges have been published recently by the Law Ministry (1980: 225–226), and most retirees receive a before-taxes pension in the range of Rs. 1600–1700 per month, less than half of their judicial salaries. No one has argued that these pensions are adequate, and there is virtual unanimity that they pose serious questions concerning the autonomous behavior of sitting judges. Although a retired judge is constitutionally prohibited from returning to the bar, he is able to go on the payroll of the Government or a private company, and these are the two largest categories of litigants who appear before the Court (Gadbois, 1970b: 40–41). Many retired judges have found post-retirement employment with the Government or as legal consultants to privately owned business houses, probably in some cases because the low pensions require them to do so. Moreover, it is clear that the Government seems to find employment for retired judges who supported the Government's position while on the bench more often than for those who acquired a reputation for being most "anti-government". Surely sitting judges who know that their standard of living will decline upon retirement cannot be too harshly faulted for thinking in terms of attractive post-retirement positions with private business or the Government. The threats to the autonomy of the Court posed by this situation are so obvious as to require no additional comment.

This section concludes unavoidably on a grim note, for the salary and pension situation is indeed grim, and the implications for the Court's autonomy ominous. If the point has not already been reached, it will soon, that only those of independent wealth, or those willing to bend some to serve the interests of those who might supplement their salaries or pensions, will be able to afford to serve on the Supreme Court. Neither of these alternatives is acceptable, but one or the other may become necessary.

AUTONOMOUS BEHAVIOR

Having sketched this discouraging picture of salaries and pensions and indicated that the low level of each all but invites corruption or otherwise unethical behavior, we hasten to emphasize that not a single Supreme Court judge has been found to have been a party to any of the wide variety of forms of corruption characteristic of Indian public and business life. By their behavior, the judges have demonstrated a high level of honesty and integrity, terms no longer applied to many ministers, MPs, bureaucrats, and businessmen. They have not subordinated their institutional roles to exogenous demands. The absence of corruption associated with the court is a strong indicator of the court's autonomy and institutional distinctiveness. Moreover, such behavior begets more autonomy and institutional strength, for it stimulates legitimacy and makes the Court as an institution less vulnerable to attack by rival institutions. Strength in the form of legitimacy is thus to a large extent earned by the "good" behavior of the judges, while the declining morality of other political institutions can be traced in considerable measure to the reputation for corruption actors in those institutions have earned.

The fact that Supreme Court judges have not succumbed to visible forms of corruption is explained in part by the judicial socialization process which, "by its very nature, places the individual within the framework of certain institutional expectations that may have a decisive influence" (Schmidhauser, 1973: 128) on the judge's behavior.

High ethical standards of behavior for judges were established by judges, both English and Indian, from the creation of the first High Courts in the 19th century to the advent of the Supreme Court in 1950. A new judge will be aware of his predecessors' reputation of independence, honesty and integrity, and even if he is a lesser man, the long tradition must fortify him, and must make him seek to maintain those high traditions. Thus, the office shapes the man, perhaps making him even better than he was.

Another behavioral indicator of autonomy would be the frequency with which other institutions lose in Supreme Court litigation. Some level of the Government is a party to about two-thirds of all Supreme Court litigation, and the Government loses about 40 percent of these cases (Gadbois, 1970a; 1970b). Since 1950, the Court has declared legislation and ordinances unconstitutional in more than one hundred decisions, and there is no evidence of any more recent hesitation on the part of the judges to cower before ministers and legislators. Of the world's apex judicial tribunals, the Indian Supreme Court ranks among the most willing to find fault with what the Government has done.

A high level of autonomy does not necessarily mean a high degree of judicial power. As Toharia (1975) has demonstrated concerning courts in Franco's Spain, an authoritarian regime and independent courts are quite compatible, providing the judges have no real power to adversely affect the regime. The formal possession of judicial power means little unless it is exercised often enough effectively to demonstrate its reality. There is no question that the Supreme Court has immense power, and exercises it often. The most obvious manifestation of such power is judicial review. The whole idea of judicial review, its very *raison d'etre,* is that the Court should act as a brake – representing a permanent law, restraining the whims of sitting legislators, if necessary resisting the outputs of the political process in the name of a higher law. Thus, judicial review places the Court in the middle of the political process, and the constitutionality of virtually all major laws and ordinances is tested in the Supreme Court.

The exercise of judicial review since 1950 has occasioned a considerable amount of institutional conflict, and various threats to the Court's autonomy. The latter include constitutional amendments, especially the 42nd, which was an institution-threatening move by the Parliament-Executive, the two supersessions, and the talk during the Emergency of creating a new body superior to the Court and more beholden to the powers that be. By one means or another, the Court has successfully met or resisted these challenges to its autonomy. But, if the judges have an interest in preventing political encroachments on their claimed turf, the Parliament-Executive can be forgiven for trying to resist what they regard as unwarranted judicial intrusions on their autonomy and domains. This draws us to the matter of judicial activism and restraint, and the question of whether the Court has, on some occasions, exercised its review and reject powers too robustly and recklessly, i.e., whether some of the political attacks on the Court's autonomy have not been wounds self-inflicted, provoked by the Court's failure to exercise proper restraint. This is not the place to try to answer this question, but it seems appropriate to observe that the Court has resisted the development of a "political questions" doctrine (Jacob and Dhavan, 1977: 362–375), and seems, on the contrary, almost to relish taking on politically-explosive issues. The Court has made little effort to evade contentious constitutional questions. A political questions doctrine – a discretionary power to determine the extent of its own involvement in weighty political issues – would serve as an escape hatch for the Court, and would make somewhat more clear and predictable boundaries between political and judicial power. The absence of a political questions doctrine, and the "basic structure" doctrine of *Kesavananda* (1973), *Indira Nehru Gandhi* (1976), and *Minerva Mills* (1981) have resulted in a situation in which these boundaries seem much less clear today than in 1950. The resulting institutional conflict may ultimately make Indian democracy tougher and more durable, but in the short run, it poses constant threats to the Court's autonomy. It would seem timely for the Court to codify procedures for dealing with constitutional questions, and for developing an Indian political questions doctrine. This would introduce some still missing stability in the relationship between the Court and rival institutions, and could result in greater institutionalization of the Court's autonomy.

IV. Coherence-Disunity

> The more unified and coherent an organization is, the more highly institutionalized it is; the greater the disunity of the organization, the less it is institutionalized. Some measure of consensus, of course, is a prerequisite for any social group. An effective organization requires, at a minimum, substantial consensus on the functional boundaries of the group and on the procedures for resolving disputes which come up within those boundaries (Huntington, 1968; 22).

So the more unity, *esprit de corps* and discipline an organization manifests, the stronger it is.

STARE DECISIS

Coherence will be enhanced when the Court follows precedent and when judges sparingly use their discretion to overrule an earlier decision. Adherence to the doctrine of *stare decisis* contributes to the stability of the law, and suggests universalistic and automatic internal decision-making, and standardized institutional procedures. The following of precedent contributes to predictability, and also the perception that the judges are impartial, i.e., that legal doctrine, rather than the whims of transient judges, controls decisions.

The Court has always emphasized its fidelity to precedent, and has stressed that overruling must be done with reluctance and caution. According to Dhavan, however, "... in practice the Court has been fairly casual in overruling earlier precedent; ... the Court has not relied on the established techniques of overruling. Instead, the Court resorted to selective referencing and ignored the decisions which they did not want to consider" (1977: 450). Dhavan's conclusion that the Court's approach is characterized by a lack of "precedent-consciousness" is shared by Baxi (1978: ii–v; 1980: 15) and Seervai (1970: 70–75).

By Dhavan's count, from 1950–75, the Court overruled itself 60 times, and on 5 other occasions overturned Privy Council rulings (1977: 41). Dhavan is alarmed by this level of insensitivity to precedent. Whether this alarm is warranted is a matter of analyst interpretation. By American standards, Indian judges have not evinced a casual attitude toward precedent. Between 1937–73, the United States' Supreme Court overruled 87 earlier decisions (Abraham, 1875: 334–335), a pace identical to that of the Indian Supreme Court. Perhaps more significant is the fact that during its formative period, i.e., prior to 1937, the American Court overruled itself only 46 times. Overruling is probably more de-institutionalizing in a young organization than in a mature one.

The raw numbers of reversals are less significant than the type of doctrine jettisoned. Many reversals of precedent go virtually unnoticed. This was not true in the landmark *Golak Nath* (1967) decision, which declared that Parliament thereafter could not, by constitutional amendment, take away or abridge any further any of the Fundamental Rights. In order to arrive at this decision, the Court had to overrule two major precedents to the contrary *(Sankari Prasad,*

1952; *Sajjan Singh,* 1965). *Golak Nath* was a watershed in Indian constitutional law, but it might also be viewed as a self-inflicted wound. It precipitated a storm of controversy in political and academic circles. Parliament had been led to believe by earlier decisions that it could overcome any Court decision by amendment of the Constitution, and the departure of the Court from these earlier precedents understandably enraged Parliament, and led to increased conflict between the Court and the Parliament-Executive.

Coherence was further eroded (and political attacks increased) when the Court appeared to depart from earlier doctrine in the *Bank Nationalization* and *Privy Purses* decision,[4] both rendered in 1970. Then in 1973 came *Kesavananda,* the apotheosis of judicial power, in which the Court overruled *Golak Nath* in order to go beyond it, ruling that any amendments altering the "basic structure" of the Constitution would be declared unconstitutional. The day following the announcement of the *Kesavananda* verdict, the Court suffered what Indians perceived to be the most pernicious political invasion of the Court's autonomy. This was the first departure from the convention of naming the seniormost puisne judge as chief justice. An enormous controversy followed, exacerbated by the resignations in protest of the three superseded judges. Of the several rationales that the Government offered for the supersession, most were relatively effectively rebutted by Court supporters and Government critics. The major exception was the charge that real or apparent departures from precedent from 1967–73 had led to instability and unsettled law, a situation the Government's spokesmen said they hoped would be alleviated by making A. N. Ray the new chief justice (Nayar, 1973; Kumaramangalam, 1973). Mrs Gandhi stressed the "frequent reversals of stand" by the Supreme Court as a major justification for the supersession (Nayar, 1973: 74). We can conclude this discussion of *stare decisis* with the observation that consistency is a political as well as legal virtue, and that the lack of coherence the Court revealed from 1967–73 provided fodder for political threats to its autonomy.

CONSENSUS-DISSENSUS

The greater the disunity of the Court, the less it is institutionalized. Thus, our attention is drawn to the solidarity of the judicial corps itself. Theoretically, the "best" decisions would be unanimous ones, although there is no empirical evidence relevant to any court that this is true. But, an organization characterized by a high degree of unity and consensus among its actors is better able to protect its own against outside attack and to advance its claims to autonomy (Fried, 1966: 45). The more hostile the Court's environment, the more important the relative absence of disunity and factionalism become. A divided decision would be easier to attack than a unanimous one, for critics could express their support for the minority opinions and be within the boundaries of acceptable criticism. And the more internally consensual, the more able the Court is to reach agreement on the formulation of new policies and the expansion of its own powers.

Compared with apex courts elsewhere (Schubert and Danelski, 1969), Indian Supreme Court judges reveal a very high degree of consensual behavior in their decisions. Gadbois (1970a: 151) found that during the Court's first two decades, approximately 92 percent of the several thousand reported decisions were reached by unanimous benches. Since 1970, the dissent rate has plummeted to just two percent of all reported decisions (Gadbois, 1984).

Although rare in general, dissensus has been a characteristic of most of the important constitutional cases. Most notable are the *Golak Nath* and *Kesavananda* decisions, where the key questions were decided by 6–5 and 7–6 majorities, respectively. These narrowest of majorities in these two landmark decisions both diminished their impact and provided critics of those decisions with much leeway for criticism. There is an even more alarming sense in which both *Golak Nath* and *Kesavananda* represent an absence of cohesion. According to Huntington (1968: 22), "an effective organization requires, at a minimum, substantial consensus on the functional boundaries of the group . . ." It was precisely the matter of the "functional boundaries" between the Court and Parliament which was the central and most contentious issue in both of these disputes, and the judges could not have been more divided over where the boundary line should be drawn.

Kesavananda also drew attention to another coherence-diminishing matter – that of a multiplicity of judgments in particular cases. During the 1950s and 1960s, the typical Court decision was a unanimous one, characterized by a single judgment or opinion – the judgment of the Court. In *Kesavananda,* however, there were no fewer than 11 separate opinions written by the 13 participating judges. This manifestation of a lack of cohesion has received widespread critical comment (Nayar, 1973: 27), and served as additional grist for those who would have objected to the *Kesavananda* outcome even if that decision had been articulated in a single judgment for a unanimous Court.

There are other indicators of the solidarity of the judicial corps. A case can be made that what was to mature into the seniority convention (the practice of naming the seniormost puisne judge as chief justice) was established in 1951 by a dramatic demonstration of unity by the seven judges who then comprised the Court. Upon Chief Justice Kania's unexpected death, Prime Minister Nehru considered naming as the new chief justice either B. K. Mukherjea (third in seniority on the Court), or M. C. Chagla, then the Chief Justice of the Bombay High Court. Upon learning that M. P. Sastri, their seniormost colleague, might not be named chief justice, *all* of the Supreme Court judges, including Mukherjea who had reason to believe that he was Nehru's choice, threatened to resign if seniority did not govern the choice of Kania's successor (Nayar, 1973: 17, 47; Anthony, 1973; Iyengar, 1973). Nehru bowed to this demonstration of solidarity, and Sastri was confirmed as chief justice. As Chief Justice M. Hidayatullah was approaching retirement age in late 1970, there was a rumor that the next-in-line, J. C. Shah, was not going to be promoted, and that an outsider, ex-Communist Mohan Kumaramangalam, was to be made chief justice. According to Hidayatullah's account, all but one of the then eleven judges said they would resign if Shah was not promoted (Palkhivala, 1973: 10). Without ever commenting on the rumor, the Government announced that Shah would succeed Hidayatullah. By 1973, however, when the first departure from the seniority convention occurred, only the superseded three resigned, and the remaining judges were mute. Exactly the same thing happened in 1977 when H. R. Khanna was superseded and resigned.

Finally, in any decision-making group as large as the Indian Supreme Court, there are bound to be discordant relations from time to time among its members over doctrinal, procedural, substantive, social, task or other matters. A measure of cohesion would be how much of this dirty linen is aired for public view, i.e., whether poor inter-personal relations among judges are an institutional secret or are shared with the public. Examples of the latter seem to be comparatively few in number, suggesting a relatively high degree of *esprit de corps*. Virtually all of the known incidents of poor inter-personal relations among the judges have occurred during the past decade. Baxi (1978: x) writes that since the 1973 supersession, "the hitherto almost socially invisible phenomenon of politics within the Court has acquired high visibility." He stressed the refusal of some judges to accept the leadership of Chief Justices Ray and Beg (the beneficiaries of the two supersessions) during the 1973–1978 period. Baxi's conclusion is that during the Ray-

Beg years, "the Indian Supreme Court almost *ceased* to be a court in the institutional sense, *It instead became an assembly of individual justices*" (1978: xi, emphasis in original). More recently, the situation has become worse rather than better. Poor relations between Chandrachud and Bhagwati, the Court's most senior judges, are an open secret, and Tulzapurkar unleashed a blistering attack on some of his colleagues in a public speech in 1982 (*India Today,* December 15, 1982: 118–120). Today's Court is characterized by more personal bickering than any of its predecessors; the day of judges presenting a united front to critics has gone.

JUDGES' TENURE-TURNOVER

As noted earlier, since 1950 76 judges have served on a Court whose maximum strength was 8 until 1956, 11 from 1956 to 1960, 14 from 1960 to 1978, and 18 since then. Thus, the Court is characterized by a rapid turnover of judicial personnel. This turnover is attributable to two factors: (i) the selection of associate judges from among the seniormost or otherwise very senior (in terms of bench experience) High Court judges, whose average age when they reached the Supreme Court is 57, and (ii) the constitutional requirement of mandatory retirement at age 65.

This rapid turnover has implications for the Court's coherence as well as its autonomy. Concerning the former, it means that lines of judicial decisions are likely to be less set as membership is more fluid, and it also means that a judge will have a relatively short time to familiarize himself with the work of the Court before he leaves office (Murphy and Tanenhaus, 1972: 102–103). However, mediating the effects of rapid turnover is the fact that all but two of these judges spent an average of some 10 years of apprenticeship on one or more of the High Courts before moving up to the Supreme Court. That is, they shared similar socialization experiences as judges on courts representing the second rung of India's unified judicial system. Although this reduces the dislocation caused by the coming and going of Supreme Court judges, turnover of this magnitude must have some adverse impact on the cohesiveness of the Court.

LEADERSHIP

During its first three decades, the Court has been headed by a succession of 16 different chief justices. One served for only 35 days, another for 105 days. Three others served for less than a year. In 1954, and again in 1966, three different men held the highest judicial office in the land. Only the most assiduous students of the Court can remember the names of all. No other constitutional court in the world changes leaders so frequently.

This parade of chief justices must have a negative effect on the coherence of the Court. The chief justiceship is a demanding and very significant office. The chief justice plays a major role in the selection of Supreme Court judges, decides which judges will sit on which benches, and is chief administrator of the Supreme Court. As we have seen, except for the two supersessions, chiefs have been selected not on the basis of leadership and management skills, but on the basis of their seniority on the Supreme Court. The seniority convention, which was restored in 1978, is valued by friends of the Court largely because it serves to eliminate political considerations in selecting chief justices. But, while serving to distance that office from executive interference, the convention involves a major trade-off in that it results in eliminating leadership skills and merit from among the criteria employed in selecting the nation's highest judicial officer.

Many students of the American Supreme Court view the 34-year chief justiceship of John Marshall as highly significant in stabilizing the role of the Court in the political system, and in enlarging the Court's influence. The same cannot be said about any Indian chief justice. However, it cannot be demonstrated that the bewildering succession of chiefs has had any disastrous effects on the Court as an institution. The fact that the Court has not only survived but has enhanced its role in the political system over the past three decades points to the conclusion that an institution can be strong without stable leadership over extended periods of time, for the need for leadership is greater when institutions are weak.

DIVISIONAL BENCHES

So significant in subtracting from institutional coherence is the divisional bench or panel system of decision-making that it merits separate consideration. Ninety-nine percent of the thousands of decisions rendered by "the Court" are in fact not rendered by the entire Court, but by small subsets of judges usually ranging from two to five members in size. Indeed the typical decision of "the Court" is today delivered by a two-judge bench, i.e., by one-ninth of the Court.

Kesavananda, Bank Nationalization, Privy Purses, and *Golak Nath* are among the small handful of decisions reached by the full Court. The best that can be said of the bench system is that it theoretically permits a Court almost literally sinking under the weight of some 40,000 cases in arrears to increase the quantity of its output.

In 1950, the Court's rules fixed the minimum number of judges on a bench at three, but later the minimum was reduced to two. With the full strength of the Court now 18, it is common for 4, 5, and often 6 or 7 separate benches to be functioning simultaneously. This may contribute to Huntington's complexity index, but this is more than offset by the deleterious effect on the Court's coherence. The bench system institutionalizes the fragmentation of the Court, and raises serious questions of coordination of functionally differentiated organizational units. This situation was decried recently by one of the current members of the Court: "... with a fragmented bench structure, the Court is in fact losing its corporate identity. There is little coherence and uniformity in its functioning and it is not possible to identify the direction in which the Court is going, because sometimes it is moving in one direction and sometimes in another" (Bhagwati, 1979: 13).

The inherently de-institutionalizing aspect of the bench system is exacerbated by the fact that not only do all the judges meet together only for ten minutes at the start of each day in the chief justice's chamber, but also there are no routine judicial conferences among even members of the same panels (Seervai, 1970: 50–51). Moreover, the various benches do not have a stable membership, i.e., a judge may be on a bench hearing criminal appeals one month, and on another bench dealing with industrial disputes the next month. Bench assignments are the prerogative of the chief justice.

There is no authoritative account of the important ramifications of the bench system, so we do not know how autonomous the various panels are, or the extent to which efforts are made to coordinate them. We do know that there have been occasions when the right hand doesn't know what the left has done. According to Baxi (1980: 16):

> It does happen ... that in the same month different benches of two or three justices reviewing death sentences reach diverse verdicts; while one bench upholds, the other commutes the sentence. The idea that review of death sentences should not fluctuate with the bench-structure has not quite registered itself; and any proposal that the Full Bench should sit in such matters is liable to dismissal on the ground that it would be too cumbersome and inefficient, especially given the problem of arrears.

The bench system, both theoretically and in fact, is a practice that poses serious threats to the Court's coherence.

Conclusions

We obviously do not wind up with a precise, composite index of institutionalization. Ben-Dor (1975: 316) was correct; Huntington "does not deal at any length with problems of concrete assessment, comparison and measurement." We are confronted with the classic dilemma of whether to conclude that the glass is half empty or half full. Perhaps it would be useful to present both a "worst case" picture and a "best case" picture, followed by an estimate as to which best represents the Court's current status. In each picture, we will deal with matters pertaining to adaptability-rigidity, complexity-simplicity, autonomy-subordination, and coherence-disunity, and in that order.

"WORST CASE"

The Court is suffocating under a backlog of cases many times larger today than just a decade ago, is having thrust upon it or admitting via its discretionary jurisdiction a deluge of new cases with which it seems increasingly unable to cope, and is unwilling or unable to devise new procedures for stemming the flow of new litigation. At the same time, it responds to external threats (e.g. constitutional amendments) to its own survival as a policy-making institution by further risking its survival and viability in a hostile (to judicial power) Westminster parliamentary system when it rejects procedurally impeccable constitutional admendments. And while willing if not also anxious to joust with the Government on the most fundamental and politically explosive questions of the distribution of power, it refuses to demonstrate the element of judicial restraint represented by a political questions doctrine.

The judges are surrounded by a surfeit of peons and lower level clerks capable of moving files around, but incapable of providing any significant intellectual assistance to the judges. Although each judge is responsible for several judgments each week and is expected to read and act upon more than 100 special leave petitions every week, the judges have no noteworthy research assistance, and perform their roles with archaic equipment and meager resources characteristic of a nineteenth century institution. They have too many functions to perform, and the largest categories of cases they decide deal with the least important (non-constitutional) disputes. At the same time, their major power (judicial review) is under constant siege by rival institutions. While the backlog of cases increases to the point of overwhelming the institution, it spent 69 working days on one case *(Kesavananada)*, an incredible inefficient use of scarce resources.

Although today's rupee bears no resemblance in buying power to the 19th century rupee, today's judges receive the same salary as their predecessors of a century earlier, and, after being forced off the bench at age 65, the pensions are so inadequate that many judges are found in the employ of those who use the Court most often. The best talent from the bar finds the emoluments of a judgeship so unattractive that they refuse to accept appointment to the Court. Judges come and go with bewildering rapidity, and every retirement provides another opportunity for rival institutions to diminish the Court's independence.

The Court has been led by so many chief justices that even careful students of the Court experience difficulty in remembering their names. These leaders are selected by criteria which eliminate leadership skills as a criterion. The organization is fractured by the divisional bench system, and there have been occasions when one bench hands down a decision at odds with that of another bench. The two decisions *(Golak Nath* and *Kesavananda)* which provoked the most critical reaction from rival institutions were decided by the leanest of majorities, underlining alarming dissensus within the Court. In reaching the conclusions they did in these and other important decision, the judges departed from precedents they had established in the recent past, suggesting instability at critical junctures. The entire membership of the Court seldom meets together for any reason. During the past decade, there is evidence of increasing disruption from within, and during the Emergency, the most serious external threat to the Court's survival, there was conflict within the Court, and it was unable to pull together.

This "worst case" picture is one of a creaky, ramshackle institution, on the threshold of collapse, malaise, or irrelevance, a decaying institution. An obituary should be prepared for the inevitable.

"BEST CASE"

The Court has obviously adapted to a variety of changes and crises, or it would not still be there. It is far more visible today as an influential actor in the political system than it was in 1950. It is the closest analogue – not just non-Western analogue – to the American Supreme Court as both a policy-making and politically important institution. It has declared over 100 laws and ordinances unconstitutional, and shows no hesitation in standing up to the Prime Minister and Parliament. Autonomous judicial institutions elsewhere usually do not survive periods of authoritarian rule, but the Indian Court adapted successfully to the 1975–77) Emergency, and in doing so, crossed a highly significant institutionalization hurdle. The Court has lost no major functions, and has in fact acquired major new ones. For 35 years, the Court has kept the Constitution in the forefront of Indian political life and, in the process, the Court itself has become the centerpiece of India's constitutional democracy. It is sustained by deep roots that go back to the middle of the 19th century. Despite inadequate staff assistance and equipment, the judges have coped remarkably well.

The Court has maintained its autonomy, integrity and morality in a society and political system in which most forms of corruption and conflicts of interest known to man have become routine facts of everyday life. It is the most trusted and legitimate institution on the landscape. This is probably a large part of the reason why so many Indians are turning to the Court and away from other institutions. The judges are an impressive lot. Indians expect an enormous amount from their judges, and the judges have struggled mightily and largely successfully to live up to these expectations.

The seniority convention, which signals that the hands of rival institutions have not contaminated the Court, was restored in 1978. The Court has survived rapid changes in the number and quality of its leaders, no doubt largely for the reasons expressed by former Chief Justice Sikri: "In our set-up, judicial leadership comes with outstanding judicial ability, not with the fact of being Chief Justice. We have had a number of Judges, who have exercised this judicial leadership without being Chief Justices or before they became Chief Justices" (Nayar, 1973: 135). With the naming of Chandrachud as chief in 1978, the Court has gained a measure of leadership continuity, for he will serve until 1985, much longer than any of his predecessors.

This "best case" picture is one of a strong, virile institution, well-equipped by past successes to cope successfully with the future. Hold the obituary; the Court is alive and well, likely to be around for the forseeable future.

Which of these radically different pictures best portrays the reality? Largely because of the Court's performance on adaptability and autonomy dimensions, the Court is stronger than it is weak. When compared with constitutional courts elsewhere, the Indian Court would have to be ranked among the most institutionalized courts on earth. This is not to say that the Court is necessarily moving inexorably toward greater structural persistence. The Court's institutionalization could start cracking tomorrow. The main message of Huntington's theory is that both political systems as well as institutions can decay as well as develop.

We will conclude with some necessarily brief comments on the adequacy of Huntington's four criteria for examining the institutionalization of courts. Application of his criteria to the Indian Court does point out some theoretical and conceptual shortcomings. The indices do not fit together as closely as one would wish; we saw that to the extent that divisional benches increase complexity, they also reduce coherence and adaptability. We found that complexity was difficult to operationalize and apply to the Court.

The major shortcoming of Huntington's scheme as applied to the Supreme Court is its failure to deal more explicitly with the Court's context and social base. Courts seem to be inherently fragile institutions, dependent upon others for various types of support, e.g. financial, and for the implementation of their rulings. Thus support, particularly from influential groups within the society, and cultural values and norms which provide succor and sustain courts, would seem to be more critical for judicial institutions than executive or legislative. Huntington was sensitive to this concern. He said that the strength of organizations "depends upon the *scope of support*... and their *level of institutionalization*" (1968: 12, emphasis in original). But, his major concern was obviously with the latter, and his four criteria focus on matters pertaining to structural persistence, dealing little with the social base of, and support for, an institution (Dominguez and Mitchell, 1977: 175). We partially resolved this shortcoming simply by occasionally bringing evidence of such support into the analysis, but much was left out, such as the evidence Sudarshan (1982) and others present of significant support for the Court from such groups as landowners and businessmen, who are increasingly well-represented in the state and national legislatures. The Court has friends in important places, and they have contributed to the Court's institutionalization.

The advantages of Huntington's institutionalization approach are considerable. He provides a systematic framework which compels one to answer questions with data not before brought together, and the result is a fresh view which provokes reconsideration of some of the conventional wisdom about the Court. His four criteria, with the partial exception of complexity-simplicity, were found to be relevant to the question of strength of the Court. Except for complexity, we were able to find two or more robust but unobtrusive empirical measures for each criterion, and experienced little difficulty in operationalizing them. This study demonstrates that the institutionalization concept can be utilized with some success to estimate the strength of judicial institutions, but underlines the need for more precise tools to cope with problems of measurement and assessment.

NOTES

1. In mid-June 1975, Mrs Gandhi was convicted by the Allahabad High Court of two counts of election campaign irregularities, the penalty for which is disbarment from holding any public office for six years. She moved the Supreme Court for an "absolute and unconditional" stay of the High Court Judgment, but on June 24th received only a partial stay. She declared the Emergency the next day, and then quickly had the by then subservient Parliament eliminate (with retrospective effect) from the election law the grounds for her own conviction, and also pushed through the 39th Amendment of the Constitution, the aim of which was to remove from judicial review the election of the Prime Minister. In November 1975, a five-judge constitution bench of the Supreme Court had little choice but to reverse her conviction, but a majority did declare unconstitutional the parts of the 39th Amendment which sought to oust judicial review.

2. In *Golak Nath*, the Court ruled that Parliament no longer could, even by procedurally correct constitutional amendments, abridge the Fundamental Rights.

3. At the current exchange rate of approximately twelve rupees to the U.S. dollar, the Court's budget was about $76,000 in 1950 and $543,000 in 1977.

4. Mrs Gandhi's government had sought to nationalize the nation's major commercial banks, and abolish the Privy Purses which had been paid to the ex-princess since their states had been absorbed into the Indian union after independence in 1947. Both actions were declared unconstitutional by the Court, a major rebuff to Mrs Gandhi. She reacted to these decision by dissolving Parliament and seeking a new mandate from the electorate. Her party captured more than two-thirds of the seats in Parliament in the 1971 national election, and then proceeded to enact constitutional amendments to reverse these Supreme Court decisions.

References

ABRAHAM, HENRY J. (1975) *The Judicial Process,* 3rd ed., New York: Oxford University Press.

ANTHONY, FRANK (1973) *Lok Sabha Debates,* May 4: 233, 292

AUSTIN, GRANVILLE (1966) *The Indian Constitution: Cornerstone of a Nation.* London: Oxford University Press.

BANK NATIONALIZATION DECISION: *R. C. Cooper v. Union of India* (1970) 3 S.C.R. 530.

BAXI, UPENDRA (ed) (1978) *K. K. Mathew on Democracy, Equality and Freedom.* Lucknow: Eastern Book Company.

BAXI, UPENDRA (1980) *The Indian Supreme Court and Politics.* Lucknow: Eastern Book Company.

BEN-DOR, GABRIEL (1974) "Corruption, Institutionalization, and Political Development". *Comparative Political Studies* **7** (April): 63–83.

— (1975) "Institutionalization and Political Development: A Conceptual and Theoretical Analysis". *Comparative Studies in Society and History* **7** (July): 309–325.

BHAGWATI, P. N. (1979) Speech Before All India Law Teachers Conference. Varanasi, December 27.

CONSTITUENT ASSEMBLY DEBATES (1946–50) 12 vols., Delhi: Government of India Press.

CONSTITUTION OF INDIA (1950) (as amended to 1980), New Delhi: Government of India Press.

DHAVAN, RAJEEV (1977) *The Supreme Court of India.* Bombay: N. M. Tripathi.

— (1978) *The Supreme Court Under Strain: The Challenge of Arrears.* Bombay: N. M. Tripathi.

— and ALICE JACOB (1978) *Selection and Appointment of Supreme Court Judges.* Bombay: N. M.Tripathi.

DHAVAN, RAJEEV (1980) *Justice on Trial.* Allahabad: Wheeler Publishing.

DOMINGUEZ, JORGE I. and CHRISTOPHER N. MITCHELL (1977) "The Roads not taken: institutionalization and political parties in Cuba and Boliva." *Comparative Politics* **9** (January): 173–195.

FRIED, ROBERT C. (1966) *Comparative Political Institutions.* New York: Macmillan.

GADBOIS, GEORGE H. Jr. (1964) "The federal court of India: 1937–1950". *Journal of the Indian Law Institute* **6** (April–September): 253–315.

— (1968–69) "Indian Supreme Court Judges: a portrait". *Law and Society Review* **III** (November–February): 317–336.

— (1969) "Selection, background characteristics, and voting behavior of Indian Supreme Court judges, 1950–59)". in Glendon Schubert and David J. Danelski [eds.] *Comparative Judicial Behavior,* New York: Oxford University Press.

— (1970a) "Indian judicial behavior". *Economic and Political Weekly* **V** (Annual Number): 149–166.

— (1970b) "The Supreme Court of India: a preliminary report of an empirical study". *Journal of Constitutional and Parliamentary Studies* **IV** (January–March): 33–54.

— (1980) "The "contribution to law" literature: dealing with inequalities of tenure, participation, and option writing of Supreme Court judges." *Banaras Law Journal* **16** (January–December): 111–121.

— (1982) "Participation in Supreme Court decision-making: from Kania to Vaidialingham, 1950–1967." *Journal of the Indian Law Institute* **24** (January–March): 1–23.

— (1984) "The Decline of Dissent on the Supreme Court, 1980-1981." in Ram Avtar Sharma (ed.) *Justice and Social Order in India.* New Delhi: Intellectual Publishing House.

GOLAK NATH V. STATE OF PUNJAB (1967) 2 S.C.R. 762.

HUNTINGTON, SAMUEL P. (1965) "Political development and political decay." *World Politics* **17** (April): 386–430.

— (1968) *Political Order in Changing Societies.* New Haven: Yale University Press.

INDIRA NEHRU GANDHI V. RAJ NARAIN (1976) 2 S.C.R. 347.

IYENGAR, H.V.R. (1973) quoted in "Jurists' charge against government." *Times of India* (Bombay), May 5: 1.

JACOB, ALICE and RAJEEV DHAVAN (1977) "The dissolution case: politics at the bar of the Supreme Court." *Journal of the Indian Law Institute* **19** (October–December): 355–391.

KESAVANANDA BHARATI V. STATE OF KERALA (1973) Supp. S.C.R. 1.

KESSELMAN, MARK (1970) "Overinstitutionalization and political constraint." *Comparative Politics* **3** (October): 21–44.

KUMARAMANGALAM, S. MOHAN (1973) *Judicial Appointments.* New Delhi: Oxford and IBM Publishing.

LAW COMMISSION OF INDIA (1958) *14th Report: Reform of Judicial Administration. I, Ministry of Law.* New Delhi: Government of India Press.

LAW COMMISSION OF INDIA (1979) *80th Report: The Method of Appointment of Judges. Ministry of Law, Justice and Company Affairs.* New Delhi: Government of India Press.

MINERVA MILLS V. UNION OF INDIA (1981) 1 S.C.R. 206.

MINISTRY OF LAW, JUSTICE AND COMPANY AFFAIRS (1980) *Judges of the Supreme Court and the High Courts.* New Delhi: Government of India Press.

MURPHY, WALTER F. and JOSEPH TANENHAUS (1972) *The Study of Public Law,* New York: Random House.

NAYAR, KULDIP (ed.) (1973) *Supersession of Judges.* New Delhi: Indian Book Company.

NWABUEZE, B. O. (1977) *Judicialism in Commonwealth Africa.* New York: St. Martin's Pres.

PALKHIVALA, N. A. (ed.) (1973) *A Judiciary Made to Measure.* Bombay: M. R. Pai.

POLSBY, NELSON W. (1968) "The institutionalization of the U.S. House of Representatives." *American Political Science Review LXII* (March): 144–168.

PRIVY PURSE DECISION: Madhav Rao Scindia v. Union of India (1971) 3 S.C.R. 9.

RUDOLPH, LLOYD I. and SUSANNE HOEBER RUDOLPH (1981) "Judicial review versus parliamentary sovereignty: the struggle over stateness in India." *Journal of Commonwealth & Comparative Politics* **XIX** (November): 231–256.

SAJJAN SINGH V. STATE OF RAJASTHAN (1965) 1 S.C.R. 933.

SANKARI PRASAD V. UNION OF INDIA (1952) S.C.R. 89.

SCHMIDHAUSER, JOHN R. (1973) "An exploratory analysis of the institutionalization of legislatures and judiciaries." in Allan Kornberg (ed.) *Legislatures in Comparative Perspective.* New York: David McKay Company.

SCHUBERT, GLENDON and DAVID J. DANELSKI (eds.) (1969) *Comparative Judicial Behavior.* New York: Oxford University Press.

SEERVAI, H. M. (1970) *The Position of the Judiciary Under the Constitution of India.* Bombay: Bombay University Press.

SEERVAI, H. M. (1978) *The Emergency, Future Safeguards and the Habeas Corpus Case: A Criticism.* Bombay: N. M. Tripathi.

SIGELMAN, LEE (1979) "Understanding political stability: an evaluation of the mobilization-institutionalization approach." *Comparative Political Studies* **12** (July): 205–228.

SUDARSHAN, R. (1982) "Law, state and society in India." in Rajeev Dhavan and Salman Khurshid (eds.) *Judges and Judicial Power: Essays in Honour of Justice Krishna Iyer.* London: Sweet and Maxwell, forthcoming.

TOHARIA, JOSE J. (1975) "Judicial independence in an authoritarian regime: the case of contemporary Spain." *Law and Society Review* **9** (Spring): 475–496.

CHAPTER 7

A CROSS-NATIONAL PERSPECTIVE ON THE STRUCTURING OF TRIAL COURT OUTPUTS: THE CASE OF THE ENGLISH HIGH COURT

BURTON ATKINS
FLORIDA STATE UNIVERSITY

To compare is to impose meaning upon objects and phenomena; no object or process has meaning in the abstract, but obtains its interpretation against some point of reference. Whether it be the archeologist examining a bone fragment, or the social scientist evaluating a political institution, what sets interpretation in motion is the ability to assess that fragment, or that institution, in relation to some other. Without the capacity to compare, reference points do not exist and our latitude for interpretation is reduced dramatically.

While this may seem obvious, the fact remains that the comparative analysis of court systems as a research strategy for enhancing our understanding of judicial politics and behavior has been anything but commonplace. Some research (e.g. Danelski and Schubert, 1969; Becker, 1970) has shown an explicit concern for transposing paradigms developed in one setting into another. Nevertheless, one would be hard pressed to argue that cross-national, or comparative, research on the politics of courts and judges has flourished. It has, instead, proceeded with fits and starts because of several barriers to conducting research. Some of these are substantial, such as not having sufficient data, not having sufficient theory upon which to establish cross-national comparability of judicial institutions imbedded in diverse political system, and the inevitable problems of language. Thus, it is all the more surprising that political scientists have not devoted more attention to the English judicial system, one which shares common ancestry with the American, and one for which language poses no barrier. It was, perhaps, the relative ease by which comparative analysis could be done in the English setting that prompted Baum (1977) to review the fruitful lines of inquiry open to investigation. With but few exceptions, little research has followed.[1]

One area Baum had suggested for analysis concerned an examination of the litigants who use English trial courts in order to obtain some benefit for themselves or impose some sanction upon another party. Related to this is the issue of what parties are supported by the English trial courts. These are among the issues that are examined in this chapter. It offers a preliminary analysis of the outputs of the High Court, an important English trial court of general civil jurisdiction. In setting the stage for this analysis, it also probes some of the factors which appear to inhibit political scientists from thinking about English Courts as political institutions.

English Courts and Politics

There appears to be an impression, deeply ingrained among both American and English political scientists, that English courts are not integrally involved in the political process and do not contribute to the making of public policy. In fact, to assume that courts are not political seems to be *de rigueur* among those who write on British politics. For example, in his preface to the first edition of *British Government and Politics,* Punnett (1969) proffers to "... give a detailed and all-embracing account of government and politics in all material ... that helps towards an understanding of British political system as it operates today." Now in its 4th edition (1980), the book still fails to include a chapter on courts and judges. In fact, the term "judges" is not contained in the index, and the term "courts" is referenced in only 8 pages of the book, six of which are in passing within non-adjacent pages. Nor is Punnett alone in his neglect of English courts and judges. Anthony Birch's *The British System of Government* also ignores courts and judges, although it devotes some attention to civil liberties in Britain (235–253). Both Beloff and Peele's (1980) *The Government of the United Kingdom: Political Authority in a Changing Society* and Carter's (1972) *The Government of the United Kingdom* have chapters on the structure of the English judiciary, but neither address the political roles performed by courts and judges.

If these examples suggest that English political scientists have been somehow socialized into believing that courts are unimportant, we might imagine that an American-trained political scientist writing about English politics would be more inclined to devote attention to the court's political roles. Consider Rose's *Politics in England,* now in its third edition. Rose's objective is to "... describe how politics in England works today" (p. 4). To accomplish this, he examines three "critical functions of any political system" – socialization, recruitment, and the communication of political information. He also examines "... how parts of the political system combine to make and implement policies ..." (p. 5) and "... the chief influences upon politics in England today" (p. 5), and does so by posing a question which organizes much of the book: "what impact does government have upon life in England today?" (p. 5). These objectives, goals and questions suggest to the reader that Rose's analysis of English politics is broadly grounded. So it is. However, as one reads further it is readily apparent that courts are not viewed as part of English politics, nor would courts, according to Rose, be relevant to answering the question about the impact of government upon English life. Like Punnett, the concepts of "courts" and "judges" are not indexed in Rose's book and the occasional references that do occur are made only to emphasize that, because the role of law is so narrowly defined (p. 94), courts exert little influence over Westminster. Similarly, if his edited volume, *Policy-Making in Britain* (1969) is used as the basis, it appears the same assumptions pertain to the policy making process in as much as the book does not contain a chapter on English courts and judges.

Whether or not characteristics unique to the English political system have stifled the pursuit of the study of judicial politics, or whether the issue is considered unimportant in a system preoccupied with Parliamentary supremacy, is hard to determine in the absence of a strong track record of interest in such matters. But if the research priorities of English political scientists provide any clues, it appears that English courts are simply not considered relevant to the political process. In some regards this is because the wrong questions have often been asked about the English judiciary. Consider, for example *The Machinery of Justice in England* (1977), R. M. Jackson's respected and comprehensive analysis of English courts. Jackson's book, although emphasizing structural and formal aspects of the English judiciary, does address the issue of whether or not judges' decisions are patterned in a politically relevant way. On this matter, Jackson argues that no relationship exists between "the political antecedents and the decisions of judges" (1977; 470). The reason for this, according to Jackson, is that little variance exists in the judges' background experiences, and thus, these political antecedents are not useful for explaining why English judges decide cases the way they do:

> English conditions tend to produce a certain measure of uniformity in the outlook of the judges . . . Judges are of different political faiths, different religions or agnostic, and have varying degrees of intelligence and cultural attainments. Yet there is something that enables us to talk about the judges almost as we do about the cabinet, tacitly postulating a body of men whose various inclinations would appear homogeneous. That is not strange when we remember that the judges have had careers that are in outline similar . . . Successful barristers, and hence the judges, are not likely to be critical of the legal order. The existing system has brought them large incomes and position has produced a disposition to resent change. (p. 472).

One might question whether Jackson's premise about the homogenizing effects of legal socialization in England should be taken as proof positive that no variance exists in the decisions of English judges, since even in the United States, the wider variance in the social backgrounds, attitudes, and values of a more diverse legal profession has not produced an inordinate amount of overt conflict on appellate courts. The relatively high dissent rate associated with the Supreme Court is a misleading indicator to levels of conflict since dissent is not common in other appellate courts. Courts of Appeals, for example, the intermediate tier of the federal judicial system, and where the bulk of American appellate law is made and interpreted, have an average dissent rate of less than ten percent. State supreme courts show about the same amount, and state intermediate appellate courts show virtually none. Paradoxically, then, a highly diverse American legal profession interacts with a judicial system that displays remarkable consensus, at least measured by the rate of dissent. Yet, we know from the American research that the lack of dissent does not mean necessarily that there is a lack of conflict (Atkins, 1972; Songer, 1982), and thus, one need not assume that to be the case in the English judiciary either.

Jackson's argument, however, skirts a more serious issue which is very much at the core of deciding if English courts can be evaluated as political institutions. Much of it alludes to a social background model of judicial decision-making. The social background model proposes that the choices made by judges in deciding cases are affected by the cognitive maps they have formed through their lives as a result of socialization and acculturation processes. These experiences, denoted by background characteristics, shape judges' values and attitudes, and these in turn affect the judges decision-making on the bench. Since, as Jackson observes in the section quoted here, judges are recruited from a cloistered, professional strata, one should not detect a relationship between political antecedents and judges decisions. In effect, Jackson proposes that because no variance exists in the independent variables, we cannot detect them in the dependent, or decision variables. That of course need not follow; nor need it follow that by proving social background theory to be inappropriate in this context one should argue the larger point about courts being unimportant political institutions.

Indeed, one might argue that social background theory has not produced a convincing body of data to verify a link between background on the one hand and on the bench behavior of American judges on the other. Some important empirical relationships have been detected. We know, for example, that Democratic presidents tend to select judges with at least nominal affiliations with the Democratic party, and Republican presidents select judges with Republican leanings. There is also some evidence that Democratic judges make more "liberal" decisions than Republicans. Yet these relationships, however useful for theory building, do not by themselves validate a comprehensive social background theory. Nor have the studies from which such findings are derived addressed the thorny problems of (1) how to disentangle the differential impact of social background factors as they evolve through time (that is, they have not captured the processes by which later socialization experiences modify, if not replace, the effects of earlier ones); or (2) how background indicators should be weighted in importance, as a comprehensive social background theory surely must assume them to be. So part of Jackson's dilemma is that he is addressing a theory for which scant evidence has been established in the first place. But assuming the theory to be sound, it does not refute the hypothesis that the narrow recruitment basis of English judges provides strong institutionally based support for the class values they represent.

Thus, Jackson really addresses two separate issues. One concerns whether or not we can detect variance in the decisions made by English judges, and particularly, whether or not such differences are structured along politically relevant lines. Another concerns what explanatory variables are proposed to account for the observed variance. Assuming that Jackson is correct that barristers represent an exceedingly narrow stratum of English society, and thus that little variance exists in their background characteristics, it may mean only that social background variables are of little use in establishing statistical relationships.

What Makes Courts Political

Apart from the problem of transposing specific theories from one context to another, there remains the issue of determining the subject matter upon which one focuses attention. In making this decision there is an inclination at times to encumber one's thinking about courts in one political system with courts in any political system. This seems very much the case when it comes to making Anglo-American comparisons.

Most observers seem to agree that English appellate courts are cut from a cloth quite unlike their American counterparts. It's claimed, for example, that English courts "do not assume the creative role out of the tradition of Holmes and Cardozo." (Stevens, 1978, p. xvi), and that the growth of creative judicial law making has been stunted in England by the doctrine of parliamentary supremacy (Horowitz, 1976, p. 2). Similarly, Cox (1977, p. 1) asserts that "Judge made law plays a much greater part in the government of the American people than of the British;" that American ". . . Judges are less attentive to the letter of the law, or to precedent," and that ". . . they move freely in wider orbits." One suspects, of course, that the United States Supreme Court is the standard by which political and policy importance is measured. But to focus upon the Supreme Court as the standard by which to evaluate the roles of courts in other political systems may be counter-productive for comparative inquiry because the evolution of the Supreme Court, from an institution for which it was difficult to recruit justices into one which many critics would claim swings in orbits dangerously out of control, has occurred within the constraints of a political theory and structural groundrules which encouraged its policy and political powers to be established. The American principle of separation of powers, for example, is more than a descriptive statement about the structure of political power and a division of responsibility. While ensuring that political conflicts will intertwine among several institutions of government, it also establishes for the federal judiciary, and the Supreme Court in particular, an independent political terrain that has been delicately nurtured over two centuries. It thus enables the Supreme Court to act as an instrument of political power because of specific responsibilities allocated to it by the architects of the American political system (Carr, 1942).

England, of course, has neither a written constitution nor a Supreme Court in the American sense of the term; not has it that peculiar instrument of limited government that its American cousins have evolved into judicial review. These differences in structure, although important, have unfortunately mesmerized those who write about English law and politics into thinking that a written constitution, the doctrine of separation of powers, and judicial review are necessary conditions for propelling a judiciary into an important political role. However important they may be for understanding the power wielded by the Supreme Court, it is erroneous to assume that a written constitution, tied with the doctrine of judicial review, accounts exclusively for why American courts are important allocators of political values. In fact the Supreme Court's power to declare Congressional statutes unconstitutional, although a substantial sanction on legislative perogative, is not used often enough to be a significant political force. Indeed, if one accepts Robert Dahl's (1957) thesis, Congress usually reasserts its policy anyway thus shifting attention to the Court's power of statutory interpretation, which is exercised by English Courts as well.

CHOICE MAKING AS POLITICAL OUTPUTS

The fact that the Supreme Court is allocated power by a written constitution says much about its roots in the American political system. The functions which emerge from this are tied to forms of policy – making which allow it to establish broad prescriptive rules directed at the future conduct of citizens and public officials. Much of the Court's work in the areas of school desegregation, reapportionment, religious freedom, separation of church and state, abortion, and criminal defendants rights fall into this category. These judicial outputs, described by Salisbury and Heinz (1970) as "structural" policies are, however, only one subset of a larger dimension of public policies made by political institutions. In reality, public policies encompass a broad array of outputs from political institutions; they include *all* of what governments and their institutions do, regardless of intent or motive (Dye, 1978, p. 3–4) and thus, most generally, all "actions taken by governments." (Sharkansky, 1970 p. 1). This broader dimension of governmental and institutional outputs has been labeled as "allocative" policies by Salisbury and Heinz. These are decisions ". . . which confer direct benefits, material or symbolic, upon individuals and groups." (1970, p. 43). In fact, Salisbury and Heinz point to "run-of-the-mill" trial court decisions as excellent examples of allocative policies. (1970, 49–54).

To speak of "allocative policies" suggests the need to look beyond the substantive rules and doctrines typically associated with structural policies of appellate courts to other important outputs and policies of trial courts. Trial courts dispose of much routine litigation where the central questions are how, and to what extent, existing rules ought to be applied to the particular parties in the law suit. However in applying the existing rules, judges inevitably make choices betwen competing interests that are represented, albeit usually informally, through the issues raised in the case. By looking at the plaintiffs and defendant's, particularly in civil cases, one can evaluate which individuals and groups use courts for their personal or collective gain. (c.f. Kenneth Dolbeare, 1967; Herbert Jacob, 1973, pp. 125–132).

These politically relevant outputs assume several forms. In many cases, private individuals or groups challenge public actions after having already lost in some other forum. Although such cases are political because they represent claims upon public resources, so too are suits involving private plaintiffs seeking relief against private defendants. The outcomes of these cases, such as personal injury, trust, wills and divorce, are political because public sanctions and constraints are being imposed upon private individuals and because enormous sums of money can be redistributed as a result of judicial intervention. Another form of trial court allocative policymaking occurs when creditors use small claims courts to collect debts, usually successfully, and when specialized trial courts are used by landlords to prevail over tenants in rental disputes. (Jacob, 1980 146–185). Support or non-support for certain classes of interests represents an important type of political choice-making that is not unrelated to the allocation of resources distributed by the larger political system. Moreover, while the choice made in a single lawsuit may not be significant except to the parties involved, a pattern of support across many cases becomes an indicator to the outputs of the political system if the structure of preference follows some hypothesized and theoretically important dimension. Thus structured choice-making among classes of litigants is an important political outcome of trial court decision-making.

Routine, or "run-of-the-mill" outputs are clearly political if we adhere to Lasswell's (1958) view that politics concerns "who get what, when and how" or to Easton's (1953) that political science focuses upon society's authoritative allocation of values. If politics encompasses such notions as these, it deals with how public institutions impose burdens and benefits and how they distribute and redistribute important societal resources such as wealth, power and freedom. Litigation raising issues of statutory and constitutional interpretation in appellate courts are certainly political by this definition. But so are torts, property and contract disputes, and divorce and family litigation, just to mention a few. How these disputes are resolved is clearly within the domain of politics because the power of public institution is used to structure private relationships concerning economic and social events. The threshold issue, then, should not be whether courts perform a creative role in the "tradition of a Holmes or Brandeis," or whether they move in wide or narrow orbits; the ability to make sweeping policy concerning school desegregation, or abortion, should not be the litmus for determining whether or not a court has a political function. If politics concerns the allocation of burdens, benefits and the imposition of sanctions, questions such as who uses courts, and which interests benefit from that use, are important ones to raise since they concern how public institutions are used to attain objectives thwarted by purely private activity.

Much attention has been paid by American social scientists to these issues as they pertain to American courts (Dolbeare, 1967; Galanter, 1974; Wanner, 1975) and there is no *a priori* reason for assuming that they are any less important for understanding the distribution of political resources in England. There seems, nevertheless, to be a hesitancy to make such assumptions about English courts, perhaps because it is taken for granted that "in England, "the law" plays a less important role than in almost any other western country" (Abel-Smith and Stevens, 1967, p. 1). Yet, if we think about judicial policy-making and political involvement in its broader context, including as we have suggested allocative as well as structural policies, we must be struck by the fact that England has an extraordinarily high civil litigation rate in comparison with other Western countries (Grossman and Sarat, 1971; Ehrmann, 1976, p. 84). This means that English courts are actively involved in dispute resolution and thus that the patterns associated with their decisional outputs should provide important information about the distribution of "allocative policies".

Choice-Making by the English High Court

The remainder of this chapter reports a preliminary analysis of data collected from 1978–1980 decisions of the High Court, the primary civil court of general jurisdiction in England. With a maximum of only 70 judges allocated for England and Wales, the High Court handles a relatively small amount of civil litigation. It is, however, generally regarded as an important civil court in as much as its jurisdiction is concurrent with the lower county courts. The High Court sits in three divisions – Chancery, Queen's Bench and Family. Chancery has jurisdiction over a variety of areas, generally affecting business, property and commercial controversies such as administering estates of decedents, partnership dissolutions, the execution of trusts, and the redemption of foreclosure of mortgages. Queen's bench "... is concerned with the ordinary business of the common law, suits for damages" (Morrison, p. 45), although it does have some limited, but rarely used criminal jurisdiction and does sometimes sit as a Divisional court with appelate jurisdiction. Family, as the name implies, deals with a variety of family related issues such as divorce, financial, maintenance, and property disputes involving spouses (Jackson, 1977, 34–80).

Two aspects of the High Court's decisions will be examined, both of which tap important output dimensions and which relate to the broader structure of its political choice making. One is the status of the litigant in the lawsuit, coded as either the petitioner/respondent or plaintiff/defendant. For our preliminary analysis we have identified a litigant's status in the lawsuit as an important variable on the grounds that those in the petitioner/plaintiff position are, in effect, urging some kind of change in, or are seeking some protection based upon, the legal status quo. They are the ones, in effect, who are requesting a judicial remedy of some type. But if we view court decisions as a form of resource allocation, or as a mechanism for providing benefits and imposing sanctions, we would not assume that law suit status, in and of itself, explains the distribution of the court's output resources. Instead we hypothesize that the distribution of political resources is dependent upon the litigant's social or economic status, where "status" refers to an implicit socio-political dominance relationship among litigants. Much research concerning the outputs of American courts have conceptualized this implicit structuring as a dichotomy between "upperdogs" and "underdogs", or as manifestation of latent societal conflicts, as for example when litigation involves a corporation and a labor union, employer and employee, or landlord and tenant. In this situation, the social or economic status of the litigant may be viewed as a microcosm of deeper, political conflicts. If this assumption is correct, litigant status as petitioner/respondent or plaintiff/defendant should interact with litigant type to establish a non-equal distribution of judicial resources.

Our data base consists of 457 cases decided by the High Court from 1978 to 1980 as reported in the *ALL England Law Reports*. Ninety-three percent of the cases that were included in our sample are from Chancery or Queens Bench (see Table 7.1). Only 7.2 percent are Family Division cases. Nevertheless, our sample of 457 cases provided a broad spectrum of disputes and litigants. These included individuals acting as spouse, tenant, aliens, taxpayers, and in some instances criminal defendants; governmental entities of various sorts, including national and local governmental administrators and agencies, and in some cases, police officers; and a broad spectrum of business and corporate interests. These, and other litigants, raised issues concerning property rights, wills, trusts, estates; domestic relations concerning marriage, divorce, and child custody; liability claims including wrongful death, personal injury and medical malpractice and negligence; public assistance claims concerning health insurance,

TABLE 7.1 Distribution of cases by division of High Court

Cases	*No.*	*%*
Chancery	209	45.7
Family	33	7.2
Queen's Bench	215	47.0
Total	457	100.0

TABLE 7.2 Litigants identified for analysis in High Bench cases

Litigant	*No.*	*%*
Individuals	68	18.1
Tenants	15	4.0
Criminal Defendants	12	3.2
Government Entity	144	38.5
Business and Professional	37	9.8
Landlords	5	1.3
Corporations	68	18.1
Foreign Corporations	13	3.4
Taxpayers	12	3.2
Total	374	100.0

housing, legal aid and widow's benefits; taxes concerning income, trusts, mortgages, donations, land, business expenses; and commercial disputes relating to articles of association, negligence, marketing infringement, contracts, and misrepresentation – just to mention a few. In order to facilitate the data analysis we recoded the litigants into a fewer number of categories as shown in Table 7.2. Some of the litigant types were not easily placed in any category and hence they were dropped from the analysis. We were, however, able to use 82 percent of the cases and thus retain a large enough data set with which to evaluate the High Court decisions.

TABLE 7.3 Petitioner success rate

	No.	%
For Petitioner	259	58.2
Against Petitioner	178	40.0
Mixed Results	8	1.8
Total	445	100.0

We begin by examining whether or not one's status in a lawsuit affects the probability of success. As data in Table 7.3 indicate, petitioners fare slightly better than do respondents, although the success rates are sufficiently balanced to suggest that one's status as petitioner or respondent does not have a great effect on whether or not one wins or loses their case. Table 7.4, however, shows that the type of litigant involved and their status in the law suit have much to do with their success. The data in this table are arranged so that we can compare the overall success rate of certain kinds of litigants against their success depending upon their positioning in the litigation. In effect, Table 7.4 compares litigant success rates when controlled for by lawsuit status. The final column in this table reports the difference in the success rates in each of the positions. The data in this final column, then, become the measure of the effect of lawsuit status; the lower the P–R (petitioner – respondent) difference, the less the impact of lawsuit status; conversely, the larger the P–R difference, the greater the impact. Using these measures we see that the success of individuals identified as criminal defendants in civil litigation is greatly dependent upon whether or not they are the complaining party; by contrast, the success rate of foreign corporations is unaffected by their lawsuit status.

TABLE 7.4 Success rates for specific litigants

	Overall percent	*Success of petitioner*	*Success of respondent*	*Difference P–R*
Government	62.5	77.7	56.0	21.7
Corporations	45.7	52.7	38.2	14.5
Business & Prof.	42.8	47.3	36.0	11.3
Individual	46.7	56.0	35.2	20.8
Criminal Def.	42.3	52.5	8.3	44.2
Foreign Corp.	41.6	43.4	38.4	5.4
Taxpayers	40.7	60.0	16.6	43.4

Overall, these data show that one litigant class, government institutions and agency representatives, fare substantially better than any other group. Simply put, government as a litigant before the High Court doesn't lose often either as petitioner or as respondent. Other litigants such as criminal defendants filing civil suits, individuals filing suit as a taxpayer, and foreign corporations, have much lower rates of success. These data indicate, however, that more is involved here than the type of litigant; they also show that litigant success is enhanced or depressed depending upon their position in the lawsuit. For example, when government represents the petitioning or complaining party it is successful in over three-quarters of the cases (77.7%); by contrast, it wins in slightly over half the time when it serves as respondent/ defendants. By contrast, corporations, while showing an overall success rate of 45.7 percent, win over 50 percent of the time as petitioner/complainant, but lose substantially more often as respondent/defendant. This interaction between litigant status and litigant type is also apparent when criminal defendants (in civil suits) and individuals involved in taxpayer litigation are parties in the lawsuit. When they were respondents, criminal defendant's success rate was only 8.3 percent and taxpayer/individuals success rate was only marginally higher at 16.6 percent. The overall impact of the differential success rates can be seen in the data presented in the last column of Table 4. It reports the difference between petitioner and respondent success rates, and thus the extent to which the law suit status exaggerates the percentage of cases in which a particular type of litigant wins. For some groups, such as the taxpayer individuals and criminal defendants, the differences are large, while for some, such as business and professional groups, they are rather small by comparison. The relatively high figure for the government probably is a reflection of its high overall rate of success and the particularly high rate when it is the plaintiff-petitioner.

The structuring of the differential support rates shown by the High Court, and the extent to which this structure parallels an implicit "upper dog"–"under dog" dimension can be examined by comparing the litigant types by litigant status and controlling again for certain combinations in which particular sets of litigants oppose each other in the same litigation. These data, in Table 7.5, report the petitioner success rates for various combination of litigants, comparing the success of litigant-type against the litigant status in the lawsuit. The data show that the government as litigant attains a high rate of success as either petitioner or respondent, but that differences exist depending upon who the opposing litigant may be. For example, when the government opposes individuals, the government wins 70 percent of the time as the petitioner, and 60 percent of the time as respondent (100 minus the individual success rate as petitioner). However, when

TABLE 7.5 Petitioner success rate by litigant status, litigant type, controlling for combinations of parties

Litigant Status Petitioner	*v. Respondent*	*Petitioner Success Rate (%)*	
I. Government vs. "lesser" interests			
Government	Individual	70	D = 30
Individual	Government	40	
Government	Prof. & Bus.	83.3	D = 51.7
Prof. & Bus.	Government	31.6	
Government	Corporations	70.6	D = 29.7
Corporations	Government	41.2	
Government	Taxpayer	83.3	D = 23.3
Taxpayer	Government	60.0	
Government	Crim. Def.	88.9	D = 34.8
Crim. Def.	Government	54.1	
II. Economic Entities v. Individuals			
Individual	Corporation	42.9	D = 57.1
Corporation	Individual	100.0	
Individual	Bus. & Prof.	50.0	D = 16.7
Bus. & Prof.	Individual	66.7	
III. Corporations v. Business and Professional Groups			
Corporation	Bus. & Prof. (8)	50.0	D = 0
Bus. & Prof.	Corporation (6)	50.0	

the suit involves an individual suing in the capacity of a taxpayer, the government fares very well winning 83.3 percent of its cases as petitioner but winning only 40 percent as respondent. And in litigation involving business and professional groups, the government wins 83.3 percent of the time as petitioner and almost 70 percent of its cases when it is the respondent. Corporations, however, appear on more equal footing in as much as the petitioning party in suits involving the government against corporations wins 56 percent of the time, a figure fairly close to the success rate of all petitioner's in our sample (51 percent).

Overall, the Government fares quite well in the High Court regardless of their status and regardless of who the opposing litigant might be. The other portion of Table 7.5 shows the same pattern. For example, when an individual sues a corporation, the individual is successful only 42.9 percent of the time. This is below the overall success rate for individuals of 46.7 percent (see Table 7.4). This means that corporations won as defendants in such suits in about 57 percent of the cases which exceeds even their overall success rates as petitioner (52.7, see Table 7.4). And corporations win all their cases when they are plaintiffs against individual-defendants. Generally, "superior" litigants prevail 61 percent of the time over "inferior litigants; and if we exclude the exceptional category of criminal defendants suing the government, the success of "superior" litigants increases to 76 percent! In fact, as a general rule, the differences in petitioner-repondent success rates for various combinations listed in Table 7.5 are greater in each instance than the differences reported in Table 7.4! In other words, while Table 7.4 indicates that litigant's success rates for various litigant types varies by their lawsuit status, Table 7.5 shows that a benefit accrues to certain litigant types – such as the government and corporations – regardless of their lawsuit status when they are matched against so-called "inferior" litigants.

Conclusion

Its apparent that a non-random structuring of litigant success rates exists in the High Court, both in terms of the relative success rate of each group and the interaction between the litigant type and lawsuit status. Why certain groups or interests fare better than others is, however, open to question. One explanation, might be that courts are instruments of dominant societal interests, and that government, corporations and to a lesser extent business and professional litigants are representative of those elite interests. Alternatively, certain parties may win more frequently than others because they bring better prepared cases, better strategies for success, or superior resources to court, all of which combine to enhance their success. In this sense, the "haves", (or at least certain types of "haves") are more successful than the "have-nots" because, as "repeat players" and not "one shotters", they are able to muster a superiority based upon resource advantage (Galanter, 1974). Of course, whether or not the benefits that accrue to repeat players can be disentangled from policy or ideological preferences shown by judges is another matter. Still, the distribution in success rates achieved by certain classes of litigants and the differentials among them, suggests some factors, whatever they may be, at work other than pure randomness.

The similarity between the outputs of the English High Court and those of American trial courts are striking to say the least. Several studies of American courts have found that certain classes of litigants win lawsuits more regularly than others when they oppose each other in the same dispute. An excellent illustration of this pattern was reported by Wanner (1975) in a study of civil trial court outputs in Baltimore, Cleveland, and Milwaukee. His data show that plaintiffs on cases more regularly than did defendants, but more importantly that the rate of success was not evenly distributed across different kinds of litigants. The most successful litigant in Wanner's study, the government, maintained a high rate of success regardless of whether it opposed business organization or private individuals. Business organizations, on the other hand, had a higher rate of success when opposed by individuals. Such findings suggest a propensity for dominant economic and societal interests – the "haves" (Galanter, 1974) so to speak – to find favorable results in civil litigation both in England and in the United States.

In probing the factors causing these patterns we return quickly to the composition of the English judiciary that our reference to Jackson's *Machinery of Justice* had highlighted. The English judiciary is staffed, on the whole, by an elite stratum of English society. It is composed of a homogenous group of barristers, 75 percent of whom are drawn from the ranks of the traditional landed upper class, professional, commercial and administrative sectors of the English upper class, and upper middle classes (J. A. G. Griffith, 1977). This distinctively "upper class bias" (Tate, 1975, p. 117) has been in effect at least during the past century. Most judges have been the product of upper middle class or upper class family backgrounds, a large proportion (a third) of them were educated at one of the prestigious "Clarendon" schools, and about 70 percent pursued their higher education at either Oxford or Cambridge Universities (Tate, 1975, page 117). It may well be that, as some have argued, few partisan appointments have occurred in this century. However, judicial politics and a judicial system involved in politics assumes forms other than those concerning partisan influences upon recruitment. It includes the political opinions of the judges, their views about how the social and economic interests in society should be structured, and the extent to which those views, consciously or unconsciously, affect their decisions.

Indeed, Jackson had perhaps chosen the wrong reason for being concerned about the utility of social background theory for understanding the decision of English judges. The homogeneity of judges' social backgrounds may, as he suggested, explain why little dissent occurs within English courts. That, however, only means that English judges hold uniform perceptions of law and policy (c.f. Robertson, 1982). However, ideological convergence does not mean that English judges are value-free and that their decisions reflect a neutral solution to disputes. Indeed, the data reported in this chapter indicate that the upper middle and upper class backgrounds of English judges encourage pro-governmental and pro-institutional bias at the expense of individual plaintiffs. To the extent that these data, preliminary to be sure, reflect more widespread support within the courts for certain litigants over others, it places English trial courts in a political posture not unlike their American counterparts. In this sense the English judiciary may be no more politically neutral or independent than the American. In a different context, this is similar to what Shapiro (1982) argues in reference to the English judiciary.

Shapiro claims that English courts are not independent judicial institutions, but have become as subordinate to parliament as they had been to the crown centuries earlier. With the fusion of authority and sovereignty in parliament, English courts, and particularly the appellate courts, do not undertake independent review of broad policy the way their American counterparts do. But, of course, lack of judicial independence, in the context used by Shapiro, does not negate English courts having an important political role; indeed being under the thumb, so to speak, of their parliamentary masters only underscores their serving to enforce and perpetuate the policies and norms of the class strata and interest served by the parliament. Courts thus may be strong anchors for the status quo and vital instruments for perpetuating the power of the "haves" at the expense of the "have-nots." Thus lack of independence may have altered the spheres of judicial activity but that does not rule out the possibility that political objectives are still served in those areas in which courts are used routinely to resolve disputes. In fact, the thrust of Shapiro's argument is that the failure of Anglo-American courts to achieve true political independence makes them distinctive from the "prototype" of courts as neutral institutions and judges as impartial disputes resolvers.

NOTE

1. David Robertson's (1982) psychometric analysis of, and Alan Patterson's (1982) application of role theory to the House of Lords represent harbingers of important and innovative future inquiry. Also important is Stevens' (1978) study of the House of Lords as a political institution. Stevens assumes that decisional differences among Law Lords reflects their divergent political, social and judicial ideologies. His thinking about the law holds decision-making as an integrated process of personality, roles and attitudes and is apparent from his description of the judicial behavior of one contemporary member:

> If Wilberforce did not always demonstrate creativity, this absence may be attributed as much to his innate modesty and to his idiosyncratic view of the goals of law . . . He was, for instance, far more willing to concur in judgments than some members of the Lords, even when he had his doubts, and he freely admitted that he had difficulty making up his mind. (p. 558).

References

ABLE-SMITH, BRIAN and ROBERT STEVENS (1967) *Lawyers and the Courts: A Sociological Study of the English Legal System, 1750–1965.* Cambridge: Harvard University Press.

ATKINS, BURTON (1972) "Decision-Making Rules and Judicial Strategy on the United States Courts of Appeals." *Western Political Quarterly* **25:** 626–642.

BAUM, LAWRENCE (1977) "Review Article: Research on the English Judicial Process." *British Journal of Political Science* **7:** 511–527.

BECKER, THEODORE, L. (1970) *Comparative Judicial Politics: The Political Functioning of Courts.* Chicago: Rand McNally.

BELOFF, MAX and GILLIAN PEEL (1980) *The Government of The United Kingdom: Political Authority in a Changing Society.* New York: Norton.

BIRCH, ANTHONY (1977) *The British System of Government.* London: George Allen and Unwin.

CARR, ROBERT K. (1942) *The Supreme Court and Judicial Review.* New York: Holt, Rinehart and Winston.

CARTER, GWENDOLYN (1972) *The Government of the United Kingdom.* New York: Harcourt, Brace, Janovich.

COX, ARCHIBALD (1976) *The Role of The Supreme Court in American Government.* New York: Oxford University Press.

DAHL, ROBERT (1957) "Decision-making in a democracy: The Supreme Court as a National Policy-Maker." *Journal of Public Law* **6:** 279–295.

DANIELSKI, DAVID and GLENDON SCHUBERT (1969) *Comparative Judicial Behavior.* New York: Oxford University Press.

DOLBEARE, KENNETH (1967) *Trial Courts in Urban Politics.* New York: John Wiley.

DYE, THOMAS R. (1978) *Understanding Public Policy.* Englewood Cliffs: Prentice Hall, Inc.

EASTON, DAVID (1953) *The Political System.* New York: Alfred A. Knopf.

EHRMANN, HENRY W. (1976) *Comparative Legal Cultures.* Englewood Cliff: Prentice Hall.

GALANTER, MARC (1974) "Why the 'Haves' Come Out Ahead: Speculations on the Limits of Legal Change." *Law and Society Review.* **9:** 95–160.

GRIFFITH, J. A. G. (1977) *The Politics of the Judiciary.* Glasgow: Fontana/Collins.

GROSSMAN, JOEL and AUSTIN SARAT (1971). "Political Culture and Judicial Research," *Washington University Law Quarterly,* 1971: 177–209.

HOROWITZ, DONALD (1977) *Courts and Social Policy.* Washington: Brookings.

JACKSON, R. M. (1977) *The Machinery of Justice in England.* 7th ed. Cambridge: Cambridge University Press.

JACOB, HERBERT (1980) *Crime and Justice in Urban America.* Englewood Cliffs: Prentice Hall.

LASSWELL, HAROLD (1958) *Politics, Who Gets What, When, How.* New York: Meridian Books.

MORRISON, FRED L. (1973) *Courts and Political Process in England.* Beverly Hills: Sage.

PATTERSON, ALAN (1982) *The Law Lords.* MacMillan: London.

PUNNETT, R. M. (1969) *British Government and Politics.* Heinemann: London.

ROBERTSON, DAVID (1982) "Judicial Ideology in The House of Lords: A Jurimetric Analyses." *British Journal of Political Science* **12:** 1–25.

ROSE, RICHARD (1969) *Policy Making in Britain: A Reader in Government.* New York: Free Press.

ROSE, RICHARD (1980) *Politics in England.* 3rd Boston: Little, Brown and Co.

SALISBURY, ROBERT and JOHN HEINZ (1970) "A Theory of Policy Analysis and Some Preliminary Applications," in Ira Sharkansky, (ed.) *Policy Analysis in Political Science.* Chicago: Markham Publishing Company. 39–60.

SHAPIRO, MARTIN (1981) *Courts: A Comparative and Political Analysis.* Chicago: University of Chicago Press.

SHARKANSKY, IRA (ed.) (1970) *Policy Analysis in Political Science.* Chicago: Markham Publishing Company.

SONGER, DONALD (1982) "Consensual and Nonconsensual Decision in Unanimous Opinions of The United States Courts of Appeals." *American Journal of Political Science.* **26:** 225–239.

STEVENS, ROBERT (1978) *Law and Politics: The House of Lords as a Judicial Body, 1800–1976.* Chapel Hill: University of North Carolina Press.

TATE, C. NEAL (1975) "Paths to The Bench in Britain: A Quasi Experimental Study of The Recruitment of a Judicial Elite." *Western Political Quarterly.* **28:** 108–129.

WANNER, CRAIG (1975) "The Public Ordering of Private Relations: Winning Civil Court Cases." *Law and Society Review.* **9:** 293–306.

PART III

MULTI—NATION ANALYSES: THE EXTENSION OF THE SCIENTIFIC FRONTIER

Introduction

Three of the four concluding chapters incorporate comparisons of the American judiciary with that of another nation, two involving perspectives on British institutions and one on Japan. In the fourth chapter Professor Glendon Schubert investigates the characteristics and behavior of judges in the non-American nations which shared in common clearly defined multi-cultural societal distinctions – Switzerland and South Africa.

In Chapter 8, Professor Robert Steamer utilizes judicial leadership as the unifying concept, functionally comparing the Chief Justice of the United States and the Lord Chancellor of Great Britain in the context of the political and institutional environment of each nation. Professor David Barnum, in Chapter 9, chooses an entirely different approach. He notes that particular institutional attributes – the presence or absence of a written constitution, a federal or a unitary structure, the maintenance or not of a system of separation of powers, or the possession or non-possession of judicial review – are frequently identified as conducive or antithetical to the protection of human rights. And he also notes that the United States and Great Britain, although different in each of these institutional particulars, are considered outstanding examples of nations strongly protective of human rights. Professors Takeo Hayakawa and John R. Schmidhauser investigate and compare the internal organization and procedures of the Supreme Courts of Japan and the United States in the context of a neo-Weberian conceptual framework. In the last substantive chapter, 11, Professor Glendon Schubert provides an incisive analysis of the significance of cultural/systemic, background attributes, attitudinal, and decisional variables in predicting higher appellate judicial decision-making in South Africa and Switzerland.

CHAPTER 8

JUDICIAL LEADERSHIP: ENGLISH AND AMERICAN EXPERIENCE

ROBERT J. STEAMER
UNIVERSITY OF MASSACHUSETTS, BOSTON

Judicial Leadership: English and American Experiences

In 1787 the American constitution makers were working within an English framework, and the American legal system is rightly called Anglo-American. As one reviews the judicial systems of the United Kingdom and the United States, however, both in their historical development and in the manner in which they currently function, their divergences appear to be greater than their similarities. To the casual foreign observer the British judiciary seems to be more complex and cumbersome than it needs to be under a unitary government, but unquestionably it has produced an efficient and fair arrangement of settling controversies and punishing criminals, second to none. If one unfamiliar with American history were shown a schematic drawing of United States courts in action, it would appear as a crazy quilt pattern of needless overlapping jurisdictions and duplication of functions. But once one becomes familiar with the nation's development, with its federal system and its huge and diverse population, the two court systems, state and federal, insulated one from the other in part, yet operating within the same common law rubric and culminating in one final court of appeals, make sense given historic necessities and political realities. Compared to the British judiciary this seems relatively inefficient, but it does produce a result that is equally fair and just.

Although both Britain and America pride themselves on their

"independent" judiciaries, that is, independent of political control, the courts in both countries are creatures of the political process, and Lord Chancellors and Chief Justices are not excepted. The occupants of both offices owe their positions to practicing partisan politicians and probably, although not necessarily, have been practicing partisan politicians themselves. The Chief Justice of the United States and the Lord Chancellor of Great Britain (their exact official titles) are not precise counterparts, but whatever leadership with respect to judicial matters is to be taken in either country, it is they who must take it. Although it was not always so, it is certainly true in the 1980s.

Before comparing the offices and duties of the Chief Justice and Lord Chancellor, it is essential that we review briefly the single most important distinction between English and American courts, namely the power of the latter and the lack of it in the former, to declare acts of the legislature unconstitutional. Although the Chief Justice has only one vote on a court of nine, his role as chief does give him an advantage over his colleagues on the United States Supreme Court in that first, he may be instrumental in persuading a majority to invalidate a state or federal law; and second, in a case involving a major question of policy his name, particularly if he writes the opinion, is forever linked with that policy.[1] Thus a leadership initiative is available to an American Chief that is not within the authority of the British Lord Chancellor. On the other hand as England's chief judicial officer and ranking in protocol above all other except the Crown and the Archbishop of Canterbury, the Lord Chancellor has many prerogatives, some of which must be the envy of any sitting American Chief Justice.

While the office of Chief Justice of the United States has been in existence for slightly less than two hundred years, the office of Lord Chancellor goes back at least to the Norman Conquest, and some historians date its beginnings in the seventh century.[2] We do know that Edward the Confessor (1042–66) was the first King to use the Great Seal and to have a chancellor to keep it.[3] Since that time there have been 232 Holders of the Great Seal, although it was not until 1562 that Parliament declared the "authority of the Lord Keeper of the Great Seal and Lord Chancellor to be one."[4] Like most British institutions the Lord High Chancellor has simply developed through custom, practice and statutory intervention from time to time, and while "no constitutional theorist would devise him in his wildest dreams," he seems typically English and is an extremely effective support to parliamentary government.[5] What makes the office suspect is that it combines executive, legislative and judicial powers in the hands of one man, a practice that is anathema to those of us who believe that dispersal of power is vital to the success and permanence of constitutional government.

Unlike the American Chief Justice who is primarily, although not exclusively, a judge; the Lord Chancellor is primarily an administrator and only minimally a judge. Currently, although the selection process is a political one in both cases, the Lord Chancellor who must be politically acceptable to his Party must also be well qualified to be a judge; he must be an experienced and capable barrister who holds the respect of bench and bar alike. The American Chief, on the other hand, although customarily a lawyer by training, may or may not have achieved any distinction as an advocate, may or may not have had any experience as a judge, may in fact, have been primarily a practising politician. Despite the lack of formal constraints on an American President when choosing a Chief Justice, the chiefs generally have been very capable men, and with few exceptions would have had the requisite qualifications by British standards for the Lord Chancellorship. Of the eight American Chief Justices who have served in the twentieth century, one (Taft) had been a former President, one (White) a United States Senator, two (Hughes and Warren) had been Governors of major states (New York and California) and two (Stone and Vinson) had served, after successful political careers, in the President's cabinet. Only two, Fuller and Burger, had not held major elective or non-judicial appointive office. All but two of the eight had seen prior judicial service, three of them (White, Hughes and Stone) having served as Associate Justices of the Supreme Court prior to being elevated to Chief. By background and training, if not by temperament, all were minimally qualified and most were very well qualified for the appointment.

Nineteen men have served as Lord Chancellor during the present century, fifteen of whom had been in the House of Commons, a not very surprising fact since the Lord Chancellor serves in the Cabinet and not only must have some affinity for the policies of the government of the day but must be able by background and training to help formulate those policies. Of the four who had never been in the Commons, the most recent, Lord Gardiner, the Labour Lord Chancellor from 1964–1970, had had extensive political experience including service as an alderman on the London County Council and membership in the House of Lords. He had also been an active crusader for law reform and was a respected member of the bar. When Winston Churchill returned to power in 1951, his choice for the job was Lord Simonds who, at the time of his election, had been a judge for fourteen years. The remaining two exceptions, Lord Sankey appointed in 1929, and Lord Maugham (1938), were selected while serving on the Court of Appeals. It has been suggested that the latter two were chosen in times of great national crisis and thus gave the public a confident sense of non-partisanship.[6] It will be readily noted that during the seven decades of the twentieth century, there were only eight Chief Justices compared to nineteen Lord Chancellors,[7] and therein lies a major distinction between the offices. The American Chief, with life tenure for all practical purposes, serves well beyond the tenure of the President who appointed him, and thus can transcend whatever political considerations surrounded his appointment, and over a period of years, he can build a record of achievement. Depending upon the nations's political climate, the Lord Chancellor's tenure may be brief or long, but on the average his time in office is considerably less than his American counterpart since he is tied to the fortunes of his Party.

DUTIES OF CHIEF AND CHANCELLOR COMPARED

Before discussing the roles in which the incumbents of the two offices may be said to have similar responsibilities, in what sense are they totally different? First, the Lord Chancellor exercises executive and legislative political powers of a kind that are absolutely removed from the constitutional duties of the American Chief Justice. As an active member of the Cabinet he must be informed on all matters of domestic and foreign policy, for he participates in the decisions of the government at the highest level. In addition to attending all meetings of the Cabinet he serves on Cabinet Committees, some of which he chairs. He is also the Chief legal adviser within the Cabinet, performing the duties of the American Attorney General.[8] Equally important are his legislative duties. He is the Speaker of the House of Lords, but he not only presides over the sessions of the Lords, he actually participates in the debates as a recognized government spokesman. This is not an easy task since he must officiate in a fair and just manner and yet espouse the incumbent government's position on legislation before the House. These roles in theory violate all the historical commands that the presiding officer of a parliamentary body be neutral, along with the potential evils of concentrating legislative and executive powers in a single office. In practice, however, the system works smoothly, in part because of the conventions that have grown up around the office, in

The two remaining roles of the Lord Chancellor, that of judge and that of judicial administrator, are also roles of the American Chief Justice, but they are exercised in a very different manner on opposite sides of the Atlantic. Prior to the development of the welfare state and corresponding roughly to the end of World War II the Lord Chancellor regularly exercised his functions as a judge. He presided over the House of Lords when it acted in its capacity as Britain's final court of appeal and he sat as an *ex officio* member of the Privy Council in hearing appeals from the colonies. He also occasionally sat in the High Court and the Court of Appeal. Today, however, his political and administrative duties are so extensive that he rarely sits as a judge even though he is empowered to do so on several levels of the judiciary.[9] And unlike the American Chief, he has no role in assigning the writing of opinions in cases at any level. In the House of Lords, the court of last resort comparable to the American Supreme Court, opinions are delivered *seriatim* and thus require no assignment as such. The Lord Chancellor is responsible, however, for selecting the panels of judges who sit on an individual case. As a matter of practice appeals are heard by eleven Lords of Appeal in Ordinary, commonly known as law lords,[10] plus any former Chancellors or former judges who happen to hold peerages. Normally the Lord Chancellor selects panels of five law lords to hear appeals, and chancellors have been known to use this power to ensure that their views prevailed in cases of public importance.[11] Usually the decision to permit an appeal to the House is made by the Court of Appeal by granting leave to appeal in those cases in which important legal questions need resolution. In some instances the law lords will grant leave after the Court of Appeal has refused, but these are given infrequently, and the Lord Chancellor has no special influence in the decision to grant or deny an appeal.[12]

Unlike that of the Lord Chancellor the American Chief's authority depends in part upon two factors that are only minimally among the duties of the former. The American Chief, like the Chancellor, is by custom a jurist whose labors are expected to command respect from his colleagues at the bar, from the faculties of law and political science in the universities and from the press and the public at large. His work as the writer of legal opinions is there for all to see, to be put under a microscope and dissected by both friendly and unfriendly critics. In this capacity he is judged as a legal craftsman, but given the fact of judicial review there is more. His opinions and the decisions of his Court have a profound impact on public policy, and for every person who is pleased with the outcome of a case there is usually one who is who is pleased with the outcome of a case there is usually one who is not. All of which means that a national debate is often swirling around the head of the Chief Justice. He is too liberal. He is too conservative. His opinions are not well reasoned. His opinions are too technical, abstruse and ineffective. More important than his reputation as a judge perhaps, is his ability to lead his Court, to present it as a hard working, intelligent, cohesive and sensitive force in American life, to convince the public that the Court is constitutionally and politically correct most of the time. He must, in short, lead internally and externally to be a successful chief. None has ever been impeached or resigned under fire, and some have touched the office with greatness. All have acquitted themselves competently.

Internal management of the Supreme Court is the Chief's most consistent challenge, and it is a role totally oustide the experience of a British Lord Chancellor. Central to the decision-making of the Supreme Court is the conference, a weekly meeting normally lasting from two to four hours in which the Justices meet, discuss and decide cases, and it is in the conference that the Chief has notable advantage over his colleagues. The conference is the "matrix of leadership of the Court," and only if the Chief can exert personal and intellectual leadership can he minimize conflict, increase social cohesion and move the work to completion.[13] Justice Rehnquist has suggested that the Chief's advantage lies in the fact that he states the case first, including an analysis of the governing legal principles. If "he cannot, with this advantage, maximize the impact of his views, subsequent interruptions of colleagues or digressions on his part will not succeed either."[14] What the Chief does initially then may at a minimum be the determining factor in convincing an uncommitted Justice to join a nucleus in forming a majority and, ideally, a unanimous Court. Generally the conference is not an occasion for conversions since each Justice has already heard oral arguments and has studied the briefs and memoranda from his law clerks and his colleagues. Nevertheless, there are always those few marginal or "hard" cases, usually the most politically sensitive in that they will trigger congressional or presidential opposition and anger or will arouse public indignation. In such cases the Chief's ability to lead will be crucial to the outcome of the decision. Only two Chiefs, John Marshall and Charles Evans Hughes, approximate the ideal in the simultaneous exertion of personal and intellectual leadership. We do not know the precise ways in which John Marshall dealt with his Court, but we do know of his warmth, his magnetism, the respect, affection and esteem in which he was held by his colleagues, and, of course, the brilliant results of his labors. The Hughes record is clear. At one time or another, virtually all of the brethren paid tribute to Hughes' leadership generally and to his conduct of the conference specifically. Hughes' penchant for order and his photographic memory brought him to each conference formidably prepared. After summarizing a case accurately and comprehensively, he would then suggest how the case ought to be decided, and in some instances that was the only discussion the case received as the Justices proceeded to vote for the disposition suggested by the Chief. When a Justice did wish to speak, he did so in order of seniority and without interruption, which meant that interchange of views was with the Chief and not with the other Justices. Most of the Chiefs have been extremely able personal leaders but more often than not they have been deferential to the intellects of others. Chief Justices Waite, Fuller, Taft, Vinson and Warren, were warm, decent human beings who possessed an ability to command; yet each could recognize and accept the superior intellectual leadership of associates like Field, Miller, Van Devanter, Holmes, Black or Frankfurter. Chief Justices White and Stone, on the other hand, while intellectually the equals of any of the brethren of their day, were incapable of running an orderly conference or orchestrating a cohesive Court. Chaos is the only word to describe the Court after Stone succeeded Hughes. The conference became a debating society with tempers out of control and tensions running high as the Justices bickered almost endlessly, with honest intellectual differences escalating into personal antagonisms.

However long it takes and by whatever route arrived at, the conference does terminate with the Justices deciding to decide, and if the Chief is in the majority, which all Chiefs have been most of the time, he then must assign the writing of opinions. For the most part this involves an equitable division of labor. Once again though, there are a few cases in which the Justice's name on the opinion has important public overtones and/or political significance. It needs to be emphasized, however, that the final opinion is a collegial affair. It has been worked and reworked after being read and commented on by those Justices in dissent as well as those who concur, and some of the most pungent and eloquent phrases may have been integrated into the opinion at the insistence of a Justice as the price to be paid for the supporting vote. Nevertheless the judge's name attached to the opinion may affect the "decision's acceptability, its value as a precedent for future guidelines, and support of other judges."[15]

In addition to equalizing the work load the Chief's reasons for matching the Justice to the case include: holding him in the majority; attracting dissenters to the majority; maximizing the desired content of the opinion; rewarding a Justice who has a particular interest in writing the opinion or conversely, preventing a colleague from placing his imprimatur on the decision; and finally, giving the opinion a public relations or political advantage.[16] Chief Justices, like all humans, have their likes and dislikes, showing preferences for some colleagues over others. Showing an obvious bias or favoritism in opinion assignment is, however, a sure way to engender disaffection, disrespect and ultimately a loss in stature and authority. And history will not be kind to the Chief whom the brethren hold in contempt.

Unlike the private nature of the Chief's role in the conference which we learn about indirectly, there is an area of official performance which the public observes directly. The Chief presides over the Court's open hearings and his behaviour is there for all to observe, including the press, an ever-present critic and not always a friendly one. During Marshall's time opposing counsel argued their cases for days, but with the gradual increase in litigation oral argument came to be limited to one hour for each side. Earl Warren introduced the summary calendar for some cases, an arrangement whereby each side was permitted only one half hour. This has now become the norm under Warren Burger, and only in cases of special importance are the litigants allotted a full hour. As is true of the presiding judge in any Anglo-American court room, the Chief Justice has absolute control over the proceedings. How the Chief conducts his Court is an individual matter and variations in style have been more a matter of degree than kind, but all Chiefs in the twentieth century have been aware of the need to conserve time within the limits of fairness to both sides in the dispute and with deference to questions from the bench. No Chief has failed to perform satisfactorily in holding court, and it is unlikely that any will in the future since the preparatory road to the Chief Justiceship, whether it be through the bench, the bar or elective office is such that the appointee will have had more experience than most in presiding over open meetings in which self-control, timing, and evenhandedness were prerequisites to success.

Certainly the lack of any political link to the executive or legislative branches after he is appointed is a strong factor in an American Chief's retaining his credibility as a truly independent judge even when deciding cases with obvious policy implications. As head of the judicial branch of government, however, he is severely handicapped in his inability to exercise political clout on behalf of efficiency and reform. In spite of theoretical injunctions against it, the union of political and judicial power in a single office where used responsibly, permits the holder to be a true head of the judiciary in every sense of the term. If the Lord Chancellor does not lead the nation's highest appellate court in the manner of an American Chief Justice, he does exercise functions that any American Chief would covet. He is in a special position to press for law reform; he is responsible for the rule-making authority of both the superior and inferior courts; he appoints court officers, fixes their responsibilities, arranges their duties; he answers to Parliament for costs and accounts for fees.[17] Most important of all, however, he determines the number of judges needed[18] and he appoints or is consulted in the appointment of all judges, high and low in the British judicial system. He also may remove second-tier judges on the ground of incapacity or misbehavior.[19]

Constitutionally, appointments to the superior courts – House of Lords (Law Lords), Court of Appeal (Lords Justices of Appeal), the Lord Chief Justice, the Master of the Rolls and the President of the Family Division – are appointed by the Queen upon the advice of the Prime Minister, and the remaining judges – High Court, Circuit; magistrates, and recorders – are appointed by the Queen upon the advice of the Lord Chancellor. In practice, however, although the Lord Chancellor consults with many people – politicians, judges and practising barristers – the final selection is his to make. In recent years the Prime Minister has perfunctorily submitted the Chancellor's choices to the Queen whose approval is a formality. There is no bar association evaluation of credentials, nor are there any confirmation hearings.[20] So much power in the hands of one man violates the American concept of checks and balances and would appear open to abuse, but given the nature and structure of the English legal profession, abuses have been rare in the past and are non-existent today. As Lord Justice Scarman maintains, the success of the English practice indicates "a firm grasp of essentials – a limited field of choice and a chooser with a personal knowledge of the field."[21] What he is referring to is: first, the superior court judges must be chosen from the ranks of barristers of which there are only 3400 in all of England and Wales; and second, the Lord Chancellor, himself a barrister, remains in touch with the profession both in his capacity as a law lord and in his continuing involvement with his Inn.[22] Furthermore, the qualifications for appointment to upper level judgeships are rigorous,[23] and while no system for promotion exists, British judges do in fact move up the ladder which means that superior court judges are men with long judicial experience.[24] However, the lower court judges and officials, unlike those at the upper levels, must apply for the office, and they are appointed only after the Lord Chancellor's Department makes inquiries about their character and professional ability, and finally after they have been interviewed and passed the requisite examinations.

This system, with the Lord Chancellor at its apex, has been remarkably free of corruption and the standards of justice have been admittedly high. But the system is not without its critics. "Almost alone," says one, "courts and lawyers have been left with many eighteenth-century practices and institutions," and radical reforms have been discouraged "by the extensive and centralized patronage system controlled by successive Lord Chancellors."[25] For the most part it is the political left and the academic sociologists who would reorder the system, but if the British look carefully at the changes the sociologists have wrought in other countries, they had better think long and hard before heeding their advice.

How an American Chief Justice allocates his time between his responsibilities as judge and his duties as head of the judiciary depends partly on the exigencies of the times but primarily on the interests of the individual occupying the office. Although the title, Chief Justice of the United States, did not appear in a statute until 1866,[26] and was not used in the language of a formal appointment until Melville Fuller was confirmed in 1888,[27] it was William Howard Taft whose political leadership entitled him to be in substance as well as name, the head of the American judiciary. As a direct result of Taft's efforts Congress enacted two major pieces of legislation dealing with the federal judicial system, one in 1922, the other in 1925. The first, in addition to creating more judges for the lower courts, gave the federal judicial system a sense of direction and a much needed administrative unity by creating the Conference of Senior Circuit Judges to advise Congress on legislation governing the judiciary and to promote effective standards of judicial administration in the lower federal courts. The second, the Judiciary Act of 1925, streamlined the entire method of appeals. Under its terms most decisions of the federal courts of appeals and of the state appellate courts were now reviewable in the Supreme Court only by a writ of *certiorari*, a writ by which the Court would have broad discretion to decide which cases should have a full hearing.

By giving the Court almost complete control over its own docket, the 1925 law added a dimension of internal strength to the Chief in that he might, depending upon his personal powers of persuasion, provide that margin of leadership that would determine which controversies were to receive a full hearing and be decided by full opinion. The Act of 1922, however, is the turning point in the expansion of the office of the Chief Justiceship. Although the establishment of the Conference of Senior Circuit Judges "constituted only a first step toward a more integrated administrative system," it "created an institutional framework with administrative leadership and informal responsibility lodged in the Chief Justice and the presiding officers of the intermediate appellate courts",[28] But if William Howard Taft became the first Chief Justice of the United States in substance, his duties in comparison to the modern day Chief were minimal. Since 1922 Congress has authorized the creation of: (1) the Judicial Conference of the United States, the outgrowth of Taft's original brainchild, which is essentially a board of directors for the federal judicial system with the Chief as its "chairman of the board";[29] (2) the Administrative Office of US Courts created in 1939 (the housekeeping agency for the federal court system); (3) the Federal Judicial Center, (a research, training and planning arm of the federal judiciary, of which the Chief Justice is chairman); and (4) the Supreme Court Historical Society (a non-profit organization conceived by Chief Justice Burger to enforce public knowledge of and interest in the Supreme Court). The Chief is designated Honorary Chairman of the Board of the latter organization, but the title adds one more dimension to his national stature as does his membership on the Board of Regents of the Smithsonian Institution and on the Board of Trustees of the National Gallery and Hirshhorn Museum.

In his role as chief executive of one of the three co-equal branches of the government the modern Chief Justice must inevitably deal with a budget and with the general procedural efficiency of the federal court system. In fiscal 1979 the Supreme Court received upwards of $11 million, the bulk of which went to pay the salaries of some 300 employees as well as those of the nine Justices. The remainder took care of the building and grounds, printing and miscellaneous expenses such as books for the Supreme Court library. It is, incidentally, a relatively small sum compared to the $83 million spent by the Executive Office of the President and the $1.2 billion appropriated for the congressional bureaucracy in that same fiscal year.

In his efforts on behalf of reforms peripheral to the Supreme Court's main tasks, Chief Justice Warren Burger has been acting more like a Lord Chancellor than any of his predecessors, including William Howard Taft. In 1969, two months after he was appointed, Burger made three proposals to the American Bar Association: first, that it create an institute to train court-manager executives; second, that it support examination and reform of the American penal system; and third, that it press for redesigning the law school curricula in order to improve the conduct of trial lawyers, to emulate insofar as it fits the American system, the British formula of training barristers at the Inns of Court. While taking action in all three areas, the Association's greatest success came in the first, and the Chief could report in 1980 that as a result of the Association's support for the Institute of Court Management, there has been a "revolution in court administration". Today, said the Chief, "there are more than 500 trained court administrators operating in the state and federal systems compared with perhaps 20 in 1969".[30] For several years Burger has been urging Congress to create a new National Court of Appeals as an intermediate tribunal between the circuit courts of appeals and the Supreme Court and he has recently proposed that Congress authorize the Judicial Conference to create judgeships as they are needed, subject to a congressional veto.

As admirable as these activities may be, some critics argue that a Chief Justice should not be spending his time in this way. As one prominent constitutional lawyer has observed: "Such behavior at worst gives the impression of attempting to circumvent the Court's own decisions by judicial and legislative politicking because he cannot command a majority on that tribunal. At best it suggests that the job of a Supreme Court Justice is only a part time effort".[31]

How a Chief Justice divides his time between his two main duties of chief judge of the nation's highest tribunal and chief executive of the judiciary is up to each individual incumbent, but however one allocates his energies, the office today, like that of the Lord Chancellor, makes extraordinary demands on its occupant and is beyond the capacities of most ordinary mortals. Back in 1895 Lord Herschell declared that the strain of holding the Lord Chancellorship was more than any man can bear for more than three years, a remark cited with approval by Lord Haldane in 1918. Yet Lord Kilmuir, apparently without complaint, held the office from 1954–1962.[32] Chief Justice Taft wrote of the "exhausting character" of his office in the 1920s and Earl Warren who worked every evening and weekends said that his schedule was "back-breaking". Chief Justice Burger has been known to work forty-two consecutive days without a break, and one of his weeks was clocked at ninety-two hours.[33] Rare indeed, however, is the man who, if offered, would decline either position; equally rare is the man who would leave it except at a very advanced age or for incapacitating illness.

Clearly the two greatest judicial offices in Britain and the United

States, although similar in some respects, are essentially of a different mold. The Lord Chancellor, his legislative and executive political roles aside, is truly the administrative head of the judiciary, and with his power to appoint virtually all the judges of the realm and to remove many of them, he exercises formidable authority over the system both in its procedures and in the substantive growth of the law. In his role as a judge, however, which he has of necessity been forced to minimize, his influence is negligible. The significance of these roles is reversed in the American Chief Justice. His primary responsibility is that of leading judge on the nation's highest court, a tribunal which, given the peculiar power of judicial review, has a major influence on some of the most crucial public policies of the nation. His role as chief executive of the judiciary is expanded or contracted, depending upon the incumbent's temperament, interests, and level of energy. The offices are identical in the sense that once a person has assumed the official status, he is free of the political pressures and entanglements that beset the executives and legislators in a democracy. In the United Kingdom the Lord Chancellor is independent because of conventions that are carefully observed after thirteen centuries of historical development. In the United States the Chief Justice is independent because of the binding force of a written Constitution plus a natural development of custom over two hundred years. In each office there are, we have suggested, strengths and weaknesses. Each has adapted to its own political environment, and neither is interchangeable with the other. Yet each is ultimately responsible for a judiciary that must be known for its integrity and fairness if it is to serve as a stabilizing force in a society that is buffeted by the winds of political change. In conclusion I should like to juxtapose the following quotations, one from a distinguished American constitutional scholar, the other from a former Lord Chancellor:

> No one function, nor all combined suffice to explain the office and power of the Chief Justice. Besides the functions themselves, the incumbent's influence depends on the use he makes of them and the manner in which they are discharged. Beyond all this is the human factor, the intangibles, the personality – the moral energy the man at the center releases. One may say of the office of Chief Justice of the United States what Woodrow Wilson said of the Presidency: his office "is anything he has the sagacity and force to make it." The Chief Justice, like the president, "is entitled to be as big a man as he can."[34]

> With his [the Lord Chancellor's] origins lost in antiquity and his functions understandable only by historical reference, yet he is by no means an

anachronism and he still performs a useful service in the modern state. His survival and the adaptability of the office owe much to the wisdom of his predecessors. Saints some of them and martyrs too: some with genius, others dishonest or toadies, or mere courtiers. But few in that long roll were incapable, and most were men who performed with devotion to their duty to their country and their office and who contributed to that cause a lifetime's experience of public and legal affairs. To them we owe much and not least indebted is their humble successor.[35]

NOTES

1. For example, Chief Justice Taney in *Dred Scott v. Sandford* 19 Howard 393 (1857); Chief Justice Fuller in *Pollock v. Farmers' Loan and Trust Co.,* 157 U.S. 429 (1859); Chief Justice Warren in *Brown v. Board of Education,* 347 U.S. 483 (1954); Chief Justice Burger in *United States v. Nixon,* 418 U.S. 683 (1974).

2. For a discussion of the development of the office of Lord Chancellor, see particularly Heuston, 1964; Schuster, 1949; Kilmuir, 1955–56.

3. For many years the Lord Keeper of the Great Seal was a separate office from that of Lord Chancellor, although at times one person held both offices. In 1532 Henry VIII directed that one man, Audley, hold both offices simultaneously and the subsequent confirmation of the practice by Parliament came in 1562. However, some twenty appointments were made therefore to the office of Lord Keeper of the Great Seal, the last in 1757.

4. Kilmuir, 1955–56: 133.

5. Kilmuir, 1955–56: 138.

6. Morrison, 1973: 201–202.

7. Some of the 19 Lord Chancellors served more than once as their political party was returned to office after an interval as the opposition. This is true of the present incumbent, Lord Hailsham, who served under Prime Minister Heath and is presently serving under Prime Minister Thatcher.

8. The English Attorney General does not sit in the Cabinet, but he may be invited to advise the cabinet on a specific issue.

9. In addition to holding his judicial position in the House of Lords the Lord Chancellor is an ex officio member and President of the Court of Appeal.

10. The law lords are generally chosen from the regular English courts since they must by statue have held "high judicial office" for a period of not less than two years in order to qualify. "High Judicial office" includes service as Lord Chancellor, judge of the High Court of Appeal. They receive life peerage upon appointment to the House, and even after retirement, they remain qualified for judicial service.

11. Shetreet, 1976: 43.

12. In 1979 the House of Lords had 57 appeals pending at the beginning of the year and entered an additional 76 bringing the total docketed to 133. They disposed of 71, affirming the lower court in 33, reversing in 35, and otherwise disposing of the remaining 3. From *Judicial Statistics for England, Wales and Northern Ireland,* 1979, Table A. 3(a).

13. See Danelski in Pritchett and Murphy, 1961: 497. Danelski uses the terms "task" and "social" leadership as the twin hooks upon which the Chief's ability to lead depends. He borrowed these terms from R. F. Bales in Maccoby et al, 1958: 437–47. I prefer the designations, "personal" and "intellectual."

14. Rehnquist, 1976: 647.

15. Ulmer, 1970: 52.

16. Ulmer, 1970: 52.

17. Kilmuir, 1955–56: 136–37.

18. The number of judges in the House of Lords, the Court of Appeal and the High Court can be increased by Order In Council requiring Parliamentary approval, but the procedure "tends to become little more than Parliamentary "rubber stamping" of the Executive [the Lord Chancellor's] decisions." Shetreet, 1976: 43.

19. Briefly the English court structure consists of the following: the House of Lords is the supreme tribunal hearing both civil and criminal appeals. Immediately below the House is the Court of Appeal consisting of the Civil Division headed by the Master of the Rolls and the Criminal Division, presided over by the Lord Chief Justice. Next in the hierarchy is the High Court of Justice headed by the Lord Chief Justice and consisting of three divisions: Queens Bench, Chancery and Family. These are essentially courts of original jurisdiction but they may take limited appeals. Brought into being in 1971 was the Crown Court which has unlimited criminal jurisdiction and hears criminal appeals from the Magistrates' Courts. Sitting on these courts are High Court judges, Circuit judges and Recorders (generally part-time judges). At the same level are County Courts, presided over by Circuit judges and exercising limited civil jurisdiction. At the bottom are the Magistrates' Courts each comprised of at least two justices of the peace (unpaid) or a "stipendiary" (paid) magistrate in London and some towns. They have jurisdiction over summary criminal offenses and over petty civil matters.

20. Morrison, 1973: 71–72.

21. Shetreet, 1976: XV.

22. The advantages of the Lord Chancellor's close personal connection with the profession of practicing barristers is that he retains a first-hand knowledge of eligible appointees to the bench. On the other hand the system is totally inbred and tends towards a traditional conservatism, a fact which the reformers, particularly the left ideologues deplore.

23. There are some 900 judicial appointments which are almost exclusively reserved to barristers. In order to be appointed to the High Court, one must have been a barrister of at least ten years standing, to the Court of Appeal, either a judge of the High Court or a barrister of fifteen years standing. To qualify as a circuit judge, one must have been a barrister for ten years or served as a Recorder for at least five

years. A solicitor of ten years standing is eligible for appointment as a Recorder or a deputy Circuit judge. The Law Society (the solicitors' spokesman) had been pressing Parliament, so far unsuccessfully, to permit solicitors to become High Court judges. Of the 334 circuit judges in 1981, only 19 are solicitors. See *The Times,* Feb. 29, 1981, p. 5.

24. Shetreet, 1976: 79.

25. Abel-Smith and Stevens, 1967: 460.

26. Act of Congress, July 13, 1866, Ch. 210 (14 Stat. L. P. 209).

27. This information was obtained from a reprint of an article in the Fuller papers in the Library of Congress. Entitled "Chief Justice of the United States or Chief Justice of the Supreme Court of the United States", it was authored by William A. Richardson and was originally published in the N.E. Historical and Genealogical Register for July, 1895.

28. Fish, 1973: 39.

29. The Conference consists of the Chief Justice and 24 members: the 11 chief justices of the U.S. Courts of Appeal, a district court judge elected by his colleagues in each circuit and the chief judges of the Court of Claims and the Court of Customs and Patent Appeals.

30. Burger, 1980: 10.

31. Kurland in Miller, 1973: 225.

32. Heuston, 1964: XX.

33. Interview with Barrett McGurn, Public Information Officer of the Supreme Court. Confirmed in letter of Dec. 16, 1980.

34. Mason, 1968: 60.

35. Kilmuir, 1955–56: 138.

References

(a) Articles:

DANELSKI, D. "The Influence of the Chief Justice in the Decisional Process." In W. F. MURPHY and C. H. PRITCHETT (eds.) (1961) *Courts, Judges and Politics.* New York: Random House.

KILMUIR, LORD. (1955–56) "The Office of Lord Chancellor." *Parliamentary Affairs* **9:** 132–139.

MASON, A. T. (1968) "The Chief Justice of the United States: Primus Inter Pares." *Journal of Public Law* **17:** 20–60.

MILLER, A. S. (1973) "Lord Chancellor Warren Earl Burger." *Society* (March/April): 18–27.

REHNQUIST, W. (1976) "Chief Justices I Never Knew." *Hastings Constitutional Law Quarterly* **3:** 637–655.

SCHUSTER, LORD (1949) "The Office of Lord Chancellor." *Cambridge Law Journal* **10:** 175–190.

ULMER S. S. (1970) "The Uses of Power In the Supreme Court: The Opinion Assignments of Earl Warren. 1953–1960." *Journal of Public Law* **19:** 49–65.

(b) Books:

ABEL-SMITH, B. and R. STEVENS, (1947) *Lawyers and the Courts.* London: Heinemann.

FISH, P. G. (1973) *The Politics of Federal Judicial Administration.* Princeton: Princeton University Press.

HEUSTON, R. G. (1964) *Lives of the Lord Chancellors, 1885–1940.* Oxford: Clarendon Press.

CHAPTER 9

CONSTITUTIONAL ORGANIZATION AND THE PROTECTION OF HUMAN RIGHTS IN BRITAIN AND THE UNITED STATES

DAVID G. BARNUM
DePAUL UNIVERSITY

I. Introduction

It is widely assumed that differences in constitutional organization will have an effect – perhaps a substantial effect – on the comparative protection of human rights in different countries. More specifically, certain constitutional characteristics – a written constitution, a federal structure, a system of separation of powers, and the institution of judicial review of legislation – are often thought to be particularly conducive to the protection of human rights. At the same time, the constitutional system of Britain – a country with an enviable record of protection of human rights – exhibits none of these characteristics. Clearly, the effects of constitutional organization on the protection of human rights are less straightforward than we sometimes assume.

The purpose of this paper is to provide a comparative examination of the effects of constitutional organization on the protection of human rights in Britain and the United States and to endeavor to derive from this comparison some broader lessons about the effects of constitutional organization on the protection of human rights. Since it is the presence of judicial review in the United States and the absence of judicial review in Britain which represents the most striking contrast between the two constitutional systems – and since the role of judicial review in protecting human rights remains exceedingly controversial –

the ensuing analysis will be organized around the key question of the role of judicial review in British and American politics. First, we will explore the question of what constitutional characteristics, if any, are particularly conducive to the existence of judicial review. Second, we will take up the question of whether the existence of judicial review is or is not particularly helpful in protecting human rights. Finally, we will endeavor to offer some overall conclusions about the comparative effects of constitutional organization on the protection of human rights in Britain and the United States.

II. Constitutional Organization and Judicial Review

The United States has a written Constitution. Among other things, this document defines a federal constitutional structure – including a single national government and several state governments – and a system of separation of powers at the national level – including a legislative, executive, and judicial branch of government. In addition, the Constitution – in the Bill of Rights and elsewhere – specifies several restrictions on the power of government and numerous rights of the individual. Britain has no written constitution. Moreover, the structure of British government is far more homogeneous or unitary than that of the United States, that is, there are no autonomous units of government below the level of Parliament equivalent to the American states. Finally, British government does not exhibit a strict or formal separation of powers, and in particular the executive in Britain is formed from amongst the members of the majority party in Parliament. What are the implications of these differences in constitutional organization for the role of the judiciary in the policy-making process – especially as it affects the rights of citizens – in Britain and the United States?

A. WRITTEN CONSTITUTIONS

There are at least two senses in which a written constitution may be conducive to the existence of judicial review. First, and most directly, the constitution may confer upon a court or courts the power of judicial review. Second, the constitution may represent "supreme law" or "basic law" – or in some other way be distinct from and superior to ordinary law. Inevitably, some institution must assume responsibility for resolving conflicts between the constitution and ordinary law. That institution is usually the judiciary, because, even if the constitution does not explicitly confer upon the judicial branch the power to review the validity of legislation, if it does contain a "supremacy clause" of some sort – as does the Constitution of the United States – it is likely to be the judiciary – whose job it is to interpret and apply the laws, including the constitution – which will assume the power to resolve alleged conflicts between constitutional norms and ordinary laws.

In at least two different senses, therefore, the existence of a written constitutional document may be seen as conducive to the development of judicial review. In addition, however, if the constitutional document is not only written, but also contains a set of fundamental rights or guaranteed rights, then the involvement of the judiciary in the process of protecting human rights will be all but inevitable. Whether the role of the judiciary will necessarily be active or salutary is a more ambiguous and controversial question. But the emergence of judicial review itself will be difficult to prevent.

B. FEDERALISM

A federal political structure is often created by a written constitutional document. Federalism, in turn, seems highly conducive to the development of judicial review. Certainly this is the lesson to be drawn from American history.

In the first place, in a federal system such as the United States, there will be numerous conflicts between the national level of government and the states over their respective powers. These conflicts will not necessarily involve issues of human rights. Nonetheless, they may present the perfect opportunity for a nationally oriented court – such as the US Supreme Court was under Chief Justice John Marshall – to enhance its own power while simultaneously supporting the legislative and executive branches of the national government in their struggles with the states (cf. McCloskey, 1960: 26–80).

Second, in a federal system composed of several autonomous or semi-autonomous states, each with the power to legislate on a wide variety of subjects, there will simply be more occasions on which legislative power may be used in ways that will provoke the intervention of a court than in a political system in which legislative power is essentially confined to a single, national institution. Moreover, if state legislatures have a subordinate status in the federal system, then their legislative results may be more vulnerable to judicial invalidation than those of the national legislature. In American history, of course, the first well-known exercise of judicial review by the Supreme Court involved a federal law,[1] while the second involved a state law.[2]

Third, in the United States, not only is there a federal constitution, but there are written constitutions in each of the states. Thus, the opportunities for courts to exercise their power to decide whether the "constitution" or "ordinary law" will govern a particular case are multiplied enormously (cf. Brennan, 1977; Linde, 1980).

Finally, there is the organization of the courts themselves to consider. In the United States, the hierarchy of federal courts – including the District Courts, the Courts of Appeals, and the Supreme Court – exists alongside the court systems of the several states. Moreover, at least one federal District Court is located in every state and may be available to litigants in constitutional cases. These arrangements have two principal consequences. The first is that citizens may be able to challenge the validity of state laws or other official actions by filing an "affirmative action" – i.e., a civil suit – in federal court. Such actions are extremely common and have produced some of the most famous decisions in American constitutional law.[3] The second consequence of the existence of a dual hierarchy of courts is that in the statute governing the appellate jurisdiction of the Supreme Court in cases coming from the state courts, the Supreme Court is given the power to review (1) state court decisions in cases in which the validity of a statute of the United States has been challenged and the decisions of the state court is "against its validity" and (2) state court decisions in cases in which the validity of a state statute has been challenged "on the ground of its being repugnant to the Constitution, treaties or laws of the United States" and the decision of the state court is "in favor of its validity".[4] Moreover, in cases coming from the federal Courts of Appeals, the Supreme Court is given the power to review cases appealed "by a party relying on a state statute held by a court of appeals to be invalid as repugnant to the Constitution, treaties or laws of the United States".[5] Thus, the Judiciary Act of 1789, on which these provisions governing the contemporary appellate jurisdiction of the Supreme Court are based, not only defines a role for the Supreme Court in supervising the political and judicial rivalry between the federal government and the state governments but also explicitly assumes that both state and lower federal courts will frequently and unabashedly exercise their power of judicial review to invalidate legislation emanating from the level of government other than that of which they themselves are a part.

It thus appears that in several ways the federal structure of the American constitutional system is highly conducive to the exercise of judicial review of legislation. A non-federal structure will not necessarily preclude the development of a system of judicial review. At the same time, a federal constitutional structure is an open invitation to courts to assert their power to review the validity of legislation and other governmental actions.

C. SEPARATION OF POWERS

The effect of a system of separation of powers on the likelihood that a constitutional system will adopt or develop the institution of judicial review is problematic. On the one hand, in a constitutional system in which powers are separated the judiciary may be encouraged to view itself as independent of the other branches of government and responsible for evaluating the constitutionality of their actions. On the other hand, in a system of separation of powers the role of the judiciary may be very strictly defined by either convention or written rules and may not include the power to review the validity of legislation. The likelihood that a constitutional system will include the institution of judicial review will probably depend on factors – such as the nature of the federal arrangements of the system and perhaps also the general degree of cultural or political independence of the judiciary – which are independent of the presence or absence of a system of separation of powers at the national level.

D. HIGHER LAW TRADITIONS

It is also problematic whether the existence of a philosophical tradition recognizing the existence of some law higher than ordinary law will necessarily be conducive to the adoption or development of a system of judicial review. Such a tradition may encourage the development among judges of a belief in the propriety and the necessity of judicial review (cf. Cappelletti and Cohen, 1979: 5–11; Ely, 1980: 48–54). However, judicial review will not necessarily result (cf. Allott, 1979). Thus, the presence of higher law conceptions in the thinking of constitutional participants is not likely to guarantee the triumph of judicial review in a constitutional system in which the political and social climate is otherwise not conducive to its acceptance.

E. CONCLUSION

The characteristics of the American constitutional system – in particular its written constitutional basis and its federal political structure – are evidently conducive to the exercise of judicial review. Beginning with John Marshall's famous statement in *Marbury v. Madison* in 1803 – that "[i]t is emphatically the province and duty of the judicial department to say what the law is"[6] – the Supreme Court, up to 1978, had struck down over 100 federal laws and over 900 state laws and state constitutional provisions because they were, in the opinion of a majority of the justices, repugnant to the Constitution (*Constitution of the United States of America: Analysis and Interpretation,* 1973: *Constitution of the United States of America: Analysis and Interpretation: 1978 Supplement,* 1979; see also Abraham, 1980: 296–7). The number of state and local laws overturned by state and lower federal courts is a matter of pure speculation. Moreover, the number of non-legislative acts and policies of governmental officials and other types of public officials declared unconstitutional by American courts is also uncounted but undoubtedly in the range of tens of thousands. Judicial review is a major component of the policy-making process in the American constitutional system.

The lesson of history, however, is that the characteristics of the British constitutional system – in particular the absence of a written constitution and the absence of a federal political structure – were not, apparently, conducive to the development of judicial review. Despite Coke's assertion in Bonham's case in 1609 that "in many cases the common law will control Acts of Parliament, and sometimes adjudge them to be utterly void",[7] the institution of judicial review never took hold in Britain, and the courts in Britain have repeatedly affirmed – as the Divisional Court did in a 1976 case alleging Parliamentary curtailment of freedom of speech – that "Parliament [is] supreme and there [is] no power in the courts to question the validity of an Act of Parliament".[8] In the words of one constitutional scholar, the courts "will endeavor to construe Acts of Parliament so as to avoid a preposterous result, but if a statute clearly evinces an intention to achieve the preposterous, the courts are under an obligation to give effect to its plain words. The safeguards against the enactment of such legislation are political and conventional, not strictly legal" (deSmith, 1981: 82). The institution of judicial review – at least for the time being – is evidently a dead letter in Britain.

II. Judicial Review and Human Rights

The United States has a written constitution, a Bill of Rights, a federal organization of its legislative, executive, and judicial institutions, and 180-year-old tradition of judicial review of the validity of legislation and other governmental actions. Britain's constitution is underwritten, its system of government is far more homogeneous and hierarchial than that of the United States, and the courts in Britain do not exercise the power of judicial review. What is the effect of these differences on the comparative protection of human rights in the two countries?

A. WRITTEN GUARANTEES AND THE PROTECTION OF HUMAN RIGHTS

A case can be made that written constitutional guarantees of individual rights are extremely important in promoting the protection of human rights. An equally strong case can be made, however, that such guarantees are not actually indispensable to the protection of human rights. The history of protection of human rights in Britain and the United States provides support for both of these theories.

1. *United States* "The very purpose of a Bill of Rights", Justice Jackson wrote in 1943, "was to withdraw certain subjects from the vicissitudes of political controversy, to place them beyond the reach of majorities and officials and to establish them as legal principles to be applied by the courts. One's right to life, liberty, and property, to free speech, a free press, freedom of worship and assembly, and other fundamental rights may not be submitted to vote; they depend on the outcome of no elections ..."[9] This passage represents perhaps the clearest judicial statement of the critical value of a Bill of Rights to the protection of human rights in a majoritarian democracy. Nevertheless, it appeared rather late in the history of judicial involvement in the policy-making process in American politics. Indeed, it was only five years earlier, in 1938, that Justice Stone, in the famous "Footnote 4" to his opinion in the non-civil liberties case of *United States v. Carolene Products Company,* had opined that "[t]here may be narrower scope for operation of the presumption of constitutionality when legislation appears on its face to be within a specific prohibition of the Constitution, such as those of the first ten amendments ..."[10] Moreover, it was not until the time of World War I, only a few years

earlier, that the Supreme Court first began handing down a significant number of decisions in the civil liberties area.

The content of these early decisions, which were based on the First Amendment, was, however, anything but protective of the constitutional rights being asserted by the individual parties to the cases.[11] These early First Amendment decisions – along with numerous decisions on civil liberties issues from other periods of the history of the Supreme Court – are therefore indicative of the important fact that despite the existence of judicial review and the existence of a specific set of constitutional rights to which the Supreme Court and other courts can refer, the decision-making activities of the Supreme Court and other courts have always taken place in a political context and are not unaffected by the social and cultural forces of the historical era in which they occur (cf. Dahl, 1957: Bickel, 1962; Casper, 1976: Choper, 1980). Thus, not only did the *absence* of specific constitutional provisions not prevent the Supreme Court from developing an elaborate jurisprudence protecting economic enterprises and property rights during the era of substantive due process, but the *presence* of specific constitutional guarantees was not sufficient to induce the Supreme Court and other courts to take an active interest in the protection of human rights until the most recent period of American judicial history. It appears, therefore, that written guarantees are not in any sense a sufficient condition of protection of human rights in a society such as the United States in which the judicial branch – for all its strength and prestige – is nevertheless an integral part of the overall political process.

2. *Britain* If Justice Jackson was a firm believer in the value of a written Bill of Rights, Professor Dicey, it is fair to say, was not. "Now, most foreign Constitution-makers", he wrote in 1908, "have begun with declarations of rights. For this they have often been nowise to blame" (Dicey, 1967: 198). There is, to be sure, a lively and growing debate in Britain over the wisdom of adopting a written set of constitutional guarantees (cf. Scarman, 1974; Wallington and McBride, 1976; Zander, 1979; Jaconelli, 1980). Nevertheless, the traditional aversion of the British to written guarantees and to judicial review has never been completely overcome, and the prevailing constitutional understanding in Britain is that "freedoms ... are residual ... To define the content of liberty one has merely to subtract from its totality the sum of the legal restraints to which it is subject" (deSmith, 1981: 447).

This does not mean, however, that civil liberties are unrespected or unprotected in Britain. Traditionally, the British have emphasized two features of their constitutional system which – in addition to the self-restraint of legislative, executive, and administrative authorities – serve to protect individual rights, even in the absence of a written set of constitutional rights or the existence of the institution of judicial review. First, they emphasize that "the courts have recognized certain fundamental rights in the form of presumptions that Parliament does not intend to restrict certain rights, or liberties, unless the words of the statute are unambiguous" (Brownlie, 1968: 144–5). In theory, at least, the English courts "lean in favour of liberty of the citizen, especially of his person: they interpret strictly statutes which purport to diminish liberty, and presume that Parliament does not intend to restrict private rights in the absence of clear words to the contrary" (Phillips and Jackson, 1978: 40).

The second point emphasized by British legal theorists is that "for every encroachment upon one's liberty there is a legal remedy awarded by an independent court of justice" (deSmith, 1981: 447). In Dicey's famous words (1967: 199),

> The Englishmen whose labours gradually framed the complicated set of laws and institutions which we call the Constitution, fixed their minds far more intently on providing remedies for the enforcement of particular rights or (what is merely the same thing looked at from the other side) for averting definite wrongs, than upon any declaration of the Rights of Man or of Englishmen. The Habeas Corpus Acts declare no principle and define no rights, but they are for practical purposes worth a hundred constitutional articles guaranteeing liberty.

Thus, while there is of course no necessary incompatibility between the existence of a written set of constitutional guarantees and the exercise of judicial review, on the one hand, and reliance on canons of statutory interpretation emphasizing the protection of rights and the provision of adequate remedies for the infringement of rights, on the other, the enduring British assumption is that the latter will suffice to protect human rights even in the absence of the former.

B. FEDERALISM AND THE PROTECTION OF HUMAN RIGHTS

There is abundant evidence that a federal constitutional structure may be conducive to the protection of human rights. On the other hand, there is no evidence that a unitary political structure is inherently unable to protect such rights. Moreover, there is even some evidence that the federal structure of the United States has inhibited the protection of human rights, while the unitary structure of Britain has promoted the protection of human rights.

1. *United States* The fact that a multitude of state and federal courts in the United States possess the power to review the validity of legislation and other governmental action on the basis of constitutional criteria has undoubtedly contributed to the development of extensive protection of human rights. There is considerable competition and mutual vigilance between the two levels of government in the United States – and between the judicial branch of government and the other branches – and this interplay of forces almost surely yields a higher level of concern for and concrete protection of human rights than would otherwise be the case. At the same time, it is clear that federalism alone – or even federalism combined with written constitutional guarantees and the institution of judicial review – has not always been completely efficacious in protecting human rights in the United States.

The best evidence of this fact emerges from the history of "incorporation" of the Bill of Rights into the Fourteenth Amendment as a restriction on the power of the states (cf. Cortner, 1981). Initially, even though the Judiciary Act of 1789 had given the Supreme Court the power to review state court decisions upholding state laws whose validity had been challenged "on the ground of their being repugnant to the constitution", the Supreme Court, in *Barron v. Baltimore* in 1833, held that the "just compensation" provision of the Fifth Amendment – even though it was part of the Constitution – was intended "solely as a limitation on the exercise of power by the government of the United States, and is not applicable to the legislation of the States. We are therefore of the opinion that there is no repugnancy between the [state's action] and the constitution of the United States".[12] Even after the adoption, in 1868, of the Fourteenth Amendment – with its restriction on the power of the states to "deprive any person of life, liberty, or property, without due process of law" – the Supreme Court was unwilling to regard the provisions of the Bill of Rights as a restriction on the states, and it was not until 1925, in *Gitlow v. New York,* that the Court first held that a provision of the Bill of Rights – the free speech guarantee of the First Amendment – was "among the fundamental personal rights and 'liberties' protected by the due process clause of the Fourteenth Amendment from impairment by the

States".[13] More recently, in the decisions of the Supreme Court under Chief Justice Earl Warren (1953–69), there was a marked acceleration of the process of incorporating the provisions of the Bill of Rights into the due process clause of the Fourteenth Amendment and marked expansion of the willingness of the Court to interpret the equal protection clause of the Fourteenth Amendment, as well as other constitutional provisions, in ways that substantially restricted the power of the states. Until that time, however, there was little evidence that the federal structure of the American polity was particularly influential in promoting the protection of human rights – as opposed to property rights and other economic rights – in the constitutional policy-making process.

There is also, it would seem, considerable evidence that the federal structure of the American polity has actually inhibited the protection of human rights in the United States. The Fourteenth Amendment prohibits the states from depriving any person of life, liberty, or property without due process of law or denying to any person the equal protection of the laws. At the same time, under American constitutional arrangements, it is the states which are primarily responsible for the passage and enforcement of legislation protecting the health and safety of their citizens. A perennial problem in American constitutional law has therefore been what to do about the situation in which a state neglects to ensure due process of law or equal protection of the laws for some citizens – in particular for racial minorities – but does so not by positive "state action" but rather by condoning the violation of the rights of citizens by private parties. In such circumstances – circumstances which have arisen repeatedly in American history, especially, but not exclusively, in the southern states – there are essentially two possible solutions to the resulting constitutional vacuum in the scope of protection of the rights of citizens. One solution is for the Supreme Court to be willing to interpret the proscriptions of the Fourteenth Amendment to include state inaction as well as state action – thus creating a *constitutional* remedy for a citizen who is deprived of due process or equal protection by a private citizen but, practically speaking, has no remedy under state law – and the other is for Congress to be willing to enact and the Supreme Court to uphold legislation providing federal civil remedies and/or federal criminal penalties for private violations of fundamental rights. The story of the struggle to implement these solutions is far too long and complex to be told here. Its obvious moral, however, is that federal constitutional structures are not necessarily conducive to the timely protection of human rights in a culturally diverse and highly litigious society.

The verdict on the effects of American federalism in promoting the protection of human rights is therefore mixed. The existence of a federal Supreme Court and the presence in every state of federal District Courts has undoubtedly been conducive to litigation aimed at vindicating constitutional rights. At the same time, the Supreme Court has not always been receptive to such litigation, and, in addition, the peculiar arrangements of American federalism have at times had an obviously inhibiting effect on the protection of human rights in the United States.

2. *Britain* The British constitution defines a unitary or non-federal system of government. While an argument can be made that such a system will be less likely to promote the protection of human rights than will a federal system, there is also ample evidence that satisfactory protection of human rights is quite possible – at least theoretically – in the absence of federalism. There is even some evidence that a unitary system of government may be more capable of devising and implementing aggressive policies for the protection of human rights than is a federal system.

Under the British constitution, the one opportunity for the courts to exercise the power of "judicial review" – apart from those occasions when a higher court is deciding an appeal from a lower court – occurs when they have been asked to overturn the legislative, executive, or administrative decision or action of an official body other than Parliament. While their power of judicial review is therefore perhaps not quite as exalted as that of the US Supreme Court, it is nevertheless extensive. Moreover, it offers the very kinds of opportunities for judicial review that are presented to *most* courts *most* of the time in a federal system such as that of the United States.

There are two principal occasions on which the courts may be asked to review and reverse the decisions or action of an official body other than Parliament or a lower court. The first is when a local byelaw or other legislative act or official action is challenged by a litigant. The two broad categories of review in such cases permit a court to overturn a challenged law or other official action if it is ultra vires – that is, if it is outside the scope of the enabling legislation (usually Parliamentary legislation) under which it has been passed – or if it violates one or more of the principles of natural justice – that is, the procedural requisites of a proper decision, the two most important of which prescribe that a man may not be a judge in his own cause *(nemo judex in causa sua)* and that one's interests may be adversely affected without providing him with an opportunity to be heard *(audi alteram partem).* The specific components of these doctrines of review are of course numerous, complex, ambiguous, and ever-evolving. For that very reason, however, they provide a fertile set of pretexts – at least in principle – for the exercise of judicial review.

The other occasion on which the courts in Britain may exercise the power of judicial review is when they are called upon to examine the decision of an administrative tribunal. There are now at least 2,000 such tribunals in Britain (Phillips and Jackson, 1978: 576), and their jurisdiction – like the legislation from which it arises – extends to virtually every area of modern life, including health, education, transport, planning, housing, income maintenance, industrial relations, and employment discrimination (cf. Jackson, 1977: 110–77). The courts in Britain are empowered to review the decision of an administrative tribunal to determine not only whether the tribunal has faithfully observed the rules of natural justice but also whether the tribunal has properly applied the law to the specific situation before it. That being the case, there is no reason why British courts will not increasingly be faced with the same issues of "equal protection" and "substantive due process" – such as the nature or importance of the right or interest of the individual allegedly violated by legislative or administrative action, the defensibility of the classifications drawn by the law, the permissible scope of legislative and administrative discretion in drafting and applying the law, and the proper degree of judicial deference to legislative and administrative decision-making power – with which American courts are often faced in contemporary constitutional litigation (cf. Prosser, 1979). In the view of one long-term analyst of the subject of judicial review of administrative action, while the courts over time have "vacillated" in their willingness to review not only the processes, but also the policies, of administrative decision-making bodies, "[w]hat is now happening is another great expansion of the common law" (Jackson, 1977: 172–4).

II Conclusion

In sum, analysis of the United States, with a written constitution, a Bill of Rights, a federal structure, and its tradition of judicial review, and Britain, without a written constitution, without a Bill of Rights, without a federal structure, and without a tradition of judicial review – does not yield any very simple answers to the question of the effects of constitutional organization on the protection of human rights. The protection of human rights is not notably deficient in either country. The question of whether one constitutional system does a better job than the other of protecting human rights – and why – is harder to answer.

It does seem, however, that on balance – Professor Dicey to the contrary notwithstanding – the presence of a written set of constitutional guarantees has a salutary effect on the protection of human rights. It provides, in the words of Professor Brownlie, "approved criteria for evaluating administrative action" (1968: 191). In the United States, the argument is sometimes made that if the Bill of Rights were submitted to the American people for ratification today, it would be rejected, and therefore it is a fortunate thing it is already in the Constitution. The additional argument might be made that if the Bill of Rights had not been part of the Constitution since 1791, the Supreme Court might have taken even longer than roughly a century and a half to begin to take seriously its responsibility for protecting human rights. In Britain, the presence of the European Convention on Human Rights and the machinery for its enforcement – the European Commission of Human Rights, the European Court of Human Rights, the right of action by one state against another, and the right of individual petition by citizens of member states –is already beginning to have concrete effects on British law and society. Not the least of these effects is that the debate over whether Britain should enact a Bill of Rights – perhaps by incorporating the European Convention into domestic law – has never been more intense.

It is also entirely possible, however, that a really satisfactory answer to the question of whether American constitutional organization or British constitutional organization is more conducive to the protection of human rights will never be forthcoming on the basis of an examination – such as that undertaken in this paper – of essentially the most obvious differences between the two societies and their legal systems, but only on the basis of an examination of a variety of more subtle and more ambiguous issues relating to the role of the judiciary in the political process of a majoritarian democracy. What is called for if that is the case is much closer scrutiny of the use by courts in Britain and the United States of prudential techniques for avoiding certain issues at certain times. In both countries, that would include a thorough examination of doctrines of standing, justiciability, ripeness, mootness, and abstention. In addition, it would require an examination of trends in judicial deference to the decision-making autonomy of non-judicial institutions – such as schools, universities, prisons, mental hospitals, and the military – and non-judicial benefit-dispensing entities – such as welfare agencies and public employers. Finally, it would necessitate an assessment of the significance for the protection of human rights of fluctuations in the willingness of the courts to confront questions implicating the emergency power and the foreign affairs prerogatives of the legislative and executive branches of government and fluctuations in the willingness of the courts to confront other so-called "political questions".

Even if we understand judicial behavior in Britain and the United States more fully than is presently the case, however, we will still not be in a tenable position to assess the comparative adequacy of protection of human rights in the two societies until we know much more about the nature of the interplay between citizens and the courts and citizens and other key decision-making bodies. It would be possible to argue, for instance, that while the courts in the United States may be more receptive that those in Britain to cases raising issues of fundamental constitutional rights, there is an all-or-nothing quality about American constitutional arrangements. It is, after all, enormously expensive and time-consuming to bring a suit in federal court or to appeal a case to the Supreme Court, and therefore these courses of action are not contemplated or undertaken very often by even the most constitutionally concerned of citizens. In Britain, on the other hand, it may be that administrative tribunals provide a more inviting and more ubiquitous point of access to the decision-making process for citizens who are interested in raising potentially important constitutional issues. Whether it really is more feasible to raise and pursue constitutional issues in Britain than in the United States, however, would depend in turn upon the availability of government-sponsored legal aid and the availability of private legal assistance from groups specializing in the representation of citizens in civil liberties cases.

Our understanding of the politics of constitutional protection of human rights is very rudimentary. A comparison of the effects of constitutional organization on the protection of human rights in Britain and the United States can substantially further our understanding of the comparative process of protection of human rights in majoritarian democracies. But a complete understanding of the politics of constitutional protection of human rights – and its comparative effects in terms of the actual protection of human rights in different societies – is still a long way off.

NOTES

1. *Marbury v. Madison,* 1 Cranch 137, 2 L.Ed. 60 (1803).

2. *Fletcher v. Peck,* 6 Cranch 87, 3 L.Ed. 162 (1810).

3. Cf. *Brown v. Board of Education,* 347 U.S. 483 (1954) (de jure racial segregation of schools unconstitutional); *Engel v. Vitale,* 370 U.S. 421 (1962) (prayers in public schools unconstitutional); *Reynolds v. Sims,* 377 U.S. 533 (1964) (state legislative apportionment unconstitutional); *Roe v. Wade,* 410 U.S. 113 (1973) (anti-abortion statutes unconstitutional); *Regents of Univ. of California v. Bakke,* 438 U.S. 265 (1978) (quota-based preferential treatment of minority students in medical school admissions unconstitutional).

4. 28 U.S.C. #1257.

5. 28 U.S.C. #1254.

6. 1 Cranch 137, 177, 2 L.Ed. 60, 73 (1803).

7. 8 Co. 113b, 118b, 77 Eng. Rep. 646, 652 (1610).

8. *R. v. Jordan,* (1967) *Crim. L. Rev.* 483.

9. *West Virginia State Board of Education v. Barnette.* 319 U.S. 624, 638 (1943).

10. 304 U.S. 144, 152 n. 4 (1938).

11. Cf. *Schench v. United States,* 249 U.S. 47 (1919) (conviction of antiwar leafleter for causing insubordination in the armed forces and obstruction of the recruiting and enlistment service of the United States not unconstitutional); *Gitlow v. New York,* 268 U.S. 652 (1925) (conviction of leftwing leafleter under the New York criminal anarchy statute for advocating overthrow of the government not unconstitutional).

12. 7 Pet. 243, 250–1, 8 L.Ed. 672, 675 (1833).

13. 268 U.S. 652, 666 (1925).

References

ABRAHAM, H. J. (4th ed. 1980) *The Judicial Process.* New York: Oxford University Press.

ALLOTT, P. (1979) "The Courts and Parliament – Who Whom?" *Cambridge Law Journal* **38** (April): 79–117.

BICKLEL, A. M. (1962) *The Least Dangerous Branch.* Indianapolis: Bobbs-Merrill.

BRENNAN, W. J. (1977) "State Constitutions and the Protection of Individual Rights". *Harvard Law Review* **90** (January): 489–504.

BROWNLIE, I. (1968) *The Law Relating to Public Order.* London: Butterworths.

CAPPELLETTI, M. and W. COHEN (1979) *Comparative Constitutional Law.* Indianapolis: Bobbs-Merrill.

CASPER, J. D. (1976) "The Supreme Court and National Policy Making". *American Political Science Review* **70** (March): 50–63.

CHOPER, J. H. (1980) *The Supreme Court and the National Political Process.* Chicago: University of Chicago Press.

Constitution of the United States of America: Analysis and Interpretation (1973) Washington: U.S. Government Printing Office.

Constitution of the United States of America: Analysis and Interpretation: 1978 Supplement (1979) Washington: U.S. Government Printing Office.

CORTNER, R. C. (1981) *The Supreme Court and the Second Bill of Rights.* Madison: University of Wisconsin Press.

DAHL, R. A. (1957) "Decision-Making in a Democracy: The Supreme Court as a National Policy-Maker." *Jornal of Public Law* **6:** 279–95.

DESMITH, S. A. (4th ed. 1981) *Constitutional and Administrative Law.* Harmondsworth, Middlesex, England: Penguin Books.

DICEY, A. V. (1967) *An Introduction to the Study of the Law of the Constitution.* London: Macmillan.

ELY, J. H. (1980) *Democracy and Distrust.* Cambridge: Harvard University Press.

JACKSON, R. M. (7th ed. 1977) *The Machinery of Justice in England.* Cambridge: Cambridge University Press.

JACONELLI, J. (1980) *Enacting a Bill of Rights.* Oxford: Clarendon Press.

LINDE, H. A. (1980) "First Things First: Rediscovering the States' Bill of Rights". *Univ. Balt. L. Rev.* **9** (Spring): 379–96.

MCCLOSKY. R. G. (1960) *The American Supreme Court.* Chicago: University of Chicago Press.

PHILLIPS, O. H. and P. JACKSON (6th ed. 1978) *Constitutional and Administrative Law.* London: Sweet & Maxwell.

PROSSER, T. (1979) "Politics and Judicial Review: The Atkinson Case and its Aftermath". *Public Law* 1979 (Spring): 59–83.

SCARMAN, L. (1974) *English Law – The New Dimension.* London: Stevens & Sons.

WALLINGTON, P. and J. MCBRIDE (1976) *Civil Liberties and a Bill of Rights.* London: Cobden Trust.

ZANDER, M. (2nd ed. 1979) *A Bill of Rights?* London: Barry Rose Ltd.

CHAPTER 10

A COMPARATIVE ANALYSIS OF THE INTERNAL PROCEDURES AND CUSTOMS OF THE SUPREME COURTS OF JAPAN AND THE UNITED STATES

TAKEO HAYAKAWA and
JOHN R. SCHMIDHAUSER
SENSHU UNIVERSITY
and
UNIVERSITY OF SOUTHERN CALIFORNIA

It is the purpose of this study to provide a comparative analysis of the internal procedures and customs of the Supreme Courts of Japan and the United States. There has been renewed interest in internal modes of operations, the role of clerks or their cross-national counterparts, and the relationship of higher appellate judges and justices to external centers of power, both public and private, because of the contemporary debates engendered by *The Brethren* (Woodward and Armstrong, 1979). But more importantly such matters are of longer range, more enduring intellectual interest because they are, of necessity, integral parts of any serious attempt at developing conceptual frameworks for comparative cross-national investigation of higher appellate judicial systems.

The Development of the Two Judiciaries

This investigation focuses upon the post-World War II experiences of the Japanese and United States Courts although a brief discussion of their development is necessary to properly frame the modern context.

Each nation had judicial systems prior to the era of political modernization, those of Japan existing for many centuries and those of colonial America reflecting centuries of English experience. Before modernization, both pre-Mejii Japan (the Shogunate) and colonial and immediate post-Revolutionary America had a variety of judicial institutions which were composites of executive, legislative, and judicial authority. The Council of Errors of New York, for example, combined executive and judicial authority *and* personnel. In Japan's Shogunate era, administrators combined administrative and judicial power. In Edo (later Tokyo), three magistrates exercised such combined power. South City Magistrate (Minami Machibugyō), North City Magistrate (Kita Machibugyō) and the highest in authority, the Temple and Shrine Magistrate (Jisha Bugyō) often rendered decisions which were specifically tailored to both administrative and judicial needs. Other magistrates in different regions did likewise. In the early Mejii era when feudal clans were abolished and prefectures were organized, combined executive and judicial power was still exercised by prefectual governors (chiji), vice governors (gonchiji), and secretaries-general (sanji). This changed in Japan with the adoption of the Constitution of 1889.

In the United States, a number of courts combined two or three functional powers, executive, legislative, and judicial such as the New York Council of Errors (manned by executive and judicial personnel) or many county courts (especially in the South where the practice continues in the county courts of Virginia). However, the Mejii era in Japan and the immediate post-independence era in the United States are generally identified as the thresholds of political modernization for each nation. The basic constitutional framework for each were the Mejii Constitution of 1889 for Japan and the Constitution of 1789 of the United States. After World War II, a new Japanese Constitution (1947) was developed under the auspices of the American Occupation Forces. Prior to 1947, the Japanese judiciary was a comprehensive national system, but differed fundamentally from the post-World War II system. The Taishinin or Court of Cessation was the final court of appeal under the governmental system of the Mejii Constitution of 1889 yet this court was not mentioned in the Constitution. Although the Constitution embodied a concept of the functional separation of the executive, legislative, and judicial branches, the fundamental principle of that system was the concept of imperial sovereignty. This was embodied in Article 4 of the Constitution of 1889 which provided that "The Emperor is the head of the Empire, combining in himself the rights of sovereignty to be exercised in accordance with the provisions of the Constitution". Its specific application to the judiciary was in Article 57: "The Judiciary power shall be exercised by the Courts of the Law according to law, in the name of the Emperor". Further, "A Commentary on the Constitution" (Kempō Gikai) by Prince Hirobumi Ito, who drafted most of the Constitution, indicated that "... the judiciary is only a part of the executive, and the executive, strictly speaking, is made up of two parts, the judiciary and the administrative, each performing distinct services". Maki pointed out that the Ministry of Justice exercised a great deal of executive authority over the courts because of its administrative and budgetary supervision and its direct control over judicial appointments and promotions (Maki, 1964: xvi–xvii). Before 1947, there were, of course, some manifestations of judicial independence such as the Otsu case in the 1890s (Takayanagi, 1963: 12; Secretariat, 1975: 19).

It was not until the Constitution of 1947 that the fundamentals of judicial independence were achieved. Seven articles in Chapter VI of the Japanese Constitution of 1947 dealt comprehensively and directly with the judiciary. Article 76 provides that "The whole judicial power is vested in a Supreme Court and in such inferior courts as are established by law." The Supreme Court consists of a Chief Justice appointed by the Emperor and fourteen justices chosen by the Cabinet. With the adoption and implementation of the Constitution of 1947, the foundation for the independence and stability of the highest appellate court in the Japanese judiciary was in the highest law itself. The inferior courts, established by statute, consist of fifty district courts with general civil and criminal jurisdiction and eight appellate courts, high courts organized to cover all of Japan divided geographically into eight contiguous regions. The Tokyo High Court has additional jurisdiction over disciplinary actions of bar associations and a number of governmental bureaus and commissions. There are fifty family courts which are combined juvenile and domestic courts (Maki, 1964: xviii–xix).

In contrast, the American higher appellate judiciary consists of a Supreme Court, constitutionally ordained in the Constitution of 1789, and a system of inferior courts the existence of which was left in that Constitution to the discretion of the Congress. In the first Congress, a separate federal inferior court system was created, but during the first century of its existence the inferior court system experienced, in periods of serious political conflict, two abolitions of components of the system. The congressional repeal of the Judiciary Act of 1801 eliminated twenty circuit judges in 1802 and the Congress eliminated the Circuit Court for the District of Columbia composed of Southern sympathizers, and replaced it with a Supreme Court for the District of Columbia manned by Union supporters in 1863. It should be noted that the Supreme Court did not have a predecessor judiciary which embodied a comprehensive national system. The Continental Congress had created a Court of Appeals in Cases of Capture which did have national scope but very limited jurisdiction (Schmidhauser, 1979: 12–16, 239–241).

In the context of the nature of and statutory or constitutional foundations of judicial authority, the post-1947 era in Japan is obviously one in which the standard for a stable and constitutionally guaranteed independent judiciary was met. Similarly, albeit for a considerably longer period, the highest appellate court of the United States, the Supreme Court, is constitutionally specified. In both post-1947 Japan and post-1789 United States the basis for the intermediate appellate judiciaries, the high courts of Japan and the courts of appeal (previously circuit courts) of the United States was statutory. In terms of the nature of the relationship of the judiciary to the other branches of government, for Japan under the post-1947 Constitution, the judicial branch was made, under the terms of that Constitution, independent of the executive and legislative branches. The previous constitutional system under the Meiji Constitution of 1889 had not provided for such independence nor had it embodied the principle of separation of powers to safeguard that independence. The Japanese Constitution of 1947 did embody that principle. In the United States, the independence of the federal judiciary was constitutionally protected and structurally designed in the Constitution of 1789. Regarding the nature of the tenure of the judges and justices, these provided the basis for some formal differences between Japanese and American higher appellate judiciaries. Article 79 of the Japanese Constitution of 1947 provided for electoral review of Justices of the Supreme Court at the first general election of members of the House of Representatives immediately following each justice's selection and at each identical election every ten years. It also provided for compulsory retirement determined by law (Maki, 1964: xx–xx1). The American Constitution of 1789 provides life tenure on good behavior for the judges and justices.

The Experience of the Legal Profession in Japan and the United States

One fundamental difference distinguishing Japan from the United States is public attitudes toward litigation. Historically, Japanese society was very negative to litigation preferring a customary form of mediation or arbitration instead. Lawyers were very few in number and were not highly respected. Historically, positive change for the legal profession in Japan came slowly. The highlights of governmental statutory responses in the 19th Century and early decades of the 20th century indicated a gradual development of professionalism. In 1872, provision was made for notaries, scriveners, and practitioners as professionals. In 1873 the qualifications for "licensed practitioners" was "good moral character and age (21)". In 1876 a bar examination system was introduced. The Attorney at Law Act of 1893 established the bar examination for the practice of law (attorneys from the old system were permited to practice under a "Grandfather" clause arrangement). The bar examination was distinct from the examination for prospective judges and prosecutors. In 1918 a new statute provided a unified bar examination as part of the High Civil Service examination but before it was to take effect (1923) another law was passed (in 1920) which retained the separate (and easier) bar examination for attorneys (as distinguished from a more rigorous examination for prospective judges and prosecutors). Approximately 700 individuals passed the attorneys examination until 1936 when a unified examination adopted by statute in 1933 went into effect. Prior to 1936 successful candidates could go into law practice without serving an apprenticeship but prospective judges and prosecutors (generally the cream of the crop of examination takers) did take such an apprenticeship, which was provided at government expense since would-be judges and prosecutors were treated as government officials. After 1936, all not only took a unified bar examination but prospective attorneys also had to work as apprentices for a year and one half before practicing law (the apprentices were not paid by the government but were informally supported by the bar association). Thus the bar examinations were unified before World War II but the training of prospective attorneys, judges, and prosecutors was not integrated until after 1947. Although the status of attorneys improved gradually after the 19th century, it did not approximate the prestige of judges and prosecutors. Even in the contemporary era there are lingering vestiges of the real or alleged inferiority of practitioners in conrast to judges and prosecutors. Some practitioner instructors in the post-World War II Legal Research and Training Institute are deemed incompetent and some justices chosen from the ranks of practicing attorneys are viewed with professional disdain by the justices chosen from the ranks of judges or prosecutors. Finally, the overall size of the legal profession is not great. The statistical report for the Japanese Bar Association (Nihon Bengoshi Rengokai) indicated that there were 10,179 lawyers in Japan in 1975.

In contrast, the United States has a very sizable lawyer population (424,908 in 1976) (Rhyne, 1978: 388, 812). Public attitudes toward the profession have not been as negative as in Japan although there were strong antiprofessional undercurrents in the Jacksonian era in the 19th century. But while the legal profession itself has not been overwhelmingly popular, many Americans are not reluctant to engage in litigation, a significant cultural difference from the Japanese. It is impossible to pinpoint a single national legislative policy sequence relating to the American legal profession because, in comparison to Japan, lawyers in the United States are governed by fifty states.

The bar examination in the states of the United States has never served as a device to screen out potential attorneys in so complete a fashion as in Japan. For example, in 1972 only 537 Japanese applicants passed out of a total of 23,425. Not all of those passing became prospective judges. In 1973, 493 applicants passed the final examination. Of these, 66 became judges, 50 became prosecutors, and 371 practicing attorneys. Newly recruited judges in Japan are frequently younger than new prosecutors or new attorneys. In 1973, for example, the average age of new judges was 26.9 years, new prosecutors 27.9 years, and new attorneys 30.3 years (Hayakawa, 1973: 2-4). For judges this also underscores a significant difference from the American system of judicial training and selection. In the United States there is a considerable variation by state in the standards for the education of lawyers, the nature of bar examinations, their accredited and non-accredited law schools, and on whether the practice of law is contingent upon membership in a state bar association (Hurst, 1950). Most importantly, there were never developed in the United States any formally accepted qualitative distinctions between practicing attorneys, judges, and prosecutors although some elitist tendencies were apparent in some historic eras (Bryce, 1891: 10–11; and Reed, 1921: 238–39).

Judicial Selection Criteria in Japan and the United States

The characteristics of justices of the Supreme Court of Japan in the post World War II era did reflect some of the changes designed to open opportunities for judicial appointments to members of the bar. But the evidence indicates that the changes have not been complete. Most importantly, the Japanese Supreme Court, which is composed of 15 justices including the Chief Justice, is very dependent upon the services of about twice as many research officials (chōsakan). Consequently, this brief appraisal of the characteristics of the personnel of the Japanese and United States Supreme Courts includes some observations about the justices of the Supreme Court of Japan and the research officials and the justices of the Supreme Court of the United States and the law clerks.[1]

The Japanese developments after World War II mark a significant change in that system. In 1947, a judicial selection committee adopted the principle (but was not required by law to do so) of devising a selection ratio of 5 judges, 5 lawyers, and 5 individuals of broad policy experience or from a scholarly career. There has been some variation in the pattern with the last group (sometimes referred to as "the men of learning and experience"). In 1979 there were (1) six judges, (2) four practitioners, and (3) one legal scholar, one diplomat, one administrator, and two prosecutors but by late 1980 the last group consisted of two legal scholars, one diplomat and two prosecutors. The Ministry of Justice has claimed that there should be at least three ex-prosecutors on the Supreme Court in order to insure that each five-justice Bench would have one ex-prosecutor to handle criminal cases. The previous rather sharp distinction between the training of lawyers and the more intensive and selective training of judges was abolished. This change was designed to help upgrade the status of attorneys (this has in part been successful) and to make the careers of attorneys and judges interchangeable (this has generally not been achieved). All who have passed a stiff bar examination, except a few who aspire, say, to an academic career, are admitted to the Supreme Court's Legal Research and Training Institute where they are trained as apprentices for two years at government expense. They pass the final examination almost automatically, when 10 to 20 percent of them should properly be flunked out. Any graduate can become a practicing lawyer, but only an excellent applicant can become a judge (hanjiho) or a prosecutor. A hanjiho is generally promoted to a full judge after 10 years, and until then he is supposed to be an associate judge in a court of three at the district court level (but by virtue of a special statute he is allowed to sit alone after 5 years because of the shortage of judges). In short, the careers of lawyers and judges are generally not interchangeable except that judges and justices may enter the practice of law at any time but generally after compulsory retirement from the bench. Perhaps one factor to account for this is the nature of law training in Japanese universities which generally deals with theories of law. Conversely the Legal Training and Research Institute, according to David Cavers, "comes closer to the American image of a law school . . ."(Cavers, 1963: xxxiv; and Oppler, 1976).

David Danelski reported that up to at least 1966, graduation from the law faculty of Tokyo University was frequently an important step towards selection as a justice of the Japanese Supreme Court and that considerable prior judicial experience is an important factor for many selectees. Such experience is enhanced by service as president of the Tokyo High Court or one of the larger of the other high courts, or the presidency of the Legal Training and Research Institute. For the lawyer component, presidency of a major urban bar association, especially in Tokyo, is helpful (Danelski, 1969: 127–132). The professional quality and overall ability of Japanese justices is generally evaluated as rather high but the competence and ability of some justices particularly from the lawyer component has been subject to criticism. In contrast to the significantly heavier influence of political participation of the American justices, most post-World War II Japanese justices are the recipients of career training which is designed to prepare them for their higher professional roles. The career ladder stages of preparation for a judicial role are considerably more clearcut in Japan than in the United States. Further the élite educational requirements are more clearly delineated in Japan as well. Justices in the United States frequently but not invariably are products of élite law schools, often Ivy League, are sons of upper middle class families, and have played political roles which permitted Presidents and key Senators to identify the political and ideological orientation of real or potential nominees (Schmidhauser, 1979: 41–99). In short, a considerably larger proportion of the Japanese justices are chosen on the basis of professional and judicial experience than that of the American justices. To this extent the Japanese system approximates the ideal of professionalism more than the American with respect to the selection of personnel based on merit.

Institutional Procedures

The criteria for fair and efficient internal procedures and institutional customs which relates to the major purposes of this investigation are threefold. First, are the institutional procedures sufficiently predictable to insure regularized access to the highest appellate court? Secondly, are those procedures designed to efficiently facilitate the orderly judicial processing of cases? Thirdly, are the standards actually applied in the processing of cases objective and insulated from public, political or private interest group pressures and influence?

In the modern post-World War II era, both Supreme Courts were confronted by the rapid increase in the number of appeals brought before them. In order to evaluate and compare the responses of these Courts to this major 20th century problem it is useful to explore both procedural adjustment to this and the adequacy of the utilization of personnel supporting and assisting the justices of each system. With respect to such supporting personnel there is a notable and major difference between the Japanese and American Supreme Courts. Both systems did, of course, have fully developed, albeit small, administrative systems for the day to day management of each court. But each Supreme Court also had more specialized systems for direct assistance to the justices. For the Japanese Supreme Court this embodies research officials (chōsakan) while for the Supreme Court of the United States it consists of law clerks.

The research officials perform a more vital role for the Chief Justice and fourteen Justices of the Japanese Supreme Court than the law clerks do for the Chief Justice and eight Justices of the United States Supreme Court. Some have suggested that the Japanese Supreme Court would be paralyzed without the research officials. Chōsakan are viewed as research officials serving the justices of the Supreme Court. This may be understood on the basis of a distinction made in Japanese society between the official status of an individual (kan) and his or her post, position, office, job or assignment (shoku). In this instance, chōsakan are considered judges or assistant judges in terms of official status (kan) and research officials in terms of job or position (shoku). The characteristics of Japanese research officials and American law clerks may be summed up as follows: (1) Research officials are chosen (on the basis of merit) from the ranks of full judges, and sometimes of assistant judges. Law clerks are not judges; they generally are selected from the top ranked students of several highly ranked law schools (often Ivy League). (2) Research officials are often recommended by the chief judges of the district courts in which they served as full or assistant judges. Law clerks are generally recommended by the few law professors who have a special advisory relationship with a particular justice such as Harvard Law Professor Felix Frankfurter's role with Justice Louis Brandeis. (3) Research officials are not assigned to any particular justice. They generally number 28 to 30. As of September,

1980, there were 29 including the chief of the research officials (Shuseki Chōsakan), 12 handling civil cases, 11 criminal cases, and 5 administrative cases. Research officials are assigned to cases in accordance with their fields of specialization while justices are assigned mechanically, as described fully below. Law clerks rarely have any specialized training and indeed generally do not have either judicial experience or experience as attorneys. They are assigned to particular justices with whom they generally serve one (sometimes two) year(s). (4) Research officials, in recent years, are called to Grand Bench or Petty Bench deliberations, and contribute information in those cases to which they had contributed (the circumstances of such attendance are discussed fully below). Law clerks do not under any circumstances attend the conference deliberations of the Supreme Court of the United States. (5) Japanese research officials and American law clerks generally have quite different career ladder profiles before and after their supporting roles in their respective Supreme Courts. The research officials are career judges both before and after such supporting roles. Some, indeed, later become justices, although none were promoted to justices directly from the ranks of chōsakan. Law clerks are not career judges and generally do not become judges or justices.

The differences in the characteristics of these supporting personnel, the research officials and the law clerks, are matched by the differences in the characteristics of the justices in each Supreme Court. Many Japanese justices are products of law training and career ladder experience clearly oriented toward a judicial or a prosecutoral career. Direct political involvement is not a significant part of the experiences of most. Conversely, American justices are not products of special judicially-oriented legal education or subsequent career experience. Virtually all have some direct political involvement in their careers. Approximately 30 percent had prior judicial experience in the post-World War II era, but such posts are acquired through the political process rather than by special career training in the United States.

Perhaps one of the most consistent and striking differences between the two Supreme Courts are those relating to age of selection and age of termination of the two sets of justices. In the Japanese system, the average age of selection is rather high, over 61 years of age, and because of compulsory retirement at age 70, the period of experience on the Japanese Supreme Court is rather short, less than ten years. Conversely, the average age of appointment of American Justices in the post-World War II era is 54 years of age and because of the constitutional requirement of tenure on good behavior, the age of termination is higher, 68 years of age. More importantly, the average years of service on the Supreme Court of the United States are considerably longer, 16 years compared to 9 on the Supreme Court of Japan (Hayakawa, 1973; and Schmidhauser, 1962: 101–134). With respect to antecedent professional career judicial training and experience, the Justices of the Supreme Court of Japan conform more closely to the criteria of a professional judicial system than the Justices of the Supreme Court of the United States. Conversely, in terms of actual experience in the unique environment of the respective Supreme Courts, the adoption of compulsory retirement at age seventy without significant understanding of the important relationships of both age of appointment and age of termination to such important institutional goals as thorough knowledge of the unique personnel and institutional requirements of each highest appellate court, seasoning and maturation in that special judicial environment, and the development of influence with and respect and rapport with judicial equals significantly abbreviates the time available to the career judges who, in the Japanese system, achieve an appointment to the Supreme Court late in life. In the American system, the Supreme Court appointees more often than not come with little or no prior judicial experience but generally, assuming good health, have a considerably longer period to gain experience and inter-personal rapport on the Supreme Court. In sum, the American system of training and selection does not fully meet the criteria for professionalized career judges. The Japanese system more closely approaches that goal. Conversely, the on-Supreme Court experience factor is greater in the American system.

Organization and Procedures

The basic organization of each Supreme Court differs. The Chief Justice and fourteen Justices of the Supreme Court of Japan are generally organized in three Petty Benches composed of five members each (three constituting a quorum). Justices are mechanically assigned without reference to their areas of specialization to Petty Bench I, II, or III. Because each justice is assigned to the particular Petty Bench vacated by the justice he succeeded, the Petty Benches are not organized by a particular set of specializations such as civil cases, criminal cases, or administrative cases. As noted earlier, the justices are assigned cases mechanically. Conversely, the research officials (chōsakan) do specialize. Some, for example, work on civil cases and work together in the same office. Cases are assigned to research officials by specialization. No research official is permanently assigned to a particular justice as is true in the case of law clerks in the United States. In Japan, a new case is first mechanically assigned to one of the three Petty Benches; within the particular Petty Bench it is mechanically assigned to a justice; but the research official is assigned to the case (and to the justice responsible for it) on the basis of his subject matter specialization.

Here is how the system works. Suppose case number 1 comes in, it may be the turn of Justice A of Bench 1 to take it. Case 2 will be assigned to Justice B of the same Bench, and so on. Assignment is made according to seniority. Case 6 will go to Justice A of Bench II until all justices have new cases assigned to them. Case II will go to Justice A of Bench III, and so on until Case 15 is assigned to Justice E of Bench III. Case 16 necessarily goes to Justice A of Bench I. This is true at least in theory, and to an extent in practice. The chief justice is often excused with the result that the Petty Bench to which he belongs gets a smaller number of case assignments: say, 4.25: 5: 5, if he is excused one time out of four.

When a vacancy happens, a retiring justice will be excused about one month before his retirement. Likewise his successor will be excused for one month, though he takes over his predecessor's cases left unfinished. This practice is getting established as a custom or a Supreme Court Justice's privilege (no chōsakan or no inferior court judge has such privilege). After one month or so he starts getting new cases, but as the last man of the five (as the new E) since the order of rotation will change because of the seniority rule.

There are three categories of cases, civil, criminal and administrative. These categories of cases are assigned mechanically as above stated independently of each other. Capital sentence cases are treated as if an independent category. Internal procedures seem to be in a state of constant flux. Instead now criminal cases are divided into two categories: those with voluminous records (thousands and thousands of pages) and those without such records.

A new chōsakan will simply take the place of his predecessor (including the order of rotation) regardless of whether cases are old or new. Assignment of cases to chōsakan is mechanical. Each chōsakan will tentatively evaluate his case before he reports to, and starts working with, the justice in charge of it (shunin saibankan). Civil and administrative cases have two ranks: meritorious (0) and less meritorious (Δ), while criminal cases have three ranks: 0, Δ, and X, the last of which stands for "totally unmeritorious". The justice in charge does in fact (or at least is supposed to) read all records, including those of X cases. He sometimes changes the chōsakan's classification. If he is convinced that a case is X, he disposes of it without even sending it for Court deliberation. The hanketsu (formal judgment) or kettei (order) is of course signed and sealed by the members of the Bench.

As a rule, the justice in charge, if he is in the majority, writes the opinion of the court with the help of the chōsakan responsible for the case (the extent of such help depends upon the justice and the case). Even if he is not in the majority, he is still responsible for the proper disposition of the case. He may write a dissenting opinion. The justices in the majority will talk among them about who should write the majority opinion.

On the Grand Bench the chief justice sits in the center, justice No. 2 in seniority (which is determined not by age, but by the date of appointment) sits on the righthand side of the Chief Justice (on the lefthand side of the Chief Justice if we see him from the floor), justice No. 3 on the lefthand side of the Chief Justice, and so on until No. 15 sits at the end of the Bench on the lefthand side of the Chief Justice. On a Petty Bench the same principle is followed. On the Grand Bench the Chief Justice is of course the presiding justice so far as the case is concerned. If he is not the justice that ranks highest in seniority, he does not sit in the center. He presides from his seat and speaks aslant, sometimes to the embarrassment of unaccustomed counsel or parties. At first there was a Petty Bench that behaved just like the Grand Bench, but there is none now.

Research officials are, as noted above, generally chosen from the ranks of new full judges who have finished 10 years as assistant judges (hanhiho), although assistant judges about to be promoted to full judges are occasionally chosen. The latter must be exceptionally competent. They are chosen on the basis of their achievements as apprentices in the Supreme Court Research and Training Institute and their ratings for competence and efficiency. Research officials (chōsakan) are appointed by the Secretary General (advised by the Director of the Personnel Bureau) but with consultation with the Chief Research Official (Shuseki Chōsakan). The selection is made from a list of candidates (some of which are recommended informally by the chief judges of the district courts where the assistant judges or full judges had served). The Chief Research Official ranks with a President of a High Court or the Director of the Supreme Court's Research and Training Institute. He supervises other research officials. Chief Research

Officials are occasionally appointed to the Supreme Court,[2] although not directly from that position.

Until the contemporary era, research officials were never called in during Grand Bench or Petty Bench deliberations. The change came in part as a result of an incident in which one justice responsible for a case could not adequately explain his own draft. The research official who worked on that case was called into the deliberations without notice, to his great embarrassment.

The entire court membership sits as the Grand Bench (nine of the fifteen constitute a quorum), in cases involving (a) the constitutionality of a law, ordinance, regulation or action, (b) a tie vote in a Petty Bench, (c) other matters deemed significant enough for such special action, or (d) Petty Bench opinions which are incompatible with Supreme Court precedents whether constitutional or statutory. The Supreme Court of the United States, consisting of a Chief Justice and eight Associates Justices, meets as a single collegial body and must handle all issues which it finds on its agenda or docket whether of necessity or by its own discretionary screening procedures.

The Japanese Supreme Court has no choice but to accept appeals when they are taken (a) in civil cases on grounds of (i) errors in constitutional construction, (ii) other violations of the Constitution, or (iii) obviously prejudicial violations of laws or ordinances (Article 394 of the Code of Civil Procedure) or (b) in criminal cases on grounds of (i) violations of the Constitution or errors in constitutional construction, (ii) incompatibility with Supreme Court procedents, or (iii) in the absence of such precedents, incompatibility with precedents of High Courts as courts of last resort (Article 405 of the Code of Criminal Procedure). In criminal cases, however, the Supreme Court has some discretion. Even if the Court finds an appeal not well grounded under Article 405, it can still hear it if it thinks that unless the judgment below is overruled, gross injustice will be done according to Article 411. A party who lost in a high court as a court of second or third instance can still petition the Supreme Court for accepting an appeal which does not fall under any one of the above three categories, but which involves important matters relating to statutory interpretation ("statutory" here means "relating to laws, ordinances or the Supreme Court's rules"). Rule 257 of the Supreme Court's Rules of Criminal Procedure is the Japanese counterpart of American *certiorari.* The Court has exercised discretion in these cases. Invocation of Rule 257 is not so frequent as invocation of *certiorari* in the United States. Most of these appeals invoke Article 405 even when appellants are well aware that their appeals are not at all grounded, in the hope that the Court may hear them in the exercise of its discretion in accordance with Article 411. That is why there are so many X criminal cases. This is not the only explanation. Dilatory tactics are, among other things, responsible especially in cases involving violations of election laws.

Each Supreme Court found it necessary to adopt procedures to screen out unimportant cases and to identify and proceed in orderly fashion with important cases. Each also was provided with certain statutory requirements regarding the sifting process. The key statutory provision for the Supreme Court of the United States was the Judiciary Act of 1925 which substituted the discretionary writ of *certiorari* for the obligatory writ of error in most appellate jurisdictions directed by the Constitution of 1789. Regardless of whether a case comes through discretionary writ of error, by means of appeal, through certificate from a federal Court of Appeals or the Court of Claims, in the infrequent actions under original jurisdiction or through invocation of one of the extraordinary writs (habeas corpus, prohibition, mandamus, or common law *certiorari*), the Supreme Court examines in preliminary fashion each case to determine which ones deserve full consideration. Approximately 87 percent of these requests are denied. Thus the Court generally provides full review of only 170 or 180 of the approximately 4,000 to 5,000 cases presented to it each year. For the Supreme Court of Japan, the post-World War II Constitution and statutes implementing that legislation provided the criteria for permitting or restricting the flow of cases. Article 7 of the Court Organization Law provides for *kokoku* appeal (essentially a complaint brought against the action of a lower court other than hanketsu, a final formal judgment) and *jōkoku* appeal (issues involving violation of the Constitution, errors in constitutional construction, or incompatibility with Supreme Court precedents). In fact, one statutory provision (Article 406 of the Code of Criminal Procedure) issues jōkoko appeal in "any cases which it (the Supreme Court) deems involve an important problem of the construction of law or ordinance". In short, the post-World II legislation in Japan, like that of the United States, facilitates rather than restricts access to the Supreme Court thus contributing significantly to increased case load (Maki, 1964: xix–xx).

In response, albeit not very successfully, each Supreme Court has attempted to screen out frivolous and unimportant cases. In each system a very heavy burden is placed on the individual justices. But each system utilizes the research officials and the law clerks, respectively, at the initial stages for thorough preliminary screening out of such cases. The Japanese Supreme Court actually utilizes three types of decisions. *Hanketsu* requires a formal announcement of a decision and generally must involve hearing oral argument and rendition of a decision in open court. In dismissing appeals hanketsu may be rendered without oral argument. Kettei requires neither oral argument nor open court announcement. And *meirei* are decisions announced by a judge or a group of judges rather than the Court. Hiroshi Itoh reported that 73% of all the criminal cases were kettei decisions in 1962, a time saving procedure, because a majority of the appeals in this area lacked proper grounds. Similarly, the Supreme Court of the United States dismisses many cases in *per curiam* decisions, a procedure far less time consuming and less demanding than full scale deliberation. However, even the heavy use of screening and time saving procedures has not reduced the burgeoning case load of each Supreme Court.

The regular, orderly processing of important cases in each Supreme Court is, of course, time-consuming. In the Japanese system once a case is on the docket, a research official initiates research on it and writes a report for the justice reponsible for the case. As noted above, the research official is assigned cases in his area of specialization; the justice is not. A justice may accept the report or ask for additional research. The research official also writes a comment in a journal called *Hōsō Jihō* (The Journal of the Legal Profession) on the Supreme Court decision for which he did research. Itoh suggests that justices write many decisions contrary to the reports of the research officials (Itoh, 1958: 80–81). Other commentators suggest that the research officials play a very significant role in the decision-making process especially because they are assigned cases in areas of their own expertise while justices often are not.

A Petty Bench sits twice or so a week. If it has no oral argument, it simply announces decisions, which will take half an hour. After that they have a conference to decide cases. The 15 justices meet once a week as a rule, but for two purposes. One is for deciding Grand Bench cases just as a Petty Bench does. The other is for deliberating on matters of judicial administration of all kinds. This conference is called Saibankan Kaigi.

Originally, Supreme Court conferences in Japan were similar to those in the United States in at least one major respect – the absolute barring of all persons other than justices from decision making conferences. But in recent years this prohibition has been lifted. In

Grand Bench deliberations, the Chief Justice acts as chairman of the total membership of the Supreme Court. He now has the chief research official and the research official in charge of the case present as well. They are sometimes asked to explain the case and answer specific questions. They stay during the deliberations because they are expected to help the Justice technically responsible for the case to write his opinion. Petty Bench deliberations are generally less formal and the Justice responsible for a particular case generally leads discussions. Petty Bench I previously never called in research officials to its deliberations but recently changed its policy. Petty Bench II has called in research officials for some time. Petty Bench III limits such invitations to important cases. In all situations, the justices and the research officials maintain conference secrecy. But in contrast to the American Supreme Court, which does not meet in divisions or panels, the Grand Bench and Petty Bench conference deliberations are held with the research official responsible for the research report in a particular case present.

Japanese justices always sit in order of seniority in conference deliberations and in open court. One of the most comprehensive assessments of the internal operation of the Japanese Supreme Court was provided by former Justice Jiro Tanaka in a lecture hosted by the Law Faculty of Kobe University, November 12, 1975. Tanaka indicated that the Chief Justice ordinarily does not participate in Petty Bench deliberations. He felt that without the contributions of the research officials the Supreme Court's functions would immediately stop. No such judgement of the contributions of American Law clerks has been made by an American justice although the clerks' contributions should not be minimized.

Tanaka's view of the ability of the Japanese Supreme Court to cope with the increased case load was pessimistic although he reported some decrease in the backlog of cases during his years on the Court. Like members of the Supreme Court of the United States the demands on the individual justices were very heavy. Tanaka served on Petty Bench I. It handled 1500 appeals annually and Tanaka was responsible for 300 civil and criminal cases. He reported working late at night and even into early morning hours. He felt this very demanding on an old man and like some of his American counterparts he was concerned that under the pressure of these demands, he might commit errors. For American justices errors are a matter of professional pride or conscience. For Japanese justices there is also an additional consideration. Technically justices guilty of errors pay fines although, in fact, this occurred only on one occasion. Tanaka estimated that about 20% of the issues coming before his bench were meritorious. All are first screened by research officials.

The Grand Bench, according to Tanaka, met rarely more than once a week generally having 10 to 20 major en banc cases for hearings. Oral argument was time consuming but was not handled in the American manner. Specifically, justices do not interrupt attorneys or ask them questions in Japanese oral argument stage.

The Supreme Court of the United States meets for nine months each year in a term generally running from the first Monday in October to the last week of June. Ordinarily, the US Supreme Court hears oral arguments on the first four days of two weeks in each month during its annual term. Decisions are also announced on those days, the courtroom sessions for oral argument and decision announcements beginning at 10:00 a.m., extending to noon and resuming at 1:00 p.m. and generally ending at 3:00 p.m. In contract to the nearly unlimited time allotted to oral argument in the early 19th century, such oral presentations are limited to one half hour per side and are not supposed to be merely repetitious of the written briefs before the Court. American justices do not hesitate to interrupt (and occasionally humiliate) attorneys presenting oral arguments that are not germane or which are poorly prepared. In comparison, oral argument in the Japanese Supreme Court generally involves an oral summary repetition or arguments provided in the written briefs. As noted, Japanese justices do not ordinarily interrupt oral argument presentations.

As in Japan, much of the preliminary screening of cases in the American Supreme Court is initially handled by auxiliary personnel. But, as was noted above, there is a considerable difference in the training, experience, and judicial ability between a Japanese research official and an American law clerk. Japanese research officials are, in effect, assigned to their areas of specialization rather than to a particular justice. In modern times, each American justice may have three clerks (the Chief Justice has four). Ordinarily, a law clerk works for one year for a single justice (Chief Justice Warren Burger has begun the practice of keeping a clerk for a number of years).

The conference begins at 9:30 on Fridays during the nine months of the annual term of the Supreme Court of the United States and generally lasts all day. Additional conference time is sometimes allotted on Wednesday afternoons. When possible, cases are decided in conference within a day to four days of its oral argument stage. The entire court acts as a single collegial body. If a majority is readily forthcoming, one of the majority will be asked to write the Court's opinion by the Chief Justice (if he is with the majority). In the event that the Chief Justice is not in support of the majority, the senior Associate Justice with the majority makes the opinion-writing assignment. The Justice assigned this task writes a preliminary draft of an opinion and circulates it among his colleagues. Frequently a considerable amount of revision and editing (often done by the Justice's clerk as well as the Justice) is necessary before the majority accepts it. In the post-World War II era, American justices have not been reluctant to give written expression to out-right rejection of a majority opinion (in a dissenting opinion) or to agreement with the result reached by the majority but choice of an alternative line of reasoning to reach that result (a concurring opinion). Historically, American justices were less willing to write many dissenting or concurring opinions although there has been considerable variation in their incidence because of either the seriousness of the issues confronting the Court (such as slavery and the other impending Civil War related issues) or the clash of strong judicial personalities (as in the post-F.D.R era).

The Chief Justice in the United States has considerable, but by no means overwhelming, influence through his case assignment capability and his ability to lead the Court in Conference. But the latter depends on the characteristics of the individual holding the position. Itoh suggests that the Japanese Chief Justice has less influence because there is no "fixed order for the expression of opinions among the justices at a conference table or for the casting of votes, there's no power advantage inherent in the discussion and voting sequence". He contrasted this to the practice in the Supreme Court of the United States where the Chief Justice states his position first in the disccussion stage and where the order of seniority is reversed in the voting stage (Itoh, 1968: 83–84). Takeo Hayakawa's data on the age of the justices provides another more compelling explanation. The actual time spent in the office of Chief Justice is generally considerably shorter than the years in office of associate justices which as noted above were only nine. The service of nine Chief Justices who served since 1947 is summarized in Table 10.1. With the exception of Tanaka, the Chief Justices generally did not hold the position long enough to develop or assert the kind of institutional leadership that several American Chief Justices developed during considerably longer periods as head of their collegial body.

Decision-making procedure and custom within the Supreme Court

TABLE 10.1 The Terms of the Chief Justices of Japan

	Chief Justice	*Appointed*	*Retired*	*Years as Chief Justice*
1.	T. Milbuchi	August 4, 1947	March 2, 1950	2 years, 7 months
2.	K. Tanaka	March 3, 1950	October 24, 1960	10 years, 7½ months
3.	K. Yokota	October 25, 1960	August 5, 1966	5 years, 9 months
4.	M. Yokota	August 6, 1966	January 10, 1969	2 years, 5 months
5.	K. Ishida	January 11, 1969	May 19, 1973	4 years, 4 months
6.	T. Murakani	May 21, 1973	May 24, 1976	3 years
7.	M. Fujibayashi	May 25, 1976	August 25, 1977	1 year, 3 months
8.	M. Okahura	August 26, 1977	March 31, 1979	1 year, 7 months
9.	T. Hattori	April, 1979	(still in office in 1979)	

of Japan has often been discussed within the context of Japanese political and social attitudes, especially the Confucian principle of harmony (Murphy and Tanenhaus, 1977: 38–39). The Court of Cassation prior to 1947 voted on each issue in controversy in each case until a majority position was developed for the case. No dissenting opinions were recorded and justices who had disagreed with the majority in conference customarily joined the majority for a unified and unanimous result. The Court of Cassation procedure of voting on each disputed issue within a case (rather than on the overall resolution of the case itself) is still followed by the post-World War II Supreme Court of Japan. But the policy of unanimous agreement with the final result has been totally abandoned by the new Court. Japanese justices quite freely and frequently record dissenting or concurring opinions. The majority opinion is drafted by the justice originally assigned the issue if a majority supports his positions on the case (Itho, 1968: 104–105). As indicated earlier, a research official whose area of specialization is related to the subject matter of the case ordinarily contributes basic research, a preliminary draft, and input in the conference.

With respect to the criteria for fair and efficient internal procedures and customs, both Supreme Courts have achieved, in their distinctive matters, the standards identified with a Weberian type ideal model. Both have developed and consistently utilized institutional procedures which are sufficiently predictable to insure regularized access to each highest appellate court, but both have found it necessary to rigorously utilize screening procedures to eliminate trivial or less important issues or summary procedures to dispose of such issues promptly. Secondly, both courts have utilized procedures designed to facilitate the orderly processing of cases and have achieved fair but not totally successful results in the face of burgeoning case loads. And thirdly, both have maintained high standards of objectivity although both sets of justices reflect conflicting judicial values in determining major public policy controversies which reach the courts as bonafide cases. Both courts have maintained high standards with regard to the secrecy of the conference and the integrity of the judicial process.

In sum the American and Japanese Supreme Courts handle some aspects of their internal procedures differently but both seek to achieve fidelity to their goals of fair and efficient procedures. They have both approximated the criteria for fairness and objectivity, but both are deeply troubled by their inability to cope adequately with their accelerating case loads. Indeed, the plaintive comments about the burdens of Supreme Court work by Justices Jiro Tanaka of Japan and Blackmun of the United States are virtually identical.[3]

NOTES

1. The data for the portions of the chapter treating the characteristics of the justices of the Japanese Supreme Court and the research officials (Chōsakan) of that court and the institutional procedures of that court, are derived from (1) preliminary interviews conducted by the authors in Tokyo with two research officials of the Japanese Supreme Court, Takashi Tojo and Toji Tao (Takashi Tojo is now judge of the Osaka District Court and Toji Tao is now chief judge of the Niigata Family Court), and (2) with former Justice Jiro Tanaka in 1977. More importantly, Takeo Hayakawa conducted more intensive and complete interviews in 1979 with them and Research Official Itsuo Sonobe (formerly Professor of Law, Kyoto University Law School).

2. The Chief Research Official of the Japanese Supreme Court at the time that several interviews for this investigation were conducted was Shuseki Chōsakan Jiro Nakamura. By 1979 he was appointed a Justice of the Supreme Court.

3. Former Justice Tanaka's lecture was provided by Takeo Hayakawa; Justice Blackmun's views are reproduced in Schmidhauser, *Judges and Justices,* 1979: 184–185. Unless other sources were cited, the basic information and analysis of the Japanese Judiciary and its personnel was provided by Takeo Hayakawa.

References

BRYCE, J. (1981) *Social Institutions in the United States.* New York: Grosset and Dunlap.

CAVERS, D. (1963) "The Japanese Program for Cooperation in Legal Studies" in A. T. van Mehren (ed.) *Law in Japan: the Legal Order in a Changing Society.* Cambridge: Harvard University Press.

DANELSKI, D. (1969) "The Supreme Court of Japan: an Exploratory Study" in G. Schubert and D. Danelski (eds.) *Comparative Judicial Behavior: Cross-Cultural Studies of Political Decision-Making in the East and the West.* New York: Oxford University Press.

HAYAKAWA, T. (1973) "Age and the Judiciary in Japan". *Kobe University Law Review* **9**.

HURST, J. W. (1950) *The Growth of American Law.* Boston: Little, Brown.

ITOH, H. (1968) "The Japanese Supreme Court: Judicial Decision-Making Analysis". Seattle: Unpublished doctoral dissertation, University of Washington.

MAKI, J. M. (1964) *Court and Constitution in Japan.* Seattle: University of Washington Press.

MURPHY, W. F. and J. TANNENHAUS (1977) *Comparative Constitutional Law: Cases and Commentaries.* New York: St. Martin's Press.

OPPLER, H. C. (1976) *Legal Reform in Occupied Japan: A Participant Looks Back.* New York: Oxford University Press.

REED, A. Z. (1921) *Training for the Public Profession of Law.* New York: Carnegie Foundation for the Advancement of Teaching.

RHYNE, C. S. (ed.) (1978) *Law and Judicial Systems of Nations.* Washington: World Peace Through Law Center.

SCHMIDHAUSER, J. R. (1962) "Age and Judicial Behavior: American Higher Appellate Judges" and "When and Why Justices Leave the Supreme Court" in W. Donahue and C. Tibbetts (eds.) *Politics of Age.* Ann Arbor: University of Michigan Press.

SCHMIDHAUSER, J. R. (1979) *Judges and Justices: The Federal Appellate Judiciary,* Boston: Little, Brown.

SECRETARIAT GENERAL OF THE SUPREME COURT OF JAPAN (1975) *Justice in Japan: The Supreme Court of Japan.* Tokyo: The Supreme Court of Japan.

TAKAYANAGI, K. (1963) "A Century of Innovation: The Development of Japanese Law, 1868–1961" in A. T. von Mehren (ed.) *Law in Japan: the Legal Order in a Changing Society.* Cambridge: Harvard University Press.

WOODWARD, B. and S. ARMSTRONG (1979) *The Brethren: Inside the Supreme Court. New York: Simon and Schuster.*

CHAPTER 11

SUBCULTURES AND JUDICIAL BACKGROUND: A CROSS-CULTURAL ANALYSIS

GLENDON SCHUBERT
UNIVERSITY OF HAWAII-MANOA

In an article presenting an excellent analysis of the significance of judicial social, professional, and political background characteristics (or "attributes", as I shall call them henceforth in this paper) to the decision-making of United States Supreme Court justices, Neal Tate (1981) has redirected the attention of political scientists to certain basic questions of theory, in judicial behavioral research, that have remained in disputation for at least sixty years (Haines, 1922 (reprinted in Schubert, 1964); and see also Tate, 1983; and Gibson, 1983). Contrary to the empirical findings of many contributors to the relevant research literature of the sixties and seventies, Tate demonstrates that selected variables measuring the attributes of Supreme Court justices combine to support predictions, of decisional behavior, that are substantially equivalent to alternative predictions of such behavior based on variables measuring judicial attitudes. Tate also (with the help of Johnston, Van Esso, and Ryan) extended in substantial part (i.e. for the content domains of the political liberalism and the economic liberalism decision-scales) earlier data sets (based primarily on the work of Pritchett [1948] and Schubert (1965, 1970, 1974; and cf. Ryan and Tate, 1974, 1981)) to include the first decade of the Burger Court. Tate (1981: 358, col. 1) reports continuing consistency in the behavior of the justices individually, as well as an excellent fit of his augmenting data to the model (Schubert, 1974) proposed on the basis of research in earlier periods of the Supreme Court; and these results provide a basis for enhanced confidence in the attitudinal theory and interpretation of Supreme Court behavior. However, Tate directs attention also (1981: 365, col. 1) to the methodological problem of validation (however it may be circumvented by longitudinal discriminations of either postdiction or prediction among data sets) inherent in the inference of latent individual attitudes, from manifest group decisions, in the absence of *independent* measurement and verification of the postulated attitudes of United States Supreme Court justices (but cf. Schubert, 1965, ch. 4).

Tate argues that the substantial isomorphism of his findings, as between attributes and attitudes as predictors of Supreme Court decisions, supports the importance of greater emphasis being placed upon work with *attributes,* which are amenable to observation entirely independent from decisions, and also because of his expressed pessimism (Tate, 1981: 366) about the chances for judicial behavioralists to gain systematic access to equivalent observations of the attitudes of justices of the United States Supreme Court. Whatever the merits of the latter presumption, the corresponding argument does not necessarily apply to any other level of the federal courts, or to the state court systems (including state supreme courts); and it demonstrably does not apply to the highest courts of other countries.

The more interesting theoretical question of the relationship in general among attributes, attitudes, and decisions of judges remains one concerning which relatively little systematic empirical evidence appears to have been discussed. In attempting to do that, it surely ought to be required that the data for all three major classes of variables (attributes, attitudes, and decisions) be derived from independent observations; and that there be at least two different such data sets so that comparative analysis can be performed. Such a test will be more rigorous if the comparative analysis is cross-cultural, especially if the judges compared are drawn from countries conventionally deemed to exhibit sharply contrasting political, social, and psychological postures in their domestic as well as in their international relationships. The study reported here meets all of these criteria; and indeed, it was designed from its inception to produce data that would *(inter alia)* bear upon the general theoretical question posited above.

That theory posits five classes of variables: cultural/systemic, attribute, interaction, attitudinal, and decisional. It states that these classes of variables are arrayed in the linear sequence depicted in Figure 11.1; and that effects will be greatest (i.e. correlationships will be strongest) between sets of variables that are adjacent in the linear sequence.

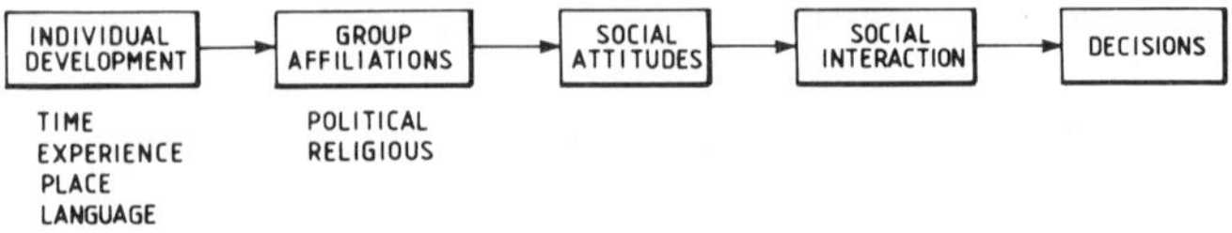

Figure 11.1 Decision-making sequence (schematic)

But interactional data are available for only one of the two countries in the present sample (but see Schubert, 1982); so that class of variables cannot be discussed comparatively as an empirical test of the theory. Figure 11.1 specifies a particular directionality of causation in the linear sequence depicted.

The two countries, whose supreme court judges are compared in the analysis below, are Switzerland and South Africa, which were given about equal time in a year of field survey research carried out by the author during 1970–71, for the purpose of making the observations on which are based the cultural, the other attribute, and the attitudinal data. The sample sizes for most analyses to be discussed here include forty-one Swiss judges and registrars and forty-seven judges from South Africa. Their published decisions could be and were observed and analyzed subsequent to the completion of the field work; and so also were other standard laboratory research operations (including transcriptions, translations, coding, computer and statistical analyses, etc.).

The complete data have been archived and accessible to other scholars for the past half dozen years (Schubert, 1977c) together with a codebook now available in an enlarged and revised second edition (Schubert, 1981) that provides detailed information, not repeated in the present chapter, about individual variables and associated data subsets. Additional information about the research design for the project and the findings for the two countries individually is provided in earlier research reports (Schubert, 1977a, 1977b, 1980, 1982, 1985a, and 1985b).

A. Attribute Variables

Within each country separately, analyses of subcultural differences were carried out with larger sets of attribute variables; but not all of those variables could appropriately be employed for cross-cultural purposes, and less than a dozen enter into the present discussion. The data were in substantial measure analyzed using SPSS computer programs; and a consequent entailment for present purposes is that acronymic, eight-alpha-numeric-character variable names became used for designation purposes in figures illustrating the principal findings; and hence appear also in the figures reported and discussed below. Such variables will be briefly identified initially with greater circumlocution in ordinary English; but thereafter reliance will be placed on the SPSS names in order to save time and space, and for consistency with the graphics.

Switzerland and South Africa are distinguished for classification of the two major data sets, by the attribute variable COUNTRY, with unimpeachable validity and reliability alike. Half a dozen other variables, which represent standard sociological concerns, presented no problems for inclusion in the cross-cultural analysis: these include the principal occupation(s) of a respondent prior to selection as a judge of the highest court (PREOC) and the principal occupation(s) of his parents (PARENTOC) usually in terms of his father; similarly, as to political experience (PREPOLEX, and FAMPOLEX); length of time since initial appointment as a judge of the highest court (JUDTENUR); and chronological life span to date of interview (AGE). These variables also are considered to be relatively non-controversial in theory-and method terms. The remaining four attributes all are of major importance; but the bases for synthesizing them for combination in variables to be compared cross-culturally are intuitively less self-evident. Of these, the basic index to subculture is provided by maternal (or primary) language: PRIMLANG. Political affiliation is POLAF; and religious, RELIGAF. Position within the status hierarchy of the court is STATUS. The author would have welcomed the opportunity, and not least in retrospect (Schubert, 1983, 1985c), to have been able to include the biocultural variable SEX; but just two of the Swiss registrars, none of the Swiss judges, and only one of the South African judges, were female.

All of the attribute variables represent ordinal scales along a dimension of ideological conservatism/liberalism. Not a single one of the eighty-eight jurists in the combined sample is classified in the first and putatively most conservative category of PREOC, which would have signified occupational experience as a banker or businessman prior to appointment or election to the supreme court. This background characteristic distinguishes this judicial elite from other political elites consisting of persons holding offices of equivalent importance in either the executive or the legislature of either country, where at least a few bankers and quite a few businessmen are certain to be found. It also appears to distinguish them from United States Supreme Court justices among whom it has not been uncommon to pursue entrepreneurial careers as directors of or consultants to various corporations or their managers prior to appointments to the Supreme Court (Schmidhauser, 1983; Shogan, 1972). Only half a dozen Swiss or South African jurists claimed experience in the most liberal category as a journalist or politician; and most of the judges clearly had experience only in other types of legal work as lower court judges, registrars, advocates, solicitors, or as teachers of law.

The occupational experience of the fathers of these judges tended to be much more conservative that that of the judges themselves. Almost half of the fathers' principal employment was in one of the two conservative categories; whereas only a dozen of the judges themselves claimed the less conservative of the two, and none was most conservative.

Judges and their fathers were much more alike in regard to previous *political* experience. A majority or more of each group categorically denied having had any at all; but twice as many judges as fathers were associated with a slight amount, while twice as many fathers as sons were identified with extensive involvement in party politics. The distribution of Swiss jurists was more liberal than that for the South African judges on three of these variables: PREOC, PARENTOC, and PREPOLEX. But the South Africans were just as markedly more liberal in regard to family politicization, with a third of them claiming "considerable" or "extensive" familial political involvement, as compared to only *two* (i.e., less than 5%) of the Swiss.

The age curve is smooth throughout most of its range. Divided into five groups, the distribution for all except the youngest category (under forty) includes 19±3 judges each; this is because the "youngest" category is populated exclusively by Swiss registrars. The South African judges tend to be older – or the Swiss tend to be younger, depending upon which way one chooses to view the matter – in all groupings except "older", for which they are about the same.

The combined distribution for judicial tenure is strongly skewed toward seniority, with two-thirds of the judges having "less" or "least" judicial experience. The South Africans tend generally, however, to be more experienced in their judicial roles than are the Swiss: over half of the Swiss fall in the category of "least" judicial tenure, whereas almost half of the South Africans range from "average" through "most". Of course this reflects the presence of the registrars in the Swiss subsample; but they are members of the Federal Tribunal, playing roles subsumed in the less specialized and less bureaucratic range of activities of the South African judge.

The status distribution also is rather strongly skewed toward seniority, although the differences between the South Africans and the Swiss are less pronounced here. There are more presiding judges in South Africa because there are more areal panels there than there are functional ones in the Federal Tribunal. In the Swiss system there are a few more registrars with minimal status, than there are "most junior" acting or ex-acting or recently appointed judges in South Africa. And even an acting judge in South Africa, who is the approximate equivalent of a substitute judge in Switzerland, has relatively higher status than even the oldest and most experienced of the Swiss registrars.

In each country PRIMLANG has as its first category the maternal language spoken by the dominant subcultural group: clearly that is German in Switzerland, and Afrikaans in South Africa. The second category represents bilingualism with equal competence in the dominant cultural language and in the language spoken by the principal subcultural population of the country. For the Swiss this implies bilingualism in German and in French; for the South Africans it implies bilingualism in Afrikaans and in English. It necessarily follows that the third category is French (for Switzerland) and English (for South Africa). The fourth category represents the second most important minority subculture's language, defining importance here in terms of weighting in the structure of the courts and legal system as well as for the primary and secondary political subcultures. This is certainly Italian for the Swiss legal system and the Federal Tribunal. No subculture other than either Afrikaner, or English-speaking (Anglican), is represented in South Africa by membership among the judges; although some recognition is accorded by the South African legal system to the large number of languages and dialects spoken by various segments of the black majority of the population of the country. Rather than to stigmatize these as the South Africans themselves do (Anonymous, 1973) as "Bantu" languages, the generic term "African" is used here to refer to the languages typically employed at the trial court level for many cases involving blacks, particularly in prosecutions for crime. Most such trials are presided over by magistrates rather than Supreme Court judges, but many of the judges in the sample here were experienced in conducting such trials, usually with the aid of interpreters.

The fifth category constitutes a logical extension of the latent scale variable: it represents the third largest minority subculture's language. This is Romansch in Switzerland, where it is one of the official languages of the country. In South Africa it is postulated to be Hindi, the maternal language of many of the emigrants from India who have settled in large ethnic colonies in Durban, Johannesburg, and elsewhere in Natal and Transvaal. Hence the latent scale variable represents deviation from the dominant language of the country's principal culture, with gradations according to the legal system's integration of various minority subcultures.

The postulated scale directs attention to the extent to which all subcultures other than the dominant one and its principal competitor remain completely or virtually unrepresented among the judges of the combined sample. Almost a majority, of 43 out of 88 jurists, are in the first and dominant subcultural group. Only slightly fewer, 37, are in the third group, that of the most important minority subculture; and here again the Anglican compositional bias of the South African sample is the cause of the no-doubt inflated size of this third group. Only five South Africans are classified in the second category as bilingual; and that leaves only the three Italian Swiss in the fourth, secondarily important, subcultural group. Neither country has any representative for the less important subcultures of the fifth group.

There is no theoretical reason why some of the Swiss respondents could not have been classified as bilingual. The fact that none was suggests far less emphasis upon becoming equally involved from infancy in two subcultures, in the early socialization of any of the Swiss jurists than there was for several of the South Africans. Both of the Italian-maternal judges could have been classified as trilingual, and possibly the registrar as well; but the logic of the latent scale here made it more important to classify these persons instead as Italian. Before the actual field work was begun in Lausanne, it was presumed that there might be at least one Romansch-maternal among the Swiss jurists, to represent the canton of Graubunden (Barber, 1974). However, it was discovered that, although the Judge-President for the entire Federal Tribunal then was indeed a citizen of Graubunden, his name (Silvio Giovanoli) is Italian while his maternal language was German. The expectation confirmed for South Africa was more realistic: that only persons classified as ethnically "European" were appointed to the Supreme Court; and hence the fourth and fifth PRIMLANG scale categories, "African" and "Hindi", are empirically empty.

The political affiliation variable has a different latent scale. It represents deviation from the most extremely conservative stance available within the country's political system, at the time when the field study was conducted. There are six empirical categories. The first two are the most extreme and the second most extreme right-wing political parties, from which members of the sample here were or might conceivably have been selected. The third category is that of the largest center-conservative party; and the fourth is for unaffiliateds and non-response. The center-liberal party is fifth, and the most important left-wing party is sixth. The empirical party equivalents for Switzerland were: (1) Farmers & Artisans & Citizens; (2) Liberal; (3) Christian Conservative; (4) Unaffiliated; (5) Radical; (6) Social Democrat. The corresponding empirical equivalents for South Africa include: (1) Republican Party; (2) Herstige Nationalist Party; (3) National Party; (4) Unaffiliated; (5) United; (6) Progressive. The empirical frequencies for the combined sample are 4, 2, 26, 9, 31, 16. There are only a handful of judicial representatives of the radical right; and only 10% are either unaffiliated or else of unknown affiliation. This leaves the largest pluralities to fall in the center-right and the center-left parties; but the larger number of representatives for the principal left-wing party, than for the right-wing alternatives, gives the joint sample a left-of-centre centroid. To the extent that political representation shows a bias in this sample, it is in the direction of liberalism.

There is no very important difference between the two countries in regard to that liberal bias; but to the extent that there is a difference, it is that the Swiss give more substantial weighting to the radical right parties for which there are twice as many representatives on the Tribunal as there are for, say, the Italian-speaking ethnic minority who constitute a much larger fraction of the population than do the right-wing political party members. Both countries give majority (and almost exactly the same proportion of) representation to the left-center plus left-wing parties: 54% for the Swiss, and 53% for South Africa. Neither the German-ethnic Farmers' Party nor the French-ethnic Liberal Party constituted a direct threat to the coalition of center-and-left parties in Switzerland; while the Herstige National Party did pose such a threat to the National Government at the time of the field survey. Jura separatists represented such a threat to the regime in Switzerland, too; but few if any of them were represented on the Federal Tribunal.

The latent scale for POLAF is the one most entitled to confidence in comparison with the scales for maternal language and religion; and RELIGAF is probably least so among these three. It is premised that there are two principal religious affiliational alternatives in each country; and that for each pair one is significantly more conservative than the other, in the sense of an attitudinal scale of psychological conservatism and liberalism. These center-right and center alternatives are associated with the second and third categories of a five-point scale of religious liberalism. Two schismatic denominations that represented viable alternatives at the time of the survey are identified with the first and most conservative category, the Swiss Christ-Catholic; and for South Africa, the "Dopper" Reformed. The fourth category is Hebrew, which in each country represents a small segment of the total population, although one with gross over-representation among lawyers and intellectuals and one that empirically had to be placed to the left rather than to the right of the two principal religious aggregations. Even further to the left, in the fifth category, are persons classified as unreligious, including those who refused to profess a religious choice.

Over four-fifths of the sample were in one or the other of the two principal denominations but there was a difference between the two countries in regard to such choices. For the Swiss, the plurality were Protestant (center) rather than Roman Catholic (centre-right); whereas for South Africa, the plurality were Dutch Reformed (center-right); rather than English Protestant (center) in affiliation. There was only one right-wing confessant for the Swiss, and this Christ-Catholic's judicial behavior was noticeably different from that of any other member of the Swiss sample. For South Africa, there are two members of the Dopper (or conservative) branch of the Dutch Reformed Church, one of whom was generally quite conservative in his judicial behavior – while the other was not. None of the Swiss jurists identified himself as Hebrew; whereas in South Africa four judges did so. The proportion of unreligious persons was precisely the same for both countries: five (of 41) Swiss, and six (of 47) South Africans.

B. Correlationships

One check upon the validity of the categories for the three basic attribute variables is to examine their cross-tabulations with some extrinsic criterion of liberalism and conservatism. The best available is COMSMATT, the first smallest space dimension for SSA-1 analysis of the Q matrix of intercorrelations among all 88 respondents, based on their replies to the 53 attitudinal inventory items common to both countries. This dimension provides a direct basis for ideological comparison of the Swiss and South African judges, in terms of their answers to the same questions – subject, of course, to certain caveats concerning the effects of differences in language, space, and time.

The limited relevant research literature provided no basis for expecting that the South Africans would appear to be more ideologically liberal than the Swiss; but that is precisely what the distribution of the common smallest-space attitudinal – hence, "COMSMATT" – dimension shows. The distribution for each country covers the entire range of the dimension, from +100 (or maximally liberal) to −100 (or maximally conservative). Those with the highest liberal scores in excess of +.69 include only 4 Swiss, 10% of their total; but it includes 9 South Africans, 19% of their total. The top quartile of the range of the dimension includes 20% of the Swiss but 28% of the South Africans; the top half, 47% and 58%; the top three-fourths, 76% and 88%; and therefore only when we come to the bottom quarter do we find proportionately more Swiss, 24%, than South Africans, 13%. On this evidence we have to conclude that the Swiss sample is more ideologically conservative than the South African, no matter what their respective culture-reputations may be.

Given the two-country subdistributions on that common dimension, the question can then be asked: what are the average COMSMATT scores, for each of the category groups and for each country, on each of the three basic attribute variables: PRIM-LANG, POLAF and RELIGAF? *If* the latent scale hypothesis is correct, then one should expect to find a scalar order of the country-group means ranging from conservative to liberal on each of these variables. As Table 11.1 shows, the sequence for the South Africans on maternal language is as expected, with the Afrikaans group slightly conservative and the English moderately liberal; and with the bilinguals in the middle although they are much closer to the Afrikaans than to the English group. The latter finding also is exactly what we should expect, because the bilinguals are persons who are ethnically Afrikaner but whose parental influence and example encouraged active participation in the then-dominant English culture. The gap between the German-maternal and the French-maternal groups is much smaller, although it too is in the expected direction. The small (three-person) Italian group is not consistent with our expectation; but that is exclusively due to the conservative ideological posture of the Italian-maternal registrar: the average for the two Italian-maternal *judges* is +18.5, which fits well with the prediction. But what is most remarkable in comparing the two cultures is the marked extent to which the Anglican group in South

TABLE 11.1 Category – Group Means on Combined Ideological Liberalism, for Maternal Language, Political Affiliation, and Religions Affiliation; by Country

PRIMLANG

	1	2	3	4	5
	German	Bilingual	French	Italian	Romansch
SW	−09.8	—	+10.1	−06.2*	—
SA	−15.6	−09.2	+46.4	—	—
	Afrikaans	Bilingual	English	African	Hindi

*+18.5, except for #64 who is −56

POLAF

	1	2	3	4	5	6
	Farmers	Liberal	Chris. Cons.	Nonpartisan	Radical	Soc. Dem.
SW	−63.0	−40.5	−38.9	+26.0	+00.5	+67.8
SA	—	—	−28.7	+12.4	+26.8	+74.7
	Republican	Herstige Nat.	National	Nonpartisan	United	Progressive

RELIGAF

	1	2	3	4	5
	Christ Cath.	Roman Cath.	Protestant	Hebrew	Unreligious
SW	−53.0	−37.3	+08.6	—	+59.7
SA	+13.0*	−22.8	+38.5	+58.0	+60.6
	"Dopper"	Dutch Reformed	English Prot.	Hebrew	Unreligious

*−28.0, except for #39 who is +54

Africa is considerably more liberal than not only the Afrikaners but all of the religious Swiss groups as well!

Both of the country-sequences on POLAF are in the expected progression, with the single exception that the Swiss non-partisans appear to be more liberal than the Swiss Radicals. It is true that the Swiss non-partisans include only two persons, both quite young registrars; but we should nevertheless conclude that the apparent sequencing of non-partisans is different for the Swiss, than for the South African, subsamples. Otherwise it appears that the two political party scales are quite similar except for the absence of representation for the radical right in the South African subsample.

The Swiss scale for religion is excellent; and the South African would be perfect except for a single judge, one of the two Doppers, who has an exceptionally liberal score. The South African scale otherwise indicates that ideological differences between avowed Hebrews and the unreligious in South Africa are virtually nil; the most important difference is between the Dutch Reformed confessants and all of the other judges. Comparing the two countries, the only other remarkable difference is that the English Protestants in South Africa appear to be substantially more liberal than do the Swiss Protestants.

A much simpler and alternative approach to understanding the extent to which the country-subsamples, for each of the ten attribute variables, are signifantly similar or dissimilar is provided by the T-test of the pairs of their respective means. This test shows that there is a highly significant difference in regard to family political experience, with the South Africans having had more of it. There is also a significant difference in age, with the South Africans older (in the light of the relative youth of the Swiss registrars). In regard to parental occupation, the Swiss and South Africans are so much *alike* that their similarity is marginally significant.

Figure 11.2 shows only the relatively higher levels of association among ten major attributes. Correlation generally is not very high, as is indicated both by the fact that only five of the coefficients indicated in the figure are larger than ±.40 and also by the simplicity of the figure. Although only fifteen associations are denoted for ten variables, twice as many possible associations were deleted from the figure because they were less than ±.20 in value. The closest relationships are among the three variables of the seniority triad, indicating that seniority is potentially an important component in any subsequent analyses between these attributes and either attitudinal or decisional variables. The next most closely associated triad consists of the three basic attributes: maternal language, political affiliation, and religion. Religion is also involved with parental occupation and family political experience, to form at a lower level of association a third triad, of *socialization:* and here it is religious *conservatism* that is linked with family politicization and relatively liberal parental socioeconomic

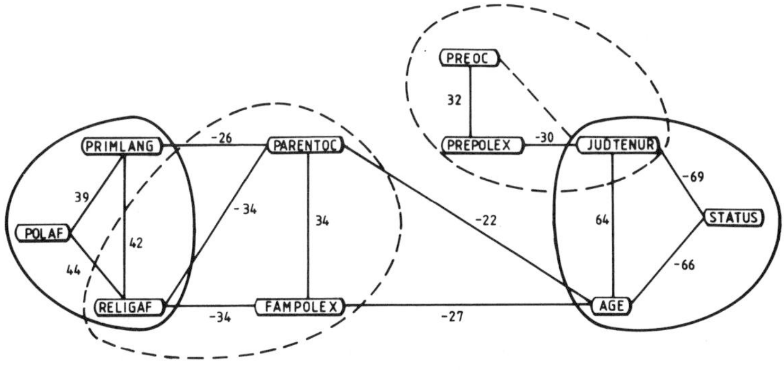

Figure 11.2 Attribute clusters

status. There are rudiments of a fourth triad, based on the associations, between previous occupation and previous political experience, and between previous political experience and judicial experience. Such a triad obviously would be one of *experience;* but it does not emerge in this figure because the association between previous occupational, and judicial, experiences is too small (at −.12).

C. Discrimant Analysis

In order to examine the multivariate effects of the attribute variables upon each other, each of the four principal ones – COUNTRY, POLAF, RELIGAF, and PRIMLANG – was discriminated from a subset of predicator variables. In each instance, the predictors included the other attribute variables (except for country) plus one or more attitudinal variables. The latter include COMSMATT, a general measure of liberal/conservative ideology; its four principal semantic components: political (POLATT), economic (ECONATT), social (SOCATT), and psychological (PSYCHATT) attitudes; and LEGORATT, the attitude of a judge, in a legal system subsuming multiple lego-cultural bases (as was true for all of these judges), toward the relative impact of those legal cultures upon decisional behavior.

In the discrimination of COUNTRY, for example, only a single discriminant function was produced (Equation 11.1), with the

SW = +.55PREOC −.48AGE −.44FAMPOLEX −.34LEGORATT −.31POLAF
+.30PSYCHATT +.28RELIGAF +.27PREPOLEX −.23PRIMLANG
−.21POLATT −.19ECONATT +.16PARENTOC −.13JUDTENUR
−.10SOCATT −.07STATUS

Equation 11.1

directionality of the Swiss sample. The directionality for both JUDTENUR and STATUS is consistent with what we observed earlier where both were positive for the South African sample; but it is remarkable how small the weightings are for these two variables in the equation, which otherwise indicates that the best predictors of the Swiss sample are liberal previous occupation, age in the sense of younger, socialization in non-politicized parental families, little appreciation of legal cultural differences in law school socialization, conservative political affiliation and psychological attitudes, liberal religious identification, previous personal political experience, and majority language-maternalism. Of lesser importance as predictors are liberalism in political and economic attitudes and in parental occupation, slight seniority, liberal social attitudes, and the slimmest indication of somewhat higher status. Evidently most of these predicators play some part, but none plays a preemptive part, in distinguishing between the Swiss and the South African samples, which is accomplished at an average rate of 75% correct with about the same success for each subsample.

The same set of predictors was used to discriminate the combined political affiliation variable, except that POLAF itself necessarily was removed from the predicator set for that purpose. The criterion for prediction here is substantially more difficult than was true for COUNTRY. That was a dichotomy; whereas POLAF has six categories, including the two right-wing Swiss parties, for which there is no empirical South African equivalent in the sample; the conservatives (Swiss Christian Conservatives, and South African Nationalists); nonpartisans for both countries; liberals (Swiss Radicals, and South African Uniteds); and the left-wing (Swiss Social Democrats, and South African Progressives). Even so and with one less predictor (POLAF itself), discrimination was just as good, with 72% correct overall and with category predictions ranging between 55% and 100%; the Swiss right-wing parties were of course easiest to predict, while the Radicals plus the Uniteds were hardest. The largest error in prediction, however, was the assignment, by the statistical procedure (and cf. Fisher, 1958), of eight of the liberal sympathizers, to the nonpartisan category – and that is hardly a strikingly irrational mistake, given the broad range of political spectrum covered by both of these two "older liberal" parties, and the fact that "nonpartisan" includes the undecideds.

With the large number of categories to be predicted, three discriminant functions were produced. The first of these is in the direction of conservative partisanship, and its best predictors are social and economic attitudinal conservatism (with SOCATT +.40, and ECONATT +.31) plus also conservative religious affilation (−.31RELIGAF). The second function is directed away from non-partisanship, with the old liberal parties also distinguished from both the conservative and the right-wing parties; the chief predictors are +.64PREPOLEX, −.57ECONATT, and +.43STATUS. These variables define non-partisanship primarily, but also liberal affiliation secondarily, as a consequence of the lack of previous personal political experience, of liberal social but conservative economic attitudes, and

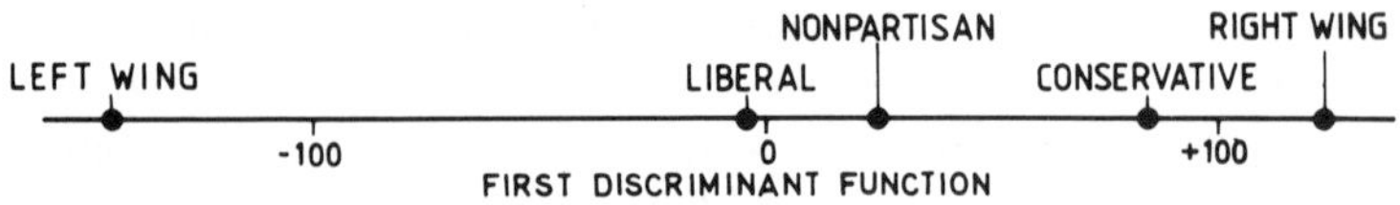

Figure 11.3 Discriminant-function principal component curve for combined political party groups: content

of high institutional judicial status. The third function acts primarily to distinguish the non-partisans from the center (liberal) party members, which it accomplishes by indicating that in this context the best predictors of non-partisanship are −.89PSYCHATT, +.70SOCATT, +.44POLATT, and −.4LEGORATT: thus non-partisans are associated with striking psychological liberalism but social and political conservatism,in their attitudes as compared to the judges identified with the center parties: and the nonpartisans also are less appreciative than the centrists of the significance of cultural effects upon legal socialization.

These three functions provide quite elegant examples of Guttman's (1954) theory of principal scale components (and see Schubert, 1965: 32–35) as Figures 11.4–11.6 illustrate. The score for "Right Wing" parties, in these figures, is estimated for the first function from available data, which do not permit corresponding estimates for the second and third functions.

RELIGAF was discriminated for the complete combined interview sample of 88 respondents, but with POLAF substituted for RELIGAF as a predictor, and with COMSMATT in lieu of the four individual

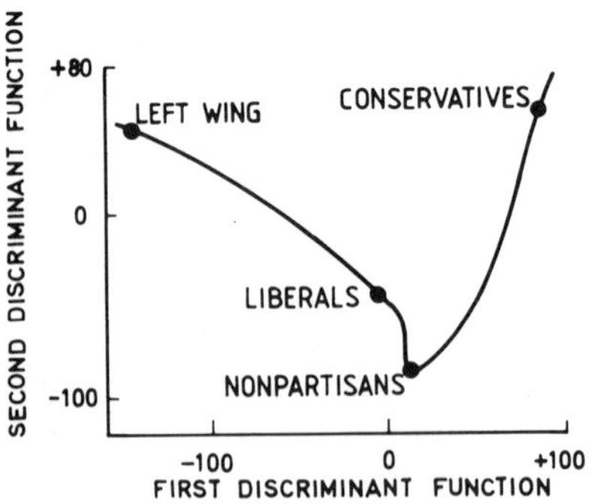

Figure 11.4 Discriminant-function principal component curve for combined political party groups: intensity

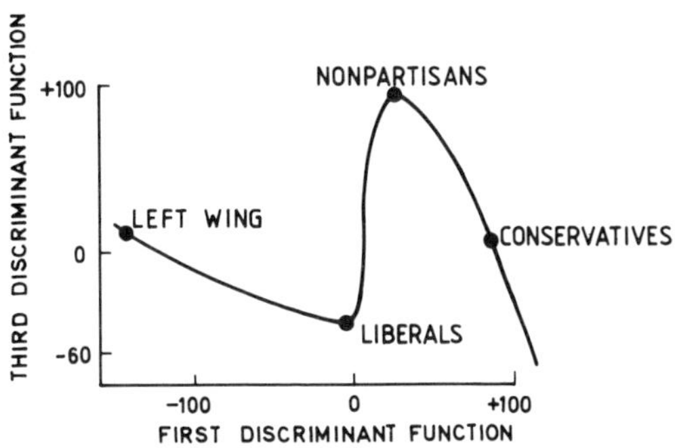

Figure 11.5 Discriminant-function principal component curve for combined political party groups: closure

attitudinal variables so that the total number of predictors was eleven. Four functions were produce for prediction to five categories; the overall rate of correct prediction was 73%, almost identical to that for POLAF. Predicting the unreligious category was least successful, and next worst was for the center group of moderates (Prostestants). COMSMATT is scaled (unlike the four individual attitudinal variables) in the direction of liberalism; and with the first discriminant function directed toward religious *conservatism,* the best predictors are −.49AGE, −.44COMSMAT, −.35POLAF, +.34PARENTOC, and −.30STATUS: religious conservatives are older, conservative in their general ideology and in their political affiliation, and of high judicial status; but they were raised by fathers engaged in relatively liberal occupations.

The final discrimination was of PRIMLANG, using the same eleven predictors used for discriminating RELIGAF (subject to the usual caveat about switching between dependent and independent variable status). But results were unsatisfactory, with an overall rate of only 48% correct predictions. Repeating the analysis using only three predictor variables (POLAF, RELIGAF, and COMSMATT) produced three functions that did exactly as well, with 48% correct: the first function attempts to discriminate the French and English maternals; the second, between bilinguals and the Italian Swiss; and the third, the bilinguals plus the Italian Swiss, from the rest of the sample.Using only three predictors improves the discrimination of the French and the English maternals, on the first dimension; but does worse on all other categories, and worst with the differentiation of majority-culture maternals. It seems clear that the combined variable

PRIMLANG is the least *internally* consistent, in its structure, of all four of the composite variables examined through discriminant analysis.

D. Conclusion

The data and analyses reported here demonstrate the importance of attributes as predictors of political behavior; and this is a finding based on comparative, cross-national research that in this respect agrees with Tate's (1981) findings for the United States Supreme Court, thereby providing at least three cases in support of the finding, as a proposition about comparative judicial politics and behavior. Moreover, these data indicate that, at least for the Swiss and South African judges included in (and at the time of) the present survey, attributes were not merely (as Tate found for the American justices) of *equivalent* importance as predictors of decisional behavior; here attributes even do somewhat better as predictors. Of course, the data here are cross-sectional, whereas those Tate used have the advantage of being longitudinal and of covering both a much longer period of time, and many more individuals who supplant each other in succession in the same institutional roles; hence, Tate's findings are based on much more reliable data than those reported here. On the other hand, the findings discussed here are comparative, and Tate's are not. The analyses discussed here are based in part on direct, independent observations of the attitudes of Swiss and South African judges; without question the attitudinal data here are much more valid that those (even though they are primarily my own) on which Tate's findings are based. This confirms further that the importance of attributal analysis can be justified, certainly for comparative research, on its own merits, and not merely as a substitute for putatively unobtainable direct observations of attitudinal data.

References

ANONYMOUS (1973) *Progress Through Separate Development.* New York Information Service of South Africa, 655 Madison Avenue; 4th ed.

BARBER, BENJAMIN R. (1974) *The Death of Communal Liberty: A History of Freedom in a Swiss Mountain Canton.* Princeton: Princeton University Press.

FISHER, FRANKLIN M. (1958) "The mathematical analysis of Supreme Court decisions: The use and abuse of quantitative methods". *American Political Science Review* **52:** 321–338.

GIBSON, JAMES L. (1983) "From simplicity to complexity: The development of theory in the study of judicial behavior". *Political Behavior* **5:** 7–49.

GUTTMAN, LOUIS (1954) "The principal components of scalable attitudes", ch. 5 in Paul F. Lazarsfeld (ed.) *Mathematical Thinking in the Social Sciences.* New York: The Free Press of Glencoe.

HAINES, CHARLES G. (1922) "General observations on the effects of personal, political, and economic influences in the decisions of judges". *Illionois Law Review* **17:** 96a–116.

PRITCHETT, C. HERMAN (1948) *The Roosevelt Court: A Study in Judicial Politics and Values, 1937–1947.* New York: Macmillan.

RYAN, JOHN PAUL, and C. NEAL TATE (1974; 2nd rev. ed. 1981) *The Supreme Court in American Politics: Policy Through Law,* Washington, D.C.: American Political Science Association.

SCHMIDHAUSER, JOHN R. (1983) "The convergence of law and politics revisited: The law firm as a case study". *Journal of Law and Politics,* **1:** 113–162.

SCHUBERT, GLENDON (1964) *Judicial Behavior: A Reader in Theory and Research.* Chicago: Rand McNally.

— (1965) *The Judicial Mind: The Attitudes and Ideologies of Supreme Court Justices, 1946–1963.* Evanston, Il.: Northwestern University Press.

— (1970) *The Judicial Mind* (Class I Data-Archive Study #7289, including codebook). Ann Arbor, Mich.: Inter-University Consortium for Political and Social Research.

— (1977a) *Political Attitudes and Ideologies: A Cross-Cultural Interdisciplinary Approach.* Beverly Hills, Cal.: Sage.

— (1977b) "Political culture and judicial ideology: Some cross and sub-cultural comparisons". *Comparative Political Studies* **10:** 363–408.

— (1977c) *Comparative Judicial Study: Switzerland and South Africa* (Class II Data-Archive Study #7365). Ann Arbor, Mich.: Inter-University Consortium for Political and Social Research.

— (1980) "Subcultural effects on judicial behavior: A Comparative analysis". *Journal of Politics* **42:** 951–992.

— (1981) *Comparative Judicial Study: Switzerland and South Africa* (Codebook for Class II Data-Archive Study #7365, 2nd rev. ed.). Ann Arbor, Mich.: Inter-University Consortium for Political and Social Research.

— (1982) "Nonverbal communication as political behavior", pp. 69–85 in Mary Ritchie Key (ed.), *Nonverbal Communication Today: Current Research.* The Hague: Mouton.

— (1983) "The biopolitics of sex: Gender, genetics, and epigenetics". In Meredith Watts (ed.) (Symposium on Biopolitics and Gender), *Women and Politics* 97–128.

— (1985A) *Political Culture and Judicial Elites: A Comparative Analysis;* Volume One of: *Political Culture and Judicial Behavior.* Lanham, MD: University Press of America.

— (1985B) *Subcultural Analysis of Judicial Behavior: A Direct Observation Study;* Volume Two of: *Political Culture and Judicial Behavior.* Lanham, MD: University Press of America.

— (1985C) "Sexual differences in political behavior." *Political Science Reviewer* **15.**

SHOGAN, ROBERT (1972) *A Question of Judgment: The Fortas Case and the Struggle for the Supreme Court.* Indianapolis, Ind.: Bobbs-Merrill.

TATE, C. NEAL (1981) "Personal attribute models of the voting behavior of U.S. Supreme Court justices: Liberalism in civil liberties and economics decisions, 1946–1978". *American Political Science Review* **75:** 35–367.

TATE, C. NEAL (1983) "The methodology of judicial behavior research: A Review and critique". *Political Behavior* **5:** 51–83.

CONCLUSION

The eleven chapters comprising this book provide a fairly representative cross-section of the variety of research investigations that have been conducted or are being completed by the one hundred and thirty active members of the Research Committee on Comparative Judicial Studies during the past decade. As suggested in the introductory chapter, the diversity of approaches is a fairly accurate approximation of the variety of conceptual perspectives and the abundance or paucity of conceptually equivalent empirical resources which characterizes the comparative judicial subfield of Political Science. Conventional area studies are appropriately absent.

Schubert demonstrated, with high methodological elegance and great analytical skill, the sophisticated use of the language of measurement as one important way in which variables derived from quite diverse legal cultures may be examined equivalently. But as Tate suggested in his challenging stock-taking, the tasks of integrating public law and political analysis are, in many respects, uncompleted. For example, as early as 1963, Banks and Textor had included the then forty-year-old classification of major legal systems provided by John Henry Wigmore (1928) among their categories of modes of national classification. Banks and Textor provided no suggestion, however, regarding the possible relationship of such a traditional family of law categorization to scientific comparative judicial and political analysis. Conventional comparative law scholars generally eschew relating families of law to political analysis on the ground that law involves dispute resolution which is impartial and neutral politically. Ironically, while Edelman's analysis of the changing role of the Israeli Supreme Court provides some basis for that position, Ehrmann's, Gadbois's, Schubert's, and Steamer's contributions provide considerable empirical evidence of the interaction of judicial behavior and national politics in Weimar, South African, Indian, Swiss, and Anglo-American experiences. The integration of conventional law approaches, such as families of law, into modern comparative politics may provide considerable impetus for far greater cross-national judicial political analysis, because such conventional approaches assume or describe attributes of legal systems which transcend single nation categorizations. Thus new perspectives on the investigation of law and politics may be recognized and scientifically investigated through reinterpretation of long established conceptual approaches.

ABOUT THE CONTRIBUTORS

Henry J. Abraham is the James Hart Professor of Government and Foreign Affairs, University of Virginia. He is the author of numerous books and articles on law and judicial politics including *The Judicial Process: An Analysis of the Courts of the United States, England, and France* and *Justices and Presidents.*

Burton Atkins, a frequent contributor to Political Science and Law Journals, is a faculty member in the Department of Government, Florida State University.

David G. Barnum is a member of the Political Science faculty of De Paul University. He is especially involved in comparative cross-national research on judiciaries and human rights and civil liberties.

Martin Edelman, a member of the Political Science faculty of the State University of New York, Albany, has written extensively on the civil and religious courts of Israel.

Henry W. Ehrmann, the distinguished author of *Comparative Legal Cultures,* is a member of the faculty of the Department of Government, Dartmouth College.

George H. Gadbois, an investigator of the judicial politics of India, is a member of the Political Science faculty of the University of Kentucky.

Takeo Hayakawa is an outstanding contributor to Political Science and Law Journals on the judicial politics of Japan. He practices law and teaches at Senshu University in Tokyo.

Edward McWhinney, a distinguished Canadian scholar and Queen's Counsel, is on the faculty of Simon Fraser University. Among his numerous publications is the seminal *Judicial Review in the English Speaking World.*

John R. Schmidhauser, a member of the faculty of Political Science at the University of Southern California has investigated judicial and legal elites and is the author of *Judges and Justices* and "The Circulation of Judicial Elites".

Glendon Schubert holds an endowed chair in the Political Science department of the University of Hawaii. He has contributed numerous books and articles in comparative judicial behavior including *The Judicial Mind* and *Comparative Judicial Behavior.*

Robert J. Steamer, a frequent contributor to journals on judicial politics published *The Supreme Court in Crisis.* He is a Professor of Political Science at the University of Massachusetts, Boston.

C. Neal Tate, a member of the faculty of Political Science at North Texas State University, has contributed significantly to the literature on comparative judicial behavior including works on British and Philippine judicial elites.